DARKNESS IN E

DARKNESS IN EDEN

The Murder of Julie Ward

JEREMY GAVRON

HarperCollins

An Imprint of HarperCollins*Publishers*

First published in Great Britain in 1991 by
HarperCollins Publishers,
77-85 Fulham Palace Road,
Hammersmith,
London W6 8JB.

9 8 7 6 5 4 3 2 1

BRITISH LIBRARY CATALOGUING IN PUBLICATION DATA

Gavron, Jeremy
Darkness in Eden: the murder of Julie Ward.
1. Kenya. Nairobi. Ward, Julie. Murder
I. Title
364.1523092

ISBN 0-00-215859-0

Photoset in Itek Galliard by Ace Filmsetting Ltd, Frome, Somerset
Printed and bound in Great Britain by Hartnolls Limited, Bodmin, Cornwall

CONTENTS

LIST OF ILLUSTRATIONS

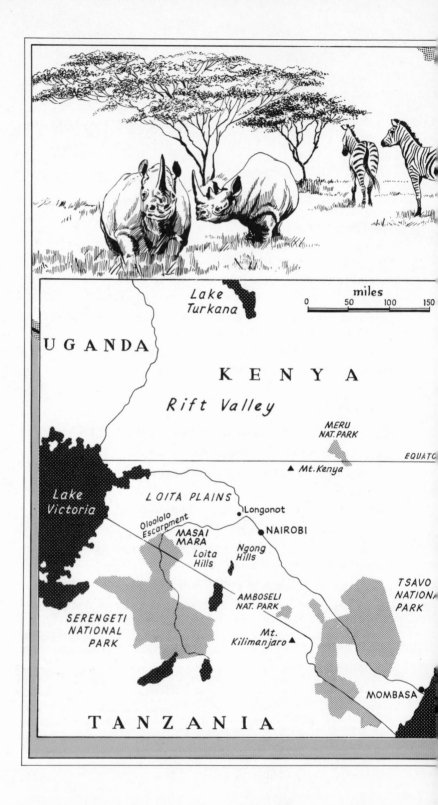

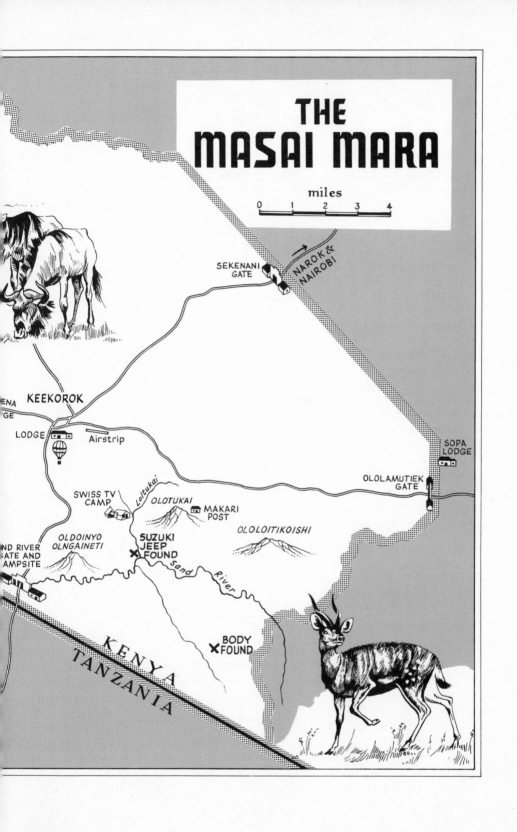

THE
MASAI MARA

miles

0 1 2 3 4

SEKENANI
GATE

NAROK &
NAIROBI

KEEKOROK

ENA
GE

LODGE Airstrip

SOPA
LODGE

SWISS TV
CAMP

Loitukai

OLOTUKAI

MAKARI
POST

OLOLAMUTIEK
GATE

OLOLOITIKOISHI

OLDOINYO
OLNGAINETI

SUZUKI
JEEP
FOUND

ND RIVER
ATE AND
AMPSITE

Sand

River

BODY
FOUND

KENYA

TANZANIA

1

A Last Safari

The Masai Mara National Reserve lies towards the south-west corner of Kenya, just one hundred and twenty miles, but a different world, from the capital, Nairobi. Its high grass plains and shimmering hills, freckled with flat-topped acacia trees, have hardly changed, tourist lodges and prowling prides of Land Rovers and minibuses apart, for a thousand years. During the day, a multitude of creatures – wildebeest, zebra, giraffe, elephant, lion, cheetah – swelter beneath the high, equatorial sun and a vast blue sky that seems to stretch up and for ever. On moonless nights, the darkness is so absolute that whole galaxies invisible in the European sky wink and glitter like dust caught in a distant shaft of light. The night's sounds, too, are unquestionably African: the saw-saw of cicadas, the long kee-ooo of the Scops owl, the grunt of lions, the howl of hyenas.

A single tarmac road, a corroded, pot-holed artery, leads from Nairobi to the Mara. The journey takes six or seven bone-rattling hours and many of the thousands of tourists who visit the reserve each year choose to fly down by small aircraft – Air Kenya's 1930s Dakotas or the newer Twin Otters – to one of half a dozen strips carved out of the bush near the main camps and lodges. But it is only by driving, climbing the lush foothills of the Central Highlands, descending the majestic escarpment of the Rift Valley and bumping, the last few miles on dirt roads, across the Loita plains, that the traveller gets a taste, albeit a dusty one, of the breathtaking scenery of East Africa and the seemingly eternal ability of this land to measure up to each new visitor's capacity for wonder.

It was on this road, in the soft, golden light of dawn, that two young travellers, Julie Ward and Glen Burns, set off on Friday 2 September 1988. Julie had woken early, while it was still dark outside the cottage she had been renting in Langata, a leafy suburb on the outskirts of Nairobi. As always, she dressed simply, in faded jeans, tee-shirt and a plain, blue sweatshirt, and then finished carefully packing her car. Although she and Glen were only planning to go to the Mara for a long weekend, two or at most three nights, Julie had prepared for the trip thoughtfully. Stacked in the back of her Suzuki jeep were a sleeping bag, a tent, a small cooking stove, methylated spirits, two boxes of food (including a tin of pilchards, some Fray Bentos steak and kidney puddings and chocolates for her sweet tooth), cigarettes, clothes, two maps, one of the Mara and one of Kenya, her treasured Olympus camera, with various lenses, and a plastic jerrycan filled with twenty-five litres of 'super' petrol. Before setting off, Julie scribbled a quick note to Doug Morey, her landlord, an American pilot who flew the Nairobi–Mara route for Air Kenya, and slipped it under the windscreen wipers of his car. It said that she was off to the Mara for a few days and joked that if, while flying over the reserve, he saw her little brown car, he should be sure to wave. Then she started the engine, waking Doug in the process, and steered the jeep down the dirt driveway and out towards Langata South Road.

Glen was staying just a couple of miles away, in the sprawling, unkempt garden of Paul and Natasha Weld Dixon, an elderly English couple who had been living in Nairobi for many years and now, in retirement, made a bit of money by allowing travellers to camp out in their grounds. Julie herself had stayed here when she first arrived in Nairobi, making friends with the old couple, and it was she who had suggested that Glen move from his run-down hotel into the airy Weld Dixon compound. Now Glen loaded his own luggage on top of Julie's – another tent, his sleeping bag, an inflatable mattress, a water bottle, binoculars and clothes. Julie had already filled the jeep with petrol and checked the water and oil, and before the Weld Dixons awoke the two companions drove out of Langata and through the suburbs of the city towards the old western road.

Like all African cities, Nairobi stirs early, taking advantage of the cool of the morning, and by the time Julie and Glen began to climb out of the city, long lines of men and women were trudging down from the cheap housing estates and shanty towns towards the centre of town. Schoolchildren too, girls in maroon and boys in blue, trooped noisily through the dust to class. Young mothers in bright dresses, with babies strapped to their backs, crouched by the roadside, washing clothes or tending tiny patches of soil. At traffic lights, newspaper hawkers in the bright red jackets of the *Standard* sold the day's news. As the car approached, scrawny, dust-coloured dogs pulled themselves wearily up from the warm tarmac and skulked away. The first shop shutters were unbolted and thrown open: Jambo Timberware, New Lucky Star butchery, the Chips Café and Zambezi Pelican Trading Centre – the latter a long, low building with a mural of swans painted across the front.

From the ragged edge of the city, the road rises more sharply, climbing into the lush tea and maize plantations first hacked out of the thick bush by white settlers, but now owned almost entirely by wealthy members of the large Kikuyu tribe. The land is high here, over seven thousand feet, and in the early morning thick, wet mists engulf the road, reducing visibility to a few score yards and making ghostly shadows out of the nearby trees. Overladen trucks and matatus – brightly coloured private buses, always full to the brim and beyond with people – hoot out of the fog, scattering smaller cars and less foolhardy drivers before vanishing again in the mists. About twenty miles from Nairobi there is a choice of routes: the main road carries on north-west along the line of the lakes – Naivasha, Nakuru and the vast waters of Lake Victoria – before turning northwards into Uganda. But Julie and Glen branched left, on to the old Naivasha road, built in the early 1940s by Italian prisoners-of-war from the Abyssinian campaign. A tiny chapel, constructed by the Italians in 1942, when the road was completed, sits at its end in the shade of a great acacia tree. But heavy trucks and the tropical climate have conspired over half a century to turn the road itself into a battlefield of craters and ridges, and Julie's old, mustard-coloured Suzuki meandered its way slowly around the potholes and past the olive trees and aloes. Although the jeep was only seven years old, it creaked and rattled like a far more antiquated vehicle. Julie had bought it in Nairobi a few weeks earlier for forty thousand shillings (about fifteen hundred pounds) from a car rental company, Cross Ways Car Hire, whose Indian owners had themselves purchased it from a building firm, Crescent Construction, and years of hard driving had taken its toll. In the few weeks Julie had owned the car, it had spent almost as much time in the garage as on the road. One act of surgery had removed its cracked four-wheel drive shaft, making it effectively a two-wheel-drive vehicle. The tyres, long overused, were as smooth as if they had been laboriously sandpapered. And there was a hole the size of an orange in the floor in front of the passenger seat, through which minor hurricanes of dust rose up now and again into the car. Underpowered to begin with, the engine groaned alarmingly when the speedometer approached fifty miles per hour.

But Julie loved the jeep and in Nairobi had happily shrugged off jokes made at its expense. She drove slowly, anyway, and she and Glen were in no particular hurry as they dropped gently away from the mists and towards the edge of the escarpment. Even from space, the Rift Valley is clearly visible as one of the most dramatic marks on the surface of the earth – a long, ragged scar that stretches from Lebanon to Mozambique. But nowhere is the view more spectacular than from the valley's forested lip, west of Nairobi. The road turns a corner, past some flowering red aloes, and there, without warning, two thousand feet below, is the great, flat bed of the valley. Black-shouldered kites ride the air currents here, at eye level, and even from the road it is a bird's eye view down the plummeting escarpment. The forest clinging to the steep slopes was one of the hideouts of the Mau Mau rebels in the 1950s, and during those troubled times vehicles had to watch out for rocks and stones pelted by unseen hands from the thick woodlands. Leopards still stalk the shadows of the forest and their favourite prey, baboons, often squat by the roadside begging corn cobs from truck drivers, or run shrieking into the trees if a matatu, swerving violently to avoid a pothole, comes too close. In the distance, the far side of the valley rises purple and grey against the blue sky and pastel clouds.

September is halfway through the long dry season in Kenya and the heat and red dust rose as Julie and Glen descended past acacias and giant Euphorbia Candelabra, cactus-like trees with flowering fingers reaching into the sky. A chain of volcanoes, most of them long dormant, runs along the floor of the Rift Valley, and the road cuts between two of them here: Mount Suswa, sacred to the Masai, on the left; and Mount Longonot on the right. This whole area was prime hunting country before shooting was banned a few years back; good for lion, oryx, buffalo and especially rhinoceros. It was on the slopes of Longonot, in the 1930s, that Kathleen Seth-Smith, one of Kenya's few professional white huntresses, lost part of her scalp to a rhino. Along with a tracker and gunbearer, she had followed two rhinos into a thicket. As she approached, the rhinos came out from either side of the bush and charged her. She dropped the female with her first shot, but was too late turning towards the male. The full weight of his charge missed her, but his horn caught the side of her head, tearing off a patch of skin and hair about five square inches in size. The huntress, then twenty-eight years old, walked for half a day to the railway line, flagged down the train, took herself to hospital in Nairobi, had her head patched up, caught the train back again, climbed up Longonot and shot the male rhino dead. The horn remains in the possession of the Seth-Smith family, mounted with its victim's scalp still impaled on the point.

Not a single rhino browses anymore on Longonot or Suswa, where once they dozed grumpily in almost every thicket, and there are now just a few hundred left in the whole of Kenya. But other creatures do still thrive here. This land belongs to he Masai: tall, languid cattle herders, notorious for their ferocity in battle and the foppish concern of their young men with their almost feminine good looks. The Masai keep cattle and occasionally kill, or are killed by, the lions which raid their herds. But they live mostly on milk and blood which they extract from their cows, and unlike most other tribes in East Africa, they seldom hunt or eat meat. Instead, they peacefully allow the plains game to graze alongside their herds, and from halfway across the Rift Valley to the Mara and beyond, a growing menagerie of beasts – zebra, kongoni, ostrich, impala and Thomson's gazelle – adorn the plains and thorn scrub stretching away from the side of the road.

Narok, the administrative capital of Masailand, sits in a dip of land halfway between Nairobi and the Tanzanian border, a frontier town and watering hole, both for the Masai and for tourists thirsty for cold drinks and petrol. Glen and Julie stopped here around midday and filled the car with petrol at the Montorosi service station. A couple of hours later, they drew up at Sekenani gate, the main entrance to the south-eastern part of the reserve. While hawkers tried to sell them Masai beadwork and leather shields, Julie paid three hundred Kenyan shillings (about twelve pounds) for two days' stay in the reserve. She wrote down the Weld Dixons' post office box number, as their address and filled in the registration number of the car, KTS 597. In return, she was given a receipt and an instruction leaflet, warning tourists, among other things, not to leave their cars when outside the safety of the lodges and camps.

From the gate, they slowly drove the dozen miles to Keekorok lodge where they ordered the speciality of the bar – fruit cocktails – and drank them overlooking the spacious gardens of the lodge. Like all the best lodges in Kenya, Keekorok has facilities fit for a city hotel: shop, swimming pool, bar, restaurant, even a radio telephone to contact Nairobi. There is also a long, wooden platform leading out from the edge of the garden to a water hole and salt lick. In the evenings, tourists drink sundowners here as the equatorial sun sets, bright red in the dark sky, and watch the buffalo or lion which have come down to the pool to slake their own thirst. Idyllic as it was, Julie and Glen had no plans to stay at Keekorok and, after an hour or two, they climbed back into the Suzuki and bumped along the dirt track for a few more miles to a campsite on the edge of the Sand river, just a couple of miles from the Tanzanian border. The campsite was simply a stretch of dry grass along either side of the river, where campers pitched their tents. The river itself was almost dry; only a small stream still meandered between sand banks and occasional deeper, stagnant pools. Glen and Julie crossed the river and found a quiet spot, away from the other campers. Previous tourists had left flat, blackened patches where they had sat around gently flaming fires at night, and by one of these Glen and Julie set up their two tents and made their supper beneath the stars, talking about their dreams. Glen had been away from home for nearly eighteen months and he told Julie that he intended to return to Australia soon. Before long, he hoped, he would meet the right girl and settle down to raise a family. Julie's plans lay, for the near future, in further adventures in Africa but she, too, wanted one day to marry and have children. Then, with an early start the next day in mind, they crawled into their separate tents and fell asleep to the sounds of the African night.

By 2 September, Julie Anne Ward had been in Africa for nearly seven months. She had celebrated her twenty-eighth birthday, on 20 April, with a truckful of other young travellers, during a five-month overland trip through north, west and central Africa. They had reached Kenya in late June, and Julie had been in Nairobi ever since. From the moment she had first flown over the city's game park into Jomo Kenyatta Airport, on a previous short holiday in 1985, Julie had fallen in love with Kenya and was now nurturing plans to stay. Due to fly home to England from Nairobi on the morning of Saturday 10 September on Ethiopian Airlines, via Addis Ababa, Cameroon and Morocco, she intended to return soon. The purchase of her jeep was a pledge of commitment to Africa and this grand new adventure and the weekend in the Mara, amid the animals and scenery she found so magical, were to be a seal on that pledge.

So far, Africa had been good to Julie. Her months under the high equatorial sun had turned her customary English pallor into a healthy, attractive tan. But while she had also filled out a little, she was still very slim – five foot seven in her bare feet and scarcely eight stone – and looked younger than her years. Apart from her one, somewhat incongruous bad habit of smoking, the way she presented herself added, without any artifice, to an impression of girlishness. She wore her dusty, blonde hair up in a simple, high ponytail. She seldom used make-up or jewellery and dressed quietly, in shorts or jeans, tee-shirts and sweat-shirts, gym shoes or flip-flops. Her face, too, was open and fresh. When serious, or upset, it took on the heavy, bearish features of her father, John Ward, a successful hotelier from Bury St Edmunds, who was built like a rugby second-row for-ward. But when she was happy, as she usually was, her whole face would crease into a broad, open grin. As her mother, Jan Ward, sometimes said, 'A light comes on in Julie's face when she smiles.'

It was also a smile full of compassion. Growing up in the country, first in Welwyn, in Hertfordshire, and later in Brockley, near Bury St Edmunds, where Julie had lived with her parents until she left for Africa, she had lavished warmth on a houseful of animals: the family's dogs; a continuous stream of stray cats; even, when she was young, a homeless donkey. The more helpless a creature, the more Julie loved it. When she went to Africa, she left behind five cats, Thomas, Kitty, Smudge, Peter, and her favourite, Sniffy – a 'fat, elderly, crotch-ety, very hairy white-and-tabby', according to Jan Ward. Sniffy was taken in much against the wishes of John Ward, who dis-liked cats, and as payment Julie gave her father one bag of fudge a week. The family also had four pedigree huskies, shipped over from Denmark, and while only one, Ben, belonged to Julie, she also showered love on Anna, Rocky and Noggins. Julie's inter-est in animals was not, however, merely sentimental. She was a keen amateur naturalist and she knew a good deal about both British wildlife and the grander game of Africa.

Although she was reasonably bright, and very practical, Julie never really took to her school, Stanborough Secondary Modern in Welwyn. When her family moved to Brockley, just after Julie had turned seventeen and had passed four 'O' levels, she decided to abandon her education and look for work. She soon found a job in a small printing firm in Bury, but she had less luck in finding friends. Likeable and easygoing, Julie had made a good circle of friends in Welwyn, some of whom, like Ken Hinson and Lynne Money, she later kept in touch with and occasionally met up with for weekends or holidays. But she was also shy, never seeking the limelight, and in a new town, working mostly with people older than herself, she was never quite able to unlock the key to a social life. It was a problem that continued for the entire ten years Julie lived in Brockley, before setting off for Africa. She sometimes went out for the evening and occasionally had dinner with young men, but throughout her twenties her life in Bury was divided almost exclusively between work and her family.

In 1979, when Julie was nineteen, she joined a small, new typesetting firm in Bury, run by a local man, Ian Rowland, who employed just a dozen people. Her first job at Rowlands was as photocopy operator, copying and binding early proofs of the books the firm was typesetting. But Julie's competence, common sense and pleasure in working hard soon impressed Ian Rowland, and he took her on as his personal assistant. The work was rewarding but time-consuming and Julie often stayed in the office until late at night and took work home at weekends. Always calm, she became a girl Friday to Rowland, a slightly nervous man, drawing up production charts and even helping to organize his private life. Rowland's daughter, Amanda, suffered from severe asthma attacks and when the little girl went into hospital, Julie would always visit her and take small presents. On one occasion, Rowland's wife had to spend the night with Amanda in hospital, and Julie came over to the Rowland house early in the morning to make breakfast for her employer and his son. Rowland's company charged high prices for its typesetting, but in return gave quality work and, aided by Julie's steadying influence on the managing director, always met its deadlines. After a few years, the firm was receiving commissions from most of the top publishing companies in Britain and had begun to earn a first-rate reputation. Soon, it moved to plush new offices in one of Bury's industrial estates and Julie was given a company car, an Escort XR3, as well as a generous salary. But while the other girls in the firm would often come to Julie if they had a problem – she was kind, always ready to listen and would go out of her way to help if she could – none became close friends. This was partly because Julie worked for the managing director, which drew a line between her and the rest of the employees. But it was also because Julie was different from the other girls, whose aspirations rarely stretched outside suburban Suffolk. Julie may have lived all her adult life in Bury, but her dreams, while still unformed, lay beyond its small-town borders.

After several years of work, Julie decided it was time to move out of the family home, and she found a small house in Bury, in a state of slight disrepair, which she bought for twenty-two thousand pounds. Rolling up her sleeves, she went down to the shops and purchased a Black and Decker 'workmate', sandpaper, paint, hammer, nails and gloves and started working on the house. But Julie's job still took up too much of her time to allow her to complete the refurbishing of her house, and after a while she came to accept that she liked living in Brockley, coming home to a hot meal and the company of her family. Eventually she divided the house in two, sold off the larger part for forty thousand pounds, a tidy profit, and planned at some point to rent out the remaining rooms.

Home life was full of small pleasures for Julie. Her father was already wealthy by the time the family moved to Brockley, and the house he bought, which he named Saxonville, was a huge modern manor, set in large grounds between farmers' fields. Julie's bedroom was a cosy den on the top floor, with a sloping roof. She had taken the legs off her bed and slept close to the floor, amid her collection of teddy bears and soft toys. A couple of large potted plants, which always seemed to grab her mother when she entered the room, stood near the door. John Ward had built bookshelves on the wall and in recent years these had filled up with books on Africa, just as Julie's own photos of animals had taken over much of the wall-space. Julie also had vague plans to go to Latin America, after she had visited Africa, and in an attempt to learn Spanish she had labelled various items in her room with their Spanish names. For most of the family's years in Bury, Julie's two brothers, Tim, two years younger than Julie, and Robert, another year younger, also lived in the house. The three children had the usual rows but became increasingly close friends as they grew older and the difference in age became less important. John Ward, a mostly benign, if rather imperious figure, presided over the house, though for two years in the early 1980s he went off to America, where he sailed and made a film about hoteliers. This period cemented a strong alliance between Jan Ward and her three children, and it was Jan who was really Julie's best friend. 'The four of us grew very close together,' Jan Ward would say of these years. 'We were less like a mother and three kids and more like friends. We worked as a committee. It became a group of four adults. The relationship changed, it was fun. That was a very special time for me.' A small, delicate woman, slightly overshadowed by her husband, but intelligent and determined nonetheless, Jan Ward shared many of the same interests as her daughter. In the evenings they would watch television programmes like 'The Waltons', which always made Julie cry. They also enjoyed nature and travel shows: the two of them, as Jan put it, were armchair travellers.

Jan and Julie were also united in their love of animals. They belonged to a small society which held huskie races and travelled all over Britain at weekends to 'runs'. A team of two huskies would be hitched to a rig (a sledge in winter and a wheeled cart in summer) with brakes and steering rod, and both Jan and Julie loved to ride behind the dogs. At meets, though, it was always Jan who would race. Julie preferred to remain in the background, helping to prepare the dogs and waiting at the finish to greet her mother. Although they always came last, Jan, Julie and the dogs thoroughly enjoyed their outings. They travelled all over Britain, but their favourite race site was in the hills above the Llyn Alwen reservoir in Wales. Here the huskie owners used a small, spartan club house and would camp out at night in sleeping bags on the club floor. Julie loved the roughness and sense of adventure, cooking meals over the little camp stove and chatting with her mother about the day's race, before falling into a snug, tired sleep.

It was a pleasant life, but as her mother said, a 'bit dull and samey and ordinary'. Julie had taken up photography and although she hated having her own picture taken, she found she enjoyed and was quite talented at taking photographs of animals. She read up on the subject, attended a couple of courses and developed her own pictures in the dark room at home in Brockley. She even bought the equipment to print colour photos, but after her first batch came out too red, she abandoned this. Then, in 1985, Julie took a major step towards independence. Animals and photography were her main interests, and she also wanted to travel, so she signed up for a fortnight's camping holiday in Kenya's game parks, with a British tour group, Guerba Expeditions. Before leaving, she was very nervous about the trip and told her mother that she had her return ticket and could always come home early if she was unhappy. But in fact, Julie immediately fell under the spell of East Africa, and making friends with an Australian couple who were very keen on bird watching, she savoured every minute of the trip. Seeing lions, elephant and other creatures in the wild felt like stepping into the television programmes she had watched with her mother with such wonder. Almost from the moment Julie returned, she began to plan another, longer safari to Africa. She bought every book she could find on the continent and its animals and subscribed to *Swara*, the magazine of the East African Wildlife Society. At this point, Julie also started sponsoring a young African girl from western Kenya, Josephine Njete, through the British charity Action Aid. For eight pounds a month, Julie was able to help Josephine through school and she regularly wrote and received letters from the girl. Because Josephine was unable to read English, Julie drew pictures on her letters to explain what life was like in England, and sent books as well. Josephine drew pictures back.

Julie took her second trip to Africa over Christmas 1986, flying out for eight weeks. She spent twenty-nine days in the Tanzanian parks: the Serengeti, one of the best places to find leopards in Africa; the Ngorongoro crater, a natural sanctuary protected by the volcanic walls of the crater; and Lake Manyara National Park, famous for its tree-climbing lions. Julie also spent a couple of weeks on her own in Nairobi, hiring a car and driving around the wildlife spots – Nairobi National Park, the Nairobi orphanage and the Giraffe Manor, an estate on the edge of Nairobi where several giraffes were kept and could be hand-fed by visitors. On this trip, Julie had time to work on her wildlife photography and she produced a collection of good animal shots. In the friendly, sharing atmosphere of a safari, Julie also began to realize how easily she could make friends and how much fun she had missed by not having a social life. She became particularly good friends with two Australian girls, Beth Symonds and Murali Varatharagan – the latter an Australian of Sri Lankan descent. Like many young Australians who travel around the world before settling down back home, Beth and Murali possessed the sort of zest for life that is often so lacking in England, and this inspired and excited Julie. After she returned to England from this second safari, she kept in touch with the Australian girls and it was with them that she was planning not only more African adventures but also a journey by Land Rover across South America. It was also through Beth and Murali that Julie met Glen Burns.

Glen and Julie woke early on their first morning in the Masai Mara, on Saturday 3 September, packed all their gear into the jeep, though leaving the two tents in place at the campsite, and before any of the park or camp staff were at their posts, drove off towards Keekorok. It was a morning filled with promise, for Julie and Glen had timed their visit to coincide with the greatest animal show on earth: the annual migration of the wildebeest from the short-grass plains of the Serengeti to the rich grazing lands of the Masai Mara. The Masai Mara National Reserve is six hundred square miles in size, encompassing hills, plains, the Oloololo escarpment in the west, and the tree-lined, muggy brown Mara river, running like a life-supplying bloodline through the western grasslands. But to many of the animals which inhabit these lands, the reserve is simply a small part of a much greater ecosystem, the tip of a creature-strewn berg whose main body lies below the Tanzanian border and is known as the Serengeti National Park. Together, the Mara and the Loita plains, to the north, and the Serengeti and the Ngorongoro game area, to the south, make up a vast, uninhabited wildlife sanctuary, unrivalled anywhere else in Africa. At the heart of this ecosystem, a sort of fast-food extravaganza on the hoof, are one and a half million of one of nature's oddest creations, the neurotic, spindle-legged, white-bearded clown of the plains: the brindled gnu or blue wildebeest. Each year, more than half a million female wildebeest drop calves in the Serengeti in the space of a few weeks. For the resident predators and scavengers this is the year's fattest time. Wildebeest calves are taken by lions on their first day, in their first hour, even as they are emerging from their mother's bloated bellies (though birth takes just a few seconds, and the calves can stand and run within minutes). But for every wildebeest calf which ends up as a quick meal for a big cat or hyena, nine more survive these first few weeks to embark upon the great wildebeest trek, following the northward path of the rains from the southern Serengeti, across the border into Kenya and the Masai Mara.

Travelling in long, winding lines, the first herds reach the Mara in early August. By September of 1988, around one million wildebeest had gathered in the Masai Mara and there were groups almost everywhere, moving from east to west and collecting in huge masses on the river banks, waiting until there were so many of their own kind pressing in from behind that those nearest the river were forced to leap into the water and scramble through flying hooves and lurking crocodiles to the far banks. Thousands died in the rivers, and thousands more fell prey to the flesh eaters. Every pride of lions seemed to be feasting on a wildebeest carcass; every vulture either flapping at a bone on the ground or sitting bloated in a tree; every hideous hyena face dripping with blood. These then, were the scenes that Glen and Julie set off to see. They stopped first at Keekorok, but found the petrol pumps dry, and decided that, as they were planning to drive to the Mara river on the western side of the park for the day, they should head for Serena lodge, on a hill near the banks of the river, and fill up with petrol there.

It was a glorious drive, from Keekorok across the plains spotted with wildebeest to the bridge over the Mara, where a family of hippos dozed in the cool brown waters after a nighttime's grazing. For Glen, as well as Julie, this was a special day. A marine biologist from Brisbane, with a doctorate from the University of New England, in New South Wales, Glen had arrived in Kenya earlier that year, on 19 July, after fifteen months of wandering through Asia. He had spent four months in Indonesia, three months in Malaysia and another four in Thailand. From there, he had island hopped to the Maldives, the Seychelles and Madagascar. In Nairobi, Glen had moved into a cheap hotel, the New Kenya Lodge, on Duruma Road, on the bad side of town. It was while staying there that he had been introduced to Julie by the two Australian women, Beth and Murali, and had taken up Julie's suggestion that he camp in the Weld Dixons' garden. During this period, Glen took a week's trip to the Kenyan coast. A few days after he came back, he agreed to join Beth, Murali and Julie for a weekend in the Mara, but at the last minute, the two Australian girls were forced to pull out. Before deciding to go alone with Glen, Julie asked her friends what they thought. 'Oh Glen,' they said, 'he's nothing to worry about.'

The road from Keekorok to Serena runs for about forty miles through dry, dusty country, and after watching the herds of wildebeest, Julie and Glen reached Serena in the early afternoon. Unlike Keekorok, which is spread out on an open plain, Serena is built on a series of ledges on the side of an escarpment.

A small swimming pool sits on one of these ledges and the chairs around the pool offer marvellous views across the plains. Julie and Glen spent a couple of hours here, sipping cool drinks and looking at the wildlife below. Around mid-afternoon, the two companions realized that if they were to reach their tents at Sand River by dark, it was time to go. They walked back to the car park, climbed into the jeep and drove around a little bush to the petrol pumps. The attendant was a slim, cheerful young man who told them that the lodge was out of 'super', the Kenyan high-grade petrol, equivalent to 'four star', but that they had plenty of 'regular'. Glen suggested that they fill up the petrol tank from their jerrycan, which contained twenty-five litres of super. But the attendant said it was fine to mix regular with super and so Julie told him to put twenty litres of regular into the car. Then, with Julie at the wheel again, they drove away.

Not far from the lodge, looking for the best way back to Sand River, Glen and Julie unwittingly took a wrong turn. After a while, they realized their mistake and turned the car round, and were just six or seven miles from the lodge when the vehicle suddenly spluttered and rolled to a halt. Glen tried to start the jeep again, but the engine wouldn't respond, and they were still stuck when a truck similar to the one in which Julie had travelled through Africa came down the track. The truck stopped and the tour leader, a young Englishman, asked what was wrong. Glen told him he thought the fuel pump had broken and the Englishman said that if the car was still not working when he and his twenty clients returned from their evening game drive, he would tow them back to the lodge. An hour or so later, the truck returned to find Glen and Julie still in the same place, and a little while later Julie's Suzuki was deposited back at Serena lodge. Just along the hilltop from Serena, past the warden's office and ranger station, was a small patch of open grass where campers were sometimes allowed to pitch their tents. The tour leader, who by now had introduced himself as Stephen Watson, had already settled in here with his group, and as he had a spare tent, he offered it to Glen and Julie, who ate

16

dinner at the lodge and then slept at the Serena campsite, while their own tents stood empty at Sand River.

The next morning was Sunday 4 September, the day Julie and Glen had intended to return to Nairobi. Anxious to be on the move again, Glen removed the fuel pump, which he was sure was the cause of their troubles, and he and Julie decided to call Paul Weld Dixon on the lodge radio phone and ask if he could send down a new pump. Weld Dixon readily agreed, but said that of course he would not be able to get hold of a new pump on a Sunday. At that point, Glen realized that if he waited for the pump he would not make it back to Nairobi in time for a conference he was attending at the Nairobi Museum. So he decided to take the daily flight from the lodge strip and leave Julie to drive back in the Suzuki on her own. Later that morning, Julie drove out with Glen, who was carrying the old fuel pump, to the airstrip. There was just one other passenger, Kennedy Mugo, a receptionist at the lodge, who had an infected tooth and was returning to Nairobi for medical treatment. Glen and Mugo climbed on the plane and Julie waved goodbye. An hour later, the flight landed at Wilson Airport in Nairobi. Mugo and Glen walked out to the Langata Road together and Mugo caught a bus into town, while Glen crossed the road and took a bus travelling in the other direction to Langata. Four days later, Glen joined another overland trip which took him through Tanzania, Rwanda, Zaire and Uganda and it was not until four weeks later, in October, that he was to return to Kenya.

Despite the fact that she was now on her own, Julie was unworried. The road from Serena to Nairobi was good, she expected a new fuel pump which would solve the jeep's problems the next day, and she was in no particular hurry. After Glen had left, she booked herself a room at the lodge and spent much of the day lying by the swimming pool, watching the creatures on the plains below. For an amateur naturalist like Julie, there was much to see. Apart from the tiny dots of animals in the distance, a troop of baboons lived much nearer, in the rocks below the lodge. Rock hyraxes, rabbit-sized creatures, which look like rodents but are in fact related to elephants, also ran around the lodge. And birds swooped and hovered in the air currents rising up the escarpment. Julie's room, number thirty-eight, was a small igloo-shaped cement structure down a bush-lined path from the main hall and restaurant. It had two beds, a bathroom, a cushioned seat in a south-facing window and a mirror decorated with Masai beadwork. The walls were painted a gaudy yellow and grey, and outside the door was a bush of little white flowers. A sign proclaimed them to be Cartharanthus Roseus, or Madagascar periwinkle.

That night, Stephen Watson brought his group to the lodge and Julie invited several of the travellers to take a much-needed shower in her room. The group decided to stay at the lodge for dinner and they invited Julie to join them. Watson was British, from Bath, and the same age as Julie. He worked for Guerba Expeditions, the company Julie had travelled with on her two previous trips to Africa, and he shared many of Julie's feelings about the continent. After dinner, Watson and Julie drifted to Julie's room and he spent the night there. It was a romantic setting and the two young travellers talked for several hours. Julie told Stephen about her life at home and her plans for the future. In the morning, Stephen tried to persuade Julie to extend her stay in Kenya until after his work was over, and while she refused, she did agree to drive up to Lake Naivasha, where Stephen was taking his group, on the coming Thursday or Friday. That day, Monday 5 September, Stephen Watson ate lunch with Julie at the lodge and, at around two-thirty in the afternoon, he left for Naivasha with his tour group.

Meanwhile, early that same morning, Paul Weld Dixon had bought a new Suzuki fuel pump and taken it to Wilson Airport to be put on the scheduled flight to Serena. Later that afternoon, the pump arrived, and Julie took it to the petrol station to see if she could find a mechanic to fit it and return her car to working order. The petrol pump attendant called over Paul Lemaiyan, a stout middle-aged mechanic, and Lemaiyan quickly screwed in the new pump. Julie put the key in the ignition but the jeep still wouldn't start. Frustrated, she asked the mechanic if the battery could be the problem. He took the battery out and tested it, but it certainly had enough power to fire the engine. Leaving it anyway to charge overnight, Lemaiyan told Julie to come back in the morning, when there would be enough time and light to fix the car.

While the mechanic was looking at the car, an American named David Weston, who worked at the lodge giving rides to tourists across the Mara in a hot air balloon, had come up and introduced himself. He asked if everything was all right, and Julie replied, 'Not really.' She told him about her car troubles and when Lemaiyan gave up for the night, Weston invited Julie for a beer at the bar. After a couple of drinks, he asked her to have dinner with him at his house, on the same compound as the lodge. Since Glen had flown back to Nairobi, leaving Julie on her own in the reserve – not something that tourist couples usually did – the staff of the lodge were convinced that the two young travellers, who were assumed to be girl and boyfriend, must have had a fight. David Weston had heard the rumour and over dinner he asked Julie if it was true. In the first place, Julie said, she and Glen were not lovers and anyway there had been no row. After dinner, Julie had a final drink and gently rejected Weston's own advances, though agreeing to join his balloon flight the following day. At around ten-thirty, she returned to her room alone.

Early on Tuesday morning Julie, David Weston and a group of five French tourists lifted off for an hour's balloon ride, drifting south-west into the Mara triangle. The grass was short and burned dry by the sun and it was easy to see not only larger animals like wildebeest and elephant, but also smaller creatures such as jackals, bustards and secretary birds. Ballooning is one of the most spectacular ways to see the Mara. It was first introduced by Alan Root, Africa's most famous wildlife cameraman, who bought a balloon himself when making a film of the wildebeest migration, and subsequently flew over the snow-capped crater of Mount Kilimanjaro, filming as he rose higher and higher. Lodge vehicles follow the tourist balloons and prepare breakfast at the landing spot before driving the balloon riders back to the lodge. Julie returned to Serena at around ten o'clock and immediately went to find the mechanic. The recharged battery was replaced in the engine, but made little difference. After a few minutes tinkering about in the car, however, Lemaiyan discovered that the problem was neither battery nor fuel pump, but simply a loose wire between the ignition and the engine. He held the wire in place and told Julie to start the car. She did and to her delight, the engine chugged into action. After a few more minutes, Lemaiyan had fixed the wire. Relieved and happy, Julie gave the mechanic a generous tip of two hundred shillings, about eight pounds, more than two days' wages. She then went into the lodge to fetch her luggage and, with her credit card, paid her bill of three thousand shillings for the two-night stay.

After the balloon ride, David Weston had accompanied Julie to her car and watched as it was fixed. Now he tried to persuade Julie not to drive off on her own. He told her it was not a good idea for a woman to drive alone in the bush, mentioning poachers and bandits. Weston said she should wait for another car and go back in a convoy, or if she was in a hurry, fly back and pick up the car another time, with a friend. He offered to lend her the money for the flight. But Julie was firm. She was keen to get back to Nairobi that day, partly because of her appointment with Stephen Watson and partly because she had affairs to conclude before flying out of Nairobi on Saturday, in just five days' time. There was no point waiting for other cars, because she had to make a diversion to Sand River camp to pick up the tents, one of which belonged to Glen Burns. She would, Julie assured Weston, be fine. Finally, dressed in white shorts, tee-shirt and flip-flops, Julie climbed into the brown Suzuki and drove out of Serena camp and on to the Keekorok road. The sun blazed high in the blue sky. It was shortly after eleven o'clock on the morning of Tuesday 6 September 1988.

2

The Search

Five days later, and more than four thousand miles away, in the spacious grounds of his home in Brockley, near Bury St Edmunds, on the morning of Saturday 10 September, John Ward was mowing his lawn. Provoked to thought by the boredom of his task, Ward's mind turned to his daughter Julie, who had been away for seven months in Africa. Throughout her journeys, Julie had written long, newsy letters home every couple of weeks, and Ward and his family knew that her main contacts in Nairobi were an elderly couple, Paul and Natasha Weld Dixon. Hundreds of young travellers camped in the Weld Dixons' grounds each year, but Julie's gentleness and her interest in their dogs had endeared the young woman to her hosts. Before long, a small friendship had grown up, with Julie invited in for meals and even house-sitting on one occasion when the Weld Dixons were briefly out of town.

From Julie's letters, Ward also knew that his daughter was due to leave Nairobi any day on her way back to England and, walking in from the garden for a cup of coffee, he decided to call the Weld Dixons and see if he could confirm her plans. When he dialled, Natasha Weld Dixon answered the phone. His daughter was not there, she said, and in fact, there was some disquieting news: Julie was several days late in returning from safari and had already missed her intended flight homewards. Although she and her husband were by now deeply concerned, Natasha belittled her own worries and told Ward that Julie had most likely changed her plans and joined up with some other young tourists. The chances were that she was simply continuing her grand adventure and would probably turn up in Nairobi within the next few hours. Despite these assurances, Ward was not comforted. His unease grew throughout the day, kindled by images of a continent he knew only through television pictures of famine, war and wild animals. At six-thirty that evening, Ward rang Nairobi again, and this time spoke to Paul Weld Dixon, who was unable to conceal his worries. He told Ward that his daughter had not been seen since Tuesday, five days earlier, when she had left a lodge in the Masai Mara game reserve intending to drive back the same day to Nairobi. Ominously, he also said that Julie's companion in the Mara had returned early to Nairobi, leaving Julie on her own in an old, unreliable jeep. Ward put down the phone and a few minutes later dialled Nairobi again, this time talking to Doug Morey, the pilot who was renting his cottage to Julie. Morey confirmed that Julie had not returned and said that efforts to look for her had already begun in the Mara. Ward was now profoundly troubled, and before he went to bed he made up his mind to fly out to Kenya. The following morning, Sunday 11 September, Ward booked himself a seat on the next available flight, leaving Heathrow that afternoon and arriving in Nairobi early the following morning.

John Ward's immediate decision to go to Kenya was typical of a man who from humble beginnings had built two separate multimillion-pound regional hotel chains. Fifty-five years old and a couple of stone overweight, Ward was still a decisive man, quick to act in business or in his personal life. He was born in Harrow in 1933, the son of a bristle buyer for a brush company called Hamiltons and a mother who, 'as people did in those days, stayed at home and looked after the kids. Marks and Spencer didn't have packaged meals back then.' After a Horlicks tablet every morning, Ward would go off to class in huge concrete drainage pipes – temporary replacements for schoolrooms destroyed in the Blitz. At fourteen, he left school and took a course at Kilburn Commercial Polytechnic. His first job was as an office boy in a shipping company, John Cockerills, which ran little tramp steamers between Tilbury, Antwerp and Ostend. The firm had two office boys, Wally

Wastell, the senior boy, and Ward, the junior. 'The difference in rank meant that I had to go out when it was raining.' Through the long, dull hours of work, Ward and Wally Wastell dreamed of running their own business, and eventually the two young men did just that, borrowing some cash and opening the El Toro, one of London's first coffee bars, on Fortis Green Road. The bar's prize drink was 'frothy coffee' which cost one penny a cup to make and sold for ninepence, 'the best profit margin I ever had'. Almost anything went in those heady days of fashion in the late 1950s, and Ward and Wastell served sugar in coconut shells and played Paraguayan harp music to their customers, who included Danny Blanchflower, captain of Tottenham Hotspur football team. It was at this time that Ward met, and then married, a delicate but determined young woman named Janet. At first, Jan worked as 'cook and chief washer-up' in the coffee shop but then, in 1960, their first child, Julie Anne, was born, and Jan 'got the sack'.

Increasingly ambitious, Ward and Wastell dreamed of moving up in the world and mapped out plans to start Britain's first motor hotel, or motel. At first, Ward looked for funding in London and made an appointment at N. M. Rothschild, a leading merchant bank in the city. 'When I arrived, I was told that the man I'd come to see wasn't there. Another young twit with a flower in his button hole came down and said, "You're the chappie who wants to open a motel. Now what exactly is a motel?"' The experience confirmed Ward's disdain for the old English establishment, and was later to convince him to send his children to local secondary modern schools rather than the private ones he could easily have afforded: 'I didn't want my kids to turn out like that twit from Rothschild,' he would explain. Instead, he went to America for money, placing an advertisement in the *Wall Street Journal*. It received ninety replies, including one from Jack Ferrell, an American businessman who owned the Ramada Inn worldwide chain of hotels. Ward spent several months with Ferrell in America, learning how to run a hotel, and came back to England to set up the first Saxon Inn in Harlow, with Wally Wastell as his partner. On

opening night, the motel's guests were a large group of salesmen from Gilbeys Gin company. Ward had run around all day
and then had to stay up until the early hours of the morning
while the salesmen drank and made merry. 'When they finally
went to bed, I thought I'd just go and check the corridors
before I went back to the office, where I was sleeping at that
stage. Outside every room was a pair of shoes, neatly placed,
awaiting cleaning. So there I was, at three o'clock in the morning, tin of shoe polish in one hand, and brush in the other. I
cleaned every last pair.'

Under Ward's shrewd, sometimes ruthless guidance, the
business steadily grew in size until there were six motels, and
both Ward and Wastell were paper millionaires. Then, in 1978,
a couple of years after the Wards had moved from Welwyn to
Brockley, Wastell died and Ward, deeply depressed, sold out his
interest in the business and took off, without his family, for
California. There he indulged in his favourite hobby, sailing,
and produced his film about hoteliers, which received no wider
audience than his friends. After a couple of years, though, Ward
grew bored and returned home to start up his new 'Butterfly'
chain of hotels. A large, confident man, full of rough charm
with a bit of bluster, but not a fellow to cross, Ward soon began
to make a success of his new venture, and by 1988, he already
had two Butterfly hotels up and running, with a third on the
way in Peterborough. Built in the easy, lounge style of the suburban American hotel, where friendliness merely masks effi-
ciency, Ward's hotels served good, simple food and provided
clean, comfortable rooms, all at reasonable prices. They also
boasted the odd touch of genius, like pinning the front pages of
the daily broadsheets to felt boards, behind glass, above the uri-
nals in the men's toilets each morning.

Just before dawn on the morning of Monday 12 September,
John Ward's plane touched down at Jomo Kenyatta Airport in
Nairobi, and emerging from the arrivals hall, Ward was met by
Paul Weld Dixon. The two men drove along roads lined with

flowering bougainvillea and thorn scrub, where giraffes were often seen, to the house in Langata where Julie herself had first stayed. Over breakfast, Ward began to piece together the events of the past few days.

Weld Dixon had first become mildly concerned on Wednesday, two days after he had sent down the new fuel pump, when he called Doug Morey and discovered that Julie had still not returned. When Glen Burns had turned up in Nairobi without Julie, Weld Dixon had been surprised and somewhat annoyed (he later called the young Australian 'an insignificant, wishy-washy person'). Although the route from Serena to Nairobi was fairly straightforward, it still lay partly through wild African country, and was not the sort of journey that Weld Dixon would have advised a foreign young woman to make on her own. He therefore asked Morey to make inquiries on his next run to the Mara and the following morning, as Morey approached Keekorok airstrip on the scheduled Air Kenya flight, he used his radio to call a friend, Sebastian Tham, a young white Kenyan who worked as a balloon pilot at Keekorok lodge. It was a casual conversation: both Tham and Morey assumed that Julie must simply have changed her plans and extended her safari, perhaps after meeting friends. It happened all the time. The wide plains and high skies of Kenya seem to breed spontaneity, and few Kenyans, black or white, are ever too worried about sticking to schedules. Tham did, nonetheless, send his crew chief up to the ranger post at Keekorok to ask about a blonde woman in a brown Suzuki. The message came back that a woman answering to this description had left the reserve on Wednesday, in company with other tourists. Tham relayed this information to Morey and the two men put the matter to the back of their minds, satisfied that there was nothing to be concerned about.

Back in Nairobi, Weld Dixon was not so sure. When Friday came, and there was still no sign of Julie, he began to fret. He knew that Julie was due to fly out of Nairobi the next day and he and his wife had, in fact, invited her to stay at his house that night. They planned to give Julie dinner and drive her to the airport the next morning. Unlike Morey and Tham, the Weld Dixons knew Julie well enough to think it unlikely she would simply change her carefully laid plans without at least sending a message. That afternoon, Stephen Watson returned to Nairobi with his group of travellers, and drove over to the Weld Dixons to look for Julie. He told Weld Dixon about Julie's failure to keep their appointment at Naivasha. Watson's news confirmed Weld Dixon's worries and he began to entertain awful visions of Julie injured in a car crash. Late in the afternoon, his patience gave out and he called the Flying Doctors organization, which sends light aircraft and medical help out to emergencies in the bush. But they had heard nothing of Julie. Shortly afterwards, Weld Dixon called the police in Nairobi, and waited while they sent out radio calls to the district police stations in the areas where it was possible Julie might have driven – Narok, Naivasha and Kiambu. But, again, there was no information. At seven o'clock, he telephoned an English friend, a former policeman, for advice, but the man was unavailable. Increasingly worried when dusk had come and then gone, Weld Dixon dialled the police once more and this time asked for a nationwide missing persons report to be issued. A little later, he called the British High Commission, eventually speaking to a man named Bryant, the duty officer, who noted down what Weld Dixon had to say.

When the next morning, Saturday 10 September, arrived with no sign of Julie, Weld Dixon made telephone calls to all the five hospitals in Nairobi, but without any luck. He then spoke to Doug Morey, who was also, by now, beginning to ponder the whereabouts of his tenant. With a spare key, Morey let himself into the cottage and found Julie's airline ticket, which confirmed she had been due to leave that morning. Morey himself then called Narok police station but they could offer little advice and no information. Later that morning, Morey flew down to the Mara and asked Sebastian Tham to check again whether Julie had left the reserve. This time, Tham personally walked over from his house near the lodge to the warden's office at Keekorok and spoke to the chief warden,

Simon Makallah, the senior official resident in the reserve. A round-faced, balding man, plump for a Masai, and quick to smile, Makallah readily agreed to help and summoning his radio operator he called around the various posts and gates. The rangers at Sekenani gate, despite the initial report a few days earlier, could not confirm that Julie had left the reserve. Tourists were checked into the Mara but not checked out again. Dozens of cars each day were just waved through by the rangers. When the Sand River staff came on the radio, however, Tham and Makallah struck lucky. The clerk at the gate said he remembered the woman arriving at the camp on the Tuesday and then leaving later that afternoon. Julie, it seemed, had reached Sand River from Serena. Over the crackling radio, they heard that Julie had left saying she was heading for Nairobi.

Sebastian Tham, known to his friends as Sambo, was a bush-wise, blond-haired young man, with a clipped, military way of speaking. He had grown up in Kenya and knew that potential dangers lurked in the bush, even for the experienced traveller. Perhaps the woman had driven off the road and got stuck or lost. 'Someone like that driving around the Mara in the dark would be like dropping me blindfold in Alaska,' he was to say. 'Anything could happen.' Tham also owned one of the few privately run helicopters in Kenya, and once he realized that the woman really might be in trouble, he decided to take his machine up and have a look around. As Sekenani gate had provided no clues, Tham decided to fly over to Ololaimutiek gate, east of Keekorok and he lifted off, cruising low above the road. When he reached the gate, he landed and spoke to the rangers, but none of them had seen the jeep or the woman. When the afternoon Air Kenya flight arrived at Keekorok, Tham told Doug Morey what he had found out and later that day, Morey passed the information on to Weld Dixon in Nairobi. Weld Dixon was by now growing increasingly frantic, and soon afterwards he had another idea and called Perez Olindo, the Director of Wildlife, the government official in overall charge of all Kenya's parks. Olindo told Weld Dixon that there was nothing that could be done that night, but suggested that they fly down together the next day and conduct an aerial search. Like many wardens and wildlife officials, Olindo knew how to fly, and as Director of Wildlife had his own plane, a four-seater Cessna 182.

The next morning, Sunday 11 September, Olindo and Weld Dixon were met at the Keekorok airstrip by Simon Makallah, who drove them down to the lodge for a cup of coffee. Makallah confirmed what Tham had told Weld Dixon: that Julie had last been seen leaving Sand River camp and that no more information had surfaced. Willing, nevertheless, to help, Olindo decided that he would make a brief search by plane while Makallah and Weld Dixon could drive down to Sand River to confirm the details of Julie's departure. Taking James Sindiyo, an assistant warden, and Abdu Wais, a field project director for the World Wildlife Fund, as spotters, Olindo took off again and flew low over the road from Keekorok to Sand River, before turning eastwards above the river. The Sand river is known locally as the Makindu river, after the makindu, or palm trees, that grow along its banks, and Olindo passed over land thick with scrub, acacia trees and palms, without any luck. When he returned to Keekorok he found that the land party had scarcely fared better. They had spoken to the clerk, David Nchoko, who had seen Julie. He said she had arrived alone, early on the Tuesday afternoon, and had collected two tents. She had then paid two hundred and sixty shillings extra camping fee and had told the clerk that she was in a hurry to get back to Nairobi. Nchoko showed them Julie's name in his books, signed at two thirty-seven on the afternoon of Tuesday 6 September. The last he had seen of her, Nchoko said, she was driving up and over the hill on the Keekorok road. On the off chance that Nchoko had been mistaken about Julie's direction, Weld Dixon and Makallah drove down to the Tanzanian border but no young white woman had passed that way. Baffled, and fretting about what to tell John Ward the next morning, Weld Dixon flew back with Olindo to Nairobi.

*

By the time Weld Dixon had outlined the events of the past few days and all his efforts to find Julie to her anxious father over breakfast in the house in Langata, Ward was desperate to start his own search for Julie. Before leaving Bury, he and Jan had talked, agonizingly, about what might have happened to Julie. Jan remembered an incident near Brockley when a cat had run across the road in front of Julie's car. She had stopped in time, but an impatient driver behind her had pulled out and hit the cat head on, killing it. Julie had been deeply upset, and had cried all day. If an animal, like a gazelle, had darted out in front of the car, Jan reasoned, then Julie might have swerved to avoid it and run off the road. The brown colour of Julie's car would easily merge with the brown dust in a gulley. Perhaps, John Ward thought, Julie was at this moment lying injured in a ditch somewhere, out of sight of passing traffic.

Hurrying into town, Ward first deposited his luggage at the Norfolk hotel, the once-notorious colonial establishment which now catered mostly to middle-aged American tourists. He then headed for the British High Commission, where he met Jenny Jenkins, a consular official. Knowing that Weld Dixon had informed all the relevant authorities, Ward immediately asked how the search for his daughter was going. Jenny Jenkins had no answer and so Ward called Police Headquarters in Nairobi. He was unable to find anyone there who had even heard of his daughter, let alone an officer co-ordinating a search. Increasingly upset, Ward arranged, with Jenny Jenkins's help, for a dark room to make one hundred copies of a photograph of Julie, which he intended to distribute. By now, Ward had also chartered a light aircraft from Wilson Airport for the rest of the day. As he was leaving the High Commission, he bumped into a young man who introduced himself as Stephen Watson and said he knew Julie. Watson was on his way to see a doctor in the High Commission building. He told Ward about waiting at Naivasha for Julie and Ward in turn said he was planning a search operation. Watson agreed to come over to the Norfolk hotel that evening.

Although Kenya has more good roads than most African

countries, much of the land is still untouched by tarmac, and on rough dirt or muddy tracks even short distances can take many hours to drive. As a result, over the past twenty years, small airplanes have become an essential part of the country's transport system, ferrying sick or wounded people to Nairobi, carrying tourists to the Mara, Samburu, Turkana and the coast and bringing fresh supplies to isolated hotels or outposts. There are thousands of airstrips around the country, most of them simply flattened stretches of earth, where someone is responsible for keeping the grass short, pulling up any thorn bushes and preventing warthogs and aardvarks from digging holes in the ground. Many politicians and businessmen have their own planes and farmers often fly into Nairobi to stock up on whisky, chocolate and other essentials. Wealthy young Kenyans, black and white, learn to fly just as teenagers in Britain pass automobile driving tests. As a result, Wilson Airport, on the outskirts of Nairobi, is one of the busiest light plane airports in the world, with aircraft landing and taking off by the score every hour. Ward had arranged for a two-seater, single-engine plane and shortly after noon, the pilot, Glen Slater, with Ward in the passenger seat, trundled along the crumbling tarmac towards the runway. With just a vague flight plan in mind, Slater asked for clearance to take off. Then, checks completed, he pushed the throttle on to full, released the brakes and accelerated along the runway. After a few seconds, the pilot eased back the stick and the plane floated effortlessly off the ground, rising and banking through the clear air.

Looking out of the window, as the plane rose away from the gleaming white buildings of Nairobi, avoiding the occasional high-flying vulture, and turned southwards over the Ngong hills and then the Rift Valley, John Ward caught his first sight of wild Africa. Somewhere in these immense lands, his daughter was lost and possibly injured. Flying below normal cruising height, and dropping lower whenever they spotted anything, Slater took the plane along the line of the same road, from Nairobi to Narok, that Julie herself had driven ten days earlier. Whenever they saw signs of a wreck near the road, they swooped down and circled. One time, they spotted something that looked just like the Suzuki, lying in the bottom of a ravine, but on closer inspection it turned out to be the remains of an old crash. Eventually, Slater steered the aircraft over the Mara, to the Keekorok area, and for another four or five hours, they flew up and down over the reserve, following every dirt road or track they could see, swinging low over clumps of trees and riding the air currents over hills. They saw elephant, giraffe, zebra and tens of thousands of wildebeest, but there was no sign of Julie or her Suzuki. Eventually, as evening approached, Ward reluctantly agreed to abandon the search and allow Slater to turn towards Nairobi, reaching Wilson Airport just as the sun dropped behind the knuckles of the Ngong hills.

On his way back into town, John Ward stopped off at the Thorn Tree café of the New Stanley hotel, at the corner of two of Nairobi's main tourist roads, Kenyatta Avenue and Kimathi Street. The Thorn Tree café, Ward had learned, was the meeting place for young travellers in Nairobi. At any time of day, there were always several groups of young people at the café, a little scruffy perhaps, backpacks resting against their chairs, sipping cold drinks and watching the city go by. Nailed into the Thorn Tree itself was a noticeboard, and here these travellers left each other messages such as: 'Carrot top, Lou in 1YH. Nairobi til Sat 4/21. Stop by or write. Happy Birthday', or 'Yo, George, we've gone to Gringo's for a drink. Then probably to the Pearl Dragon. Join us if you like.' There was still a chance that Julie had merely changed her plans: that she was safe and happy on some unscheduled safari. Perhaps on the message board of the Thorn Tree café, Ward would find a carefree solution to the looming tragedy of his daughter's disappearance. Scanning the board, Ward suddenly saw his daughter's name. He opened the paper, but the message held no answers. It was simply a quick note from some friends who had arrived back in town. It gave their new address and said if Julie was around she should get in touch. There was nothing else.

Wearily, Ward returned in the dark to the Norfolk hotel. There, he was soon informed of the other events of the day.

31

Weld Dixon had driven to Narok to try to drum up help from the District Commissioner. He had been directed to the Narok police chief, Superintendent Charles Issika, who offered him men but said that he could not spare a car – a common refrain in Kenya, where reports of robberies to police stations are often met with requests for a vehicle to pick up the investigating policemen. Desperate for any help, Weld Dixon hired a jeep for a day from a local Indian garage owner and announced a five thousand shillings reward for information about Julie. The police trip, like everything else so far, proved fruitless. The policemen drove down to Sand River and then repeated Weld Dixon's own visit to the Tanzanian post. They alerted their Tanzanian counterparts and then drove back to Narok. The next day, the Indian garage owner did call Weld Dixon to tell him that a couple of Masai had seen Julie driving to Narok with an African in the car, but the information was vague and from the garage owner's keen questions about the reward, Weld Dixon drew the conclusion that this was a 'red herring'. From his hotel room, John Ward also spoke to his wife, who was finding being at home, without any news, hard to take. That day she had visited Ian Rowland, Julie's employer, whom she also worked for part-time. They talked, Jan said, about inconsequential things while all the time she had a vision in her head of Julie lying injured underneath her car.

Later that evening, John Ward, Stephen Watson and Doug Morey met at the Norfolk hotel to plan out the following day's search. Morey noticed that Watson seemed deeply distracted and ill at ease. The father, on the other hand, was still authoritative and businesslike. Ward also now had some idea of the geography of the area in which his daughter was missing. The far, southerly edge of the Mara ran for about forty-five miles along the Tanzanian border with just one exit, past Sand River, into Tanzania. This route had twice been checked now, and Ward was pretty sure that Julie had not gone this way. To the west of the reserve lay the Oloololo escarpment, the western border, which climbed a thousand feet up to the Siria plateau. There was no road this way. The third, eastern edge of the reserve, past

32

Ololoitikoishi hill, at almost seven thousand feet the highest peak in the reserve, was also hard to cross and it seemed unlikely that Julie would have driven far in this direction. Two possibilities therefore remained. On the one hand, after driving away from Sand River, Julie might have left the Masai Mara, passing unchecked through one of the five gates leading out of the northern boundary of the reserve. Oloololo and Musiara in the far west, beyond Serena, seemed the least likely routes. Talek, Sekenani and Ololaimutiek looked more credible. But all five roads, after twists and turns, finally joined up at Narok, and Ward realized he could concentrate on searching the area directly between Nairobi and the reserve. The other possibility was that after leaving Sand River and before arriving at one of the gates, something had gone wrong. Perhaps Julie was still somewhere inside the reserve, hidden in the thick vegetation, about to spend another night in the company of the lions, leopards and hyenas that roamed the bush in the darkness.

Within the Mara, there were a limited number of all-weather roads. The main ones ran from Oloololo and Musiara gates in the west to Serena and then on to Keekorok, and from there in three further directions, to Sand River, Sekenani gate and Ololaimutiek. But, unlike in many other parks in East Africa, it was perfectly legal in the Masai Mara to drive off the road, and the entire reserve was criss-crossed with hundreds of dirt roads, tracks and faint trails, carved into the grasslands by the thousands of tourists' minibuses and jeeps. Some of these tracks ran across open plains. But others followed the winding, riverine courses of small rivers or threaded their way, unseen, through dense, low thorn bush. If Julie was still in the Mara, she could have been anywhere on or near one of these routes, either out in the open or hidden by foliage even from the keenest eyes peering down from an aircraft.

The area in which Julie might be lost seemed immense and the problems facing a search team were almost as huge. But Ward had always thrived on overcoming obstacles in business and he applied the same principles here. With Morey's help, he arranged for five charter planes to meet early at Wilson Airport

33

the next day, and he and Morey sat down with a map on the verandah of the Norfolk hotel to divide the area between Nairobi and the Masai Mara into a series of blocks. Morey also sent out word that spotters would be needed the next day, and early on the morning of Tuesday 13 September, exactly one week since Julie Ward had last been seen, more than forty people, including Stephen Watson, met at the airport, offering to help. The five aircraft, all four-seater Cessnas, took off one after the other, heading south-west to their allotted blocks, four pairs of eyes in each, scanning the dusty landscape below. By now, most of the pilots at Wilson Airport knew that someone was missing and anyone flying in the Mara was asked to keep an eye open for a brown Suzuki. One of the pilots to hear this plea was Andy Stepanowich, a rugged Canadian working for the Kenya government survey department who was flying a training session near Keekorok that day. At ten forty-five that morning, flying a loop south of Keekorok not usually taken by the scheduled Air Kenya flights or charters from Nairobi, something caught Stepanowich's eye. He banked sharply and came in lower, searching the ground for the glint of metal he had seen. Suddenly, there it was, a brown Suzuki, lying in a gully a few miles south-east of Keekorok. Stepanowich circled and could see no sign of any person, but he was able to make out, quite clearly, three letters written in mud on the roof of the car. They spelt out SOS.

Continuing to circle, Stepanowich used the radio to alert the search planes and Ward, flying with Glen Slater, heard the message. Slater turned back and landed at Keekorok and Ward, filled with elation, jumped out of the plane and asked for a car. Sebastian Tham, whom Ward now met for the first time, offered to drive Ward to the site in his Range Rover, and they set off on the road towards Sand River. In order to help Tham find the car, Stepanowich continued to fly tight circles over the gully. The car appeared to be stuck in the muddy bed of a small, almost dry stream. It was facing west to east and Stepanowich could see a rough track winding down from the Sand River–Keekorok road, which he assumed the car had followed. The stream, marked as Loltukai on the map, was a tributary of the main Sand river, which lay one hundred yards away to the south. The Sand River camp was four miles to the west, Keekorok lodge a little further to the north-west. The nearest main road, running between Sand River and Keekorok, passed within two miles of the car. In the other direction, one and a half miles away, lay a small rangers post of five green metal huts in a clump of trees. Even closer, Stepanowich could just make out a tented camp pitched at a division in the Loltukai stream, directly north of the car. This, it emerged later, was being used by a Swiss film team. Before long, Tham had turned off the main road and started following a faint track down to the Loltukai stream. He crossed above the Swiss camp, skirting it on the way down, and drove southwards along the east bank of the stream. Ward and Tham were just a few yards from the Suzuki when they saw it through the trees and stopped. It was shortly after eleven, and Stepanowich dipped his wings before peeling away and landing at Keekorok strip.

Slipping down the ditch to the car, Ward called out Julie's name, but there was no answer. The car lay at an angle in the bed of the stream. A small trickle of water ran under one wheel while another wheel was raised off the ground, free to spin in the air. There was a thick patch of churned mud around the car and the sides of the vehicle were splattered with brown spots. 'She'd obviously got stuck and had tried to get out, slewed a bit and got stuck even more,' Ward decided. But what had she been doing here, in the middle of nowhere? Why, when she was heading back to Nairobi, had she turned off the road? Peering into the car, Ward saw a bundle of tents and sleeping bags in the back. Perhaps Julie might be underneath this, asleep. The car was locked, so Tham picked up a rock and smashed the right-hand, back window, and Ward reached in and pulled aside the cotton and canvas. Nothing. Ward's hopes, which had risen so sharply upon the finding of the car, fell flat against the burned earth.

The car was still full of assorted belongings. Apart from the sleeping bag, there were two tents, one neatly packed, the other seemingly hastily folded and tossed into the car. There were clothes, a pair of tennis shoes, a camp cooking stove, two bottles of Premium beer, one half drunk, and various packages of food including a tin of Fray Bentos steak-and-kidney pudding and a box of chocolates. Lying on the floor was a jack, covered in mud. Ward's attention was particularly drawn to a pair of binoculars, a pen and two maps, one of the Mara and one of Kenya. If Julie had become stuck and decided to walk away from the car to find help, as seemed possible, why had she not taken the maps and the binoculars? And, more importantly, where was the note? Julie was a habitual note-leaver and she would surely have scribbled a few words explaining what the car was doing there and where its owner had gone. Bewildered and deeply disturbed by Julie's absence from the site, Ward walked away from the car, calling out to his daughter. With Tham, he walked in a circle around the car, looking for footprints or any kind of sign that might show where Julie had gone. Tham found a palm frond, shaped much like an arrow, and for a moment they wondered whether Julie had set this down as a pointer. But they dismissed the idea: why use palm fronds when there were pen and paper in the car? The two men also found an empty orange juice carton and a cigarette butt. Up on the bank, they came across the remains of a small fire, about ten inches wide and a foot long, which had left a yellowish, plastic residue. Ward broke off a small piece of the plastic and put it in a match box in his pocket. Looking further afield, Ward noticed a small hill nearby and reasoning that Julie might have walked up here to scan the countryside for help, Ward began to climb the hill himself. But after a few minutes, Tham called him back. There was no point adding to all their troubles by Ward running into a lioness with cubs or a grumpy buffalo and getting hurt or killed himself.

As they stood in the gully, working out what to do next, three cars appeared. First, a dark-green Toyota Landcruiser, with Ker & Downey, the name of one of Kenya's most exclusive safari companies, painted in white on the side, drove slowly across the gully just a couple of yards upstream from the Suzuki. The passengers and driver looked across but carried on. A little later, two open Land Rovers, belonging to the Ministry of the Environment and Natural Resources, drew up near Tham's Range Rover. They were led by Police Inspector Anthony Mwaura, from Narok. He had been sent down to the reserve after Weld Dixon's visit to Narok and had arrived at Keekorok shortly after the message had come through that the jeep had been found. Commandeering the two jeeps, Mwaura had driven to Sand River and picked up Police Constable Namora, who knew the area and was able to guide them to the jeep. Mwaura walked up to Tham and Ward and asked who had broken the window of the jeep. At the same time, the Ministry men piled out of the jeeps and started walking around the Suzuki, some of them actually clambering on to it to avoid the mud. Mwaura then instructed Namora to collect the items in the car, and Namora gathered them in the sleeping bag, which he tossed into the back of one of the Land Rovers. The two Land Rovers then drove away.

Julie's absence from the car was a mystery, but Ward and Tham now realized that if for some reason she had wandered off and was alone in the bush, without the protection of the vehicle, every minute might be important. The best way to find her still seemed to be from the air. So Tham and Ward hurried back to Keekorok and, before long, the five aircraft took off again from the strip, scattering wildebeest and zebra near the runway as they roared into the air. At least they could now concentrate on a much smaller area, the south-east corner of the Masai Mara. Stepanowich, who had put off work for the rest of the day to help search, agreed to go up with Tham in the helicopter and they decided to head south-east, on the premise that if Julie had walked in any other direction she would have hit either a road or a camp. Directly west from the car was the Sand River–Keekorok road. North lay first the Swiss camp and then the Keekorok–Ololaimutiek road. To the east was the nearby rangers post and beyond that a spot where the Ker & Downey party which had passed the car earlier that day was camped. So, kicking up a swirl of dust as they took off, Tham turned the helicopter on a south-easterly course from Keekorok, over the deserted Suzuki and on towards the Tanzanian border. Twelve or so miles from the lodge, near the edge of the reserve, they spotted a small Masai village, or manyatta, where Tham brought down the helicopter. The mud-and-stick huts stood in a mire of cow dung, and when the helicopter landed a few desultory Masai, wrapped in red cloth, came out to look. Tham, as he put it, 'asked the Masai if they'd seen a blonde bird wandering around the bush on their own.' But the Masai had seen no one.

John Ward, meanwhile, was back up in the air with Glen Slater. By now, he was possessed with a hardening feeling of dread. Desperate to do anything he could, he sent a message to Doug Morey, back in Nairobi, for any more helicopters that could be found to be sent down. Morey called Safari Air at Wilson Airport, searching for Lars Svensson, the only licensed pilot with a helicopter in town. But Svensson was out, actually in the middle of an aviation medical examination necessary before he could renew his licence, which had expired. When Svensson returned to the office and received Morey's request, he rapidly contacted the Director of Civil Aviation for permission to fly without a valid licence. By mid-afternoon, Svensson and Morey were given clearance and lifted off from Wilson Airport, headed directly for the Mara. For Doug Morey, used to flying this route in his Air Kenya Dakota, it was a strange, moody trip, and he too was now full of foreboding about the pleasant young Englishwoman who had lived in his cottage. These feelings grew stronger as the Keekorok strip came into sight, shortly after four o'clock, and Morey could see a large group of people standing on the tarmac, talking disconsolately or simply staring into the air. Svensson quickly landed the helicopter, and Morey jumped out to ask what was happening.

Shortly before, he learned, while the planes were still searching, a brief, crackling message had come over the earphones. John Ward was listening in and the report was everything he had most been dreading: rangers searching on the ground had found a body. Waves of despair swept through the various aircraft. Slater muttered, 'It can't be her,' and banked sharply, pushing the throttle on to full before landing low and fast at Keekorok. Neither of the two helicopters was at the strip, so Ward asked for a car, and accompanied by Stephen Watson and two rangers he set off across country. Ward had little idea where to go and before long it became clear that the rangers did not know either. Frustrated and angry, Ward told them to turn back to Keekorok, but they explained that Makari outpost, the rangers camp Stepanowich had seen from the air, was just nearby. There they would be able to use the radio and call for a helicopter. The car bumped down the track for a few more minutes and then turned a bend before arriving at the post. It was an idyllic spot, set in a sheltered and secluded valley between two hills, near the banks of the Olosidam stream, another tributary of the Sand river. The camp itself was simple, containing five prefabricated green metal huts and two wooden toilet shelters surrounded by barbed wire. Everything was green or brown, except one splash of colour from an orange bush of bougainvillea. One of the rangers in the camp used the radio to contact Keekorok and ask for Tham to fly over with the helicopter. A few minutes later, the radio crackled into life again and this time the rangers called Ward over. The message was for him. More horror. Apparently a complete body had not been found: just a leg, separated from the rest of the body and partially burned.

While waiting for the helicopter to arrive, Ward paced around the camp and came across a small button battery of the type used almost exclusively in cameras. It was carefully placed on a coin, as if to recharge in the sun and Ward, though deeply distracted, picked up the battery. He turned it over in his hand, wondering for a moment what it was doing there. Then, the drone of the helicopter filled the air, and Ward put the battery back in its place, thinking no more about it. Finding a flat spot nearby, Tham landed, and as the helicopter could take only one passenger, Watson stayed behind at Makari while Ward climbed in beneath the whirling blades. Tham had only a general idea as to where the remains had been found, so he took the helicopter higher and higher, until the search party who had located the leg could see it and direct him down again on the radio. Just before five o'clock, they sighted the rangers standing in a patch of thick, croton bush, near a large tree. Tham landed and sat in the helicopter for a few seconds, waiting for it to cool down, while Ward jumped out and strode towards the group of Kenyans in official uniform.

The next few seconds were to remain engraved on John Ward's mind for ever. From the group of a dozen or so people, a tall man in green combat gear walked forward and said, simply, 'Come. This is what we have found.' He led the way through the bushes and then stopped, pointing down into the grass at the lower part of a bare leg, severed at the knee and partially burned around the joint. Ward's eyes fell on the pink skin, the toes and toenails, the curve of the ankle. Almost at once, Ward knew with horror that this was his daughter's leg. Julie, he now had to accept, was dead. The tall man beckoned Ward on and a few steps away he showed him two parts of a jawbone, broken in half. Most of the teeth were still attached. Beyond lay the ashes of a fire and, as Ward approached it, the gut-wrenching stench of burned human flesh, sweet and sickly, rose up. The father turned away from the fire, tears finally released and rolling down his heavy cheeks.

The tall man was, Ward later discovered, Police Inspector George Othiambo, from the Mara Bridge Police Post, at the crossing of the Mara river between Keekorok and Serena. The other senior official was Simon Makallah, the chief warden, and he told Tham his story of the day's events. That morning Makallah had met Othiambo to work out their own plan of action over the missing woman. While they were talking, a message had come through that Julie's jeep had been found and they drove back to Makallah's office. From there, they arranged to drive in two cars to the site, with a dozen rangers, a police constable, and James Sindiyo, one of Makallah's assistant wardens. They found the Suzuki without too much trouble and, as Tham and Ward had done, looked around for clues to the woman's whereabouts. They found the remains of the plastic fire and saw, Makallah said, twigs and pieces of wood underneath the tyres of the car, as though someone had been trying

40

to give the bald wheels traction in the mud or divert the trickle of water that was still running under the car. They also saw tyre tracks, leading northwards along the west side of the stream, and Makallah followed them for about half a mile. When he returned, one of the rangers said that they had found something more important: footprints, leading across the Sand river. Makallah and Othiambo followed the single pair of prints southwards across the dry, sandy bed of the river until they faded away in the undergrowth, about one hundred yards from where they had started.

Reasoning, as Tham and Stepanowich had done, that Julie must have walked south, Makallah sent Sindiyo, in one car, on a south-westerly route along the northern bank of the Sand river towards the Sand River gate. He and Othiambo, in the other car, headed south-east, following the direction of the footprints. 'It was ninety-nine percent luck,' Tham later said, to explain Makallah's subsequent discovery. 'Makallah trusted to his instincts, but he was lucky.' At around four-thirty, Makallah and Othiambo saw vultures sitting on the branches of a tree. Driving closer, more vultures rose up from the ground and the car stopped. The men climbed out and a few yards away, they found the first part of the jawbone. Soon, they had discovered the other part of the jawbone, the leg and the fire. At this point, the search horribly successful, Makallah and Othiambo realized that they must call Keekorok on the radio and tell the rangers to contact John Ward.

The site lay, Tham and Ward had seen when they flew down, in the far south-east corner of the reserve, miles from the nearest road but close to the Tanzanian border. It was, in fact, less than a mile from the Masai manyatta where Tham and Stepanowich had landed earlier that afternoon. The remains were, Ward was sure, those of his daughter. But the scene posed as many questions as it answered. The lower leg, lying in a patch of short grass between bushes, had a four inch gash down the calf but was otherwise almost untouched. There were no signs, apart from a few red insect bites, that vultures, animals or insects had been at the flesh. Instead, the area around the knee

41

joint was charred. The two parts of the jawbone were about fifteen feet away. Unlike the leg, they were bare of flesh and muscle, as though they had lain longer in the grass and been picked clean by insects. A little further on lay the remains of the fire and beyond that, the tree. Two torn pieces of orange towel hung from the tree. An open tin sat on one branch, the remains of some fish inside. Written on the tin, apparently in Julie's handwriting, was the word 'pilchards'.

By the side of the fire were more belongings – a pair of flip-flops, a camping tin, a small bottle of shampoo and some charred sunglasses. There was also a lock of blonde hair, which Ward picked up. It looked like Julie's. While Ward looked around, Othiambo, Makallah and their men stood silently, watching the father. They made no attempt to gather any of the items or offer Ward condolences. The girl was dead. In Africa, death is more readily accepted than in Western culture. It has to be. So many more people die young. Touching the dead is also a taboo for many Kenyans and among some tribes the dying are traditionally put out into the bush to be finished off by the hyenas and lions. It is far easier than having to carry out the body and also spares houses from the curse of the dead – although such a practice is now frowned upon and is increasingly rare.

Steeling himself, John Ward bent down and plunged his fingers into his daughter's ashes. They were about three inches deep. Searching around, he found two burned film cassettes, two metal rings from a bag and a piece of denim, with a zip atta-ched. Realizing, through his sorrow and confusion, that he was getting little help from the officials, Ward then embarked with Tham's assistance on the gruesome task of gathering Julie's few, burned remains. Tham brought over a plastic seat cover from the helicopter and they wrapped the leg and pieces of jawbone in toilet paper and then put them inside the plastic. At this point, the deed done, Othiambo came over and said he would have to take the remains to Narok to hand over to his superiors. Ward began to argue, but Othiambo explained that he was a police officer and he wrote down his name on a piece of paper.

Reluctantly, Ward handed over the plastic cover and its contents, and as dusk was now approaching, Othiambo and Makallah decided to return to Keekorok. With the rangers, they climbed back inside the Land Rover and drove off, leaving Tham and John Ward alone, in the screaming silence, as the sun began to set over the African bush.

Numbed by the horror of the day, Tham and Ward stayed a few more minutes and then climbed into the helicopter and took off. Shaking himself out of his weary reverie, Ward asked Tham if he would be able to find the spot again. Tham circled, took his bearings, and then turned the helicopter towards Keekorok. It was now too late to fly back to Nairobi, and Doug Morey had booked the last available room for Ward at the lodge. Morey took Ward's arm and led the grieving father, who by now had succumbed to uncontrollable shakes, to his room. Ward's hands were still black from the ashes, and he muttered over and over again, as they walked, 'I can't believe there was nothing left.'

More than a year later, in the *Daily Telegraph*, Ward related his feelings as the awful reality began to sink in. 'Doug left me in a room with a verandah which overlooked the bush. There was some scotch on the dressing table and, at last, in privacy, I could vent some of my pent-up emotions. Later, in the darkness, I sat out on the verandah with the remains of the whisky. In the open-sided restaurant a native show was on: drums beat continually, dancers with spears stamped and pranced, and out beyond the lights, in the bush, animals snarled, roared and screamed through the darkness. To me, it was a prehistoric hell on earth.' The following night, he flew back to London to share the tragedy with his family.

Five days later, on Monday 19 September, a copy of Julie's dental records reached Nairobi and a police pathologist confirmed what John Ward and his family already knew. The remains of the lower jawbone and, in all probability, the bottom half of the left leg, belonged to Julie Anne Ward. A few days later, Julie's last letter fell silently through the post box in Brockley. She was just about to drive down to the Masai Mara to see the migration, it said, full of excitement. Then she was heading home. See you all soon.

3

✦✦✦✦✦

Shangri-la

It had been seven and a half months earlier, on a cold English winter morning, that John and Jan Ward had said goodbye to their daughter for the last time. Since returning from her second holiday in East Africa, in early 1987, Julie had been talking about and preparing for another, grander safari to Africa. Ian Rowland, her employer, had reluctantly, but with all good wishes, granted her a year's leave from her job, well aware that she might never come back to the fairly humdrum life of a personal assistant in Bury St Edmunds. Over the year, she had added to her library of books on Africa and sent off for brochures of companies running overland trips across the continent. Eventually, she had discovered a small adventure outfit, Hobo Trans Africa Expeditions, which was based in Halesworth, Suffolk, not too far from her home in Brockley. Julie telephoned and went to see a woman named Jo Jordan who, with her husband, Nick Fisher, a local farmer, ran the company.

At first glance, there was little in Jo Jordan's appearance to suggest an African adventurer. In her life in Halesworth, she was a solicitor and dressed the part, in business suit, make-up and elegantly styled hair. But a more off-beat image soon emerged. She drove an old black Morris Minor with yellow trimmings and lived in a farmhouse crammed with African art – grimacing Ivorian masks, beaten metal statues from Mali, ebony Makonde carvings, brightly coloured Nigerian cloth, dark clay lamps, patterned carpets – and hundreds of books on African art, history, travel and wildlife. Sitting in front of the fire in the farmhouse living room, with the bitter East Anglian winter raging outside, Jordan explained how she had joined an

45

African expedition in 1974, while only a little younger than Julie, and had fallen in love with both Africa and the expedition leader. Before long, she had married the leader, Nick Fisher, and they had begun running trips together. More recently, Jordan had been concentrating on the law and Fisher on his farm, and they had taken to hiring guides to run the expeditions for them. The next trip, starting on 7 February 1988, would be guided by two old friends, Dave Tree, the leader, and Nick King, as assistant. Jordan and Fisher would provide the truck, equipment, food, passengers and suggested route – the rest was up to the guides. Hobo's charge was £995 but extras such as food, visas, spending money and flight home would raise the amount of money Julie would need to three thousand pounds. That was no problem. The money Julie had saved from work, the profit on her house and her share of the family wealth added up to well over one hundred thousand pounds. For Julie, the main attraction of Hobo was that it pledged to follow the least beaten tracks and provide the sort of adventurous hardships that she so enjoyed. 'Julie wanted to rough it,' as her father said. 'She had the ideal temperament to deal with mosquitoes and other problems. The more the better, she loved overcoming problems.' By the end of the afternoon, Julie had signed up for the last place on the February trip. A few days later, she sent in a cheque and a completed form, not typed but handwritten in her round, girlish script. Modestly, she described herself as a secretary rather than personal assistant. She also ordered, for collection when the trip began, one Hobo tee-shirt and a mosquito net.

As the departure date approached, Julie grew increasingly excited and nervous. Somehow, she had to fit her clothes, books, maps, torch, water bottle, insect spray, sunglasses, medicines, photographs of home and other vital possessions into one backpack and a shoulder bag. She reorganized the backpack at least twenty times, trying to squeeze everything in, according to her mother. Each time it was so heavy she could hardly lift it. Finally, when the day came, Julie threw half the contents of the pack out and Jan and John Ward drove her over to Jo Jordan's house. The other travellers were meeting at Ramsgate, but because Julie lived nearby, Jordan had suggested she join the truck at Halesworth. When the Wards arrived, Jordan was sitting in the middle of the living-room floor, surrounded by several small mountains of tinned food and tents. John and Jan Ward stayed for a while, asking questions about the forthcoming trip, but soon felt they were only getting in the way. There were a few tears when it came time to say goodbye and Julie hugged her parents. Then they were gone, driving back to Bury St Edmunds.

Julie was soon caught up in the preparations for the trip. Before long, Dave Tree and Nick King turned up and they all proceeded to load the huge Leyland truck. Over the years, Nick Fisher had improved and modified dozens of similar trucks, and the vehicle Julie and her companions were to travel in was well suited to the rough roads that lay ahead. The back of the truck, where the passengers were to sit – facing inwards on cloth-covered seats – had been almost entirely opened up and thick plastic flaps were fitted as windows for when it rained. There was also a viewing seat fixed to the roof of the driver's cabin and a wooden rack for unspoilable goods behind that. Attached to the back and side of the vehicle were a row of shovels, six spare tyres, a dozen sand mats and water containers with capacity for one hundred and fifty gallons. The main storage, for the thousands of pounds of food, tents, sleeping bags and truck spares, including a complete engine, axles and radiator, lay in a huge compartment beneath the seats. This rolling behemoth was to be home to Julie and her twenty-five companions for the next five months.

It was cold and drizzling when the truck arrived in Ramsgate. The other travellers, waiting at the ferry port, were greeted by a wild-eyed Dave Tree shouting in a thick Birmingham accent, 'Anyone for Africa?' As well as Tree and Nick King, there were fifteen women and ten men, of whom nineteen were British and six from New Zealand and Australia. Their ages ranged from twenty to forty-eight, their occupations from barmaid through labourer to teacher and quantity surveyor. Apart from

47

one couple, all the rest had joined the trip individually. Over the next few months, they would travel across some of the roughest places on earth, through the desert heat and forest mud, rising before dawn to cook breakfast and load the truck, washing from a bucket or a puddle and fending off pickpockets, mosquitoes and rats. For many of them, Julie included, this journey was to prove the happiest time of their lives, and Julie in particular was to thrive on sharing her days and adventures with bright, lively people her own age. On the truck, she found herself sitting next to a slight, dark-haired girl called Lucy Brewer. Julie and Lucy readily agreed to share a tent and by the time they reached Nairobi, the two had become the firmest of friends: the best each had ever had.

The first part of the journey, through France and Spain, camping out by the roadside in the cold, was the most miserable time. From Spain, they took the boat across to Tangier and then drove down to Rabat, before turning east again and back along the northern coast route to Algiers. They explored the Moroccan and Algerian markets, bargaining over leather, silver and silk goods and eating cous-cous and almond pastries. 'We spent about ten days in Morocco, visiting Marrakesh, Meknès and Fez,' Julie wrote from Algeria on 3 March. 'Marrakesh was an unplanned "holiday" due to a wait for visas. Fez is a giant rabbit warren of little alleyways – you go in, get totally lost, then pay a guide to get out again! We met two other groups like us from England on a beach in Algiers, which knocks the intrepid explorer bit on the head! It's still quite cold for camping – but we're headed south now so it should get better.'

From Algiers, they took the road leading directly south, through Ghardaia and then El Golea, an oasis town of palm trees and glistening fields of sand. After El Golea, the usual overland route continues straight on towards In Salah, Tamanrasset and eventually the Niger border. But the Hobo expedition forked right here and followed the much less beaten track to Adrar and finally Reggane, where they filled up with petrol for the last time for eight hundred miles. From here, they embarked on a genuine desert crossing: drinking only what they could carry and driving as much by instinct as on tracks; occasionally passing ancient trucks bringing goats to market; and sleeping without tents, under the stars. Dave Tree and Nick King, old hands at the journey, were good at keeping spirits up during the hot, dusty days; teasing and ragging, turning every problem into a laugh and every disaster into a black joke. Every now and again, the truck would sink into soft sand and stick, forcing everyone to jump down, grab the spades and dig until they could slide the sand mats under the soft tyres and painstakingly begin moving again. Sometimes, the digging beneath the burning sun proved too much and they would give up and settle in for the night, brewing huge pots of tea and serving it first to whoever had been quick enough to get their cups to the front of the tea queue. Julie and Lucy both loved the group camaraderie, though they tended to fall silent when everyone gathered together; they listened and laughed, but seldom made jokes themselves. Julie soon became truck nurse and whenever anyone suffered cuts or fell sick they turned to her. She also seemed, somehow, to keep an everlasting supply of sweet food and cigarettes. At the hungriest and most uncomfortable moments in the desert, she would produce a box of butterscotch toffee or a pack of biscuits from her pack and share it around.

After the most desolate stretch of the Sahara, the truck crossed into Mali and eventually arrived in Timbuctu. The legendary city of gold and ivory is now a dull, brown, dusty town, with little to recommend it apart from its name. Several hundred years ago the Niger river changed its course and stranded the city a dozen miles from its banks. Mungo Park, the great explorer, paddled up the Niger in 1807 and passed Timbuctu without realizing the city lay just beyond a field of sand dunes. Park met his death upstream a few weeks later, in a hail of poisoned arrows. Timbuctu was not a particularly happy city for the Hobo group either and one of the girls had a bad case of sunstroke and had to be tended by Julie for a few days before the truck could carry on. From Timbuctu, Dave Tree drove westwards along the northern banks of the Niger river until he reached his favourite crossing point. A group of local Malian boys, wading and swimming through the sluggish brown water, waved the truck into the river and it was half-way across when one wheel slipped into a deep hole and the entire vehicle slewed and stuck, leaning at an angle of forty-five degrees. Emaciated cattled drifted past the truck and laughing children swam up for a look. Worried about water-borne diseases such as bilharzia, Julie and her companions lowered themselves gingerly into the river. But by the time they had unloaded the truck, they were thoroughly soaked and were happy to splash about in the cooling, if filthy water. That night, they slept in a kraal of tents pitched in a circle on the bank, with all their goods piled safely in the centre. The next day, and the day after that, they tried pulling and pushing the truck but it refused to move an inch. In the end they were stuck by the Niger for five days. 'It was great, really wonderful,' Lucy said. 'It was so relaxed, it didn't matter. We didn't have to go anywhere, be anywhere. We just sat back and took it easy. We made scones and everyone had their hair cut by Glenys. We spent the whole day watching Africans and they spent most of their time watching us. We also spent lots of time in the water. The little Africans were amazed at the colour of our skin and they kept washing us.' Eventually, another overland truck arrived and after much preparation, winched the Hobo truck out.

After this enforced rest, the expedition continued to follow the Niger downstream, visiting Mopti, famous for its riverside market and mosque, and the Dogon cliff-villages of the Falaise de Bandiagara. Next, the truck cut across the edge of Burkina Faso, meaning 'Land of the Upright Men' and changed from its old name of Upper Volta by Thomas Sankara, a dashing young soldier who took power in a military coup in 1983 and was himself killed a few years later when his best friend, Blaise Campoare, overthrew him in turn. By now, the travellers had all but left Arab Africa behind and were in black, tribal, animist country. They finally reached the coast at Abidjan, the gleaming modern capital of the Ivory Coast, dotted with Hiltons and other grand hotels; the Hobo group camped on the beach. But it was neighbouring Ghana that enchanted Julie and Lucy most. The first English colony to gain independence, in a blaze of glory in 1957, Ghana had fallen from wealth in colonial times to absolute poverty by the time the Hobo party arrived in April 1988. But the untouched beaches were perfect and the people, even in poverty, charming and welcoming. One night, the group decided to hold a fancy-dress party on a Ghanaian beach, and Lucy and Julie dressed up as South Sea island girls, in black bikinis and brightly coloured sarongs, with garlands of flowers round their necks. Two of the party (one male) turned up dressed as prostitutes. Glenys came as a ghost, Phil as a teabag and Alastair, a salesman from Stoke Newington, as a French letter. They drank cheap Ghanaian beer and slept, drunkenly, on the sand.

After Ghana, the group drove through Togo, Benin, Nigeria and Cameroon until they reached the Central African Republic, whose leader in the 1970s, the self-styled Emperor Jean Bokassa, had been as notorious to the French as Idi Amin was in Britain. He personally beat schoolchildren to death and was said to have kept human remains in the refrigerator for his meals. 'You won't believe I was up at four-thirty this morning trying to get the fire lit for breakfast – and finally managed – with the help of a cup of diesel,' Julie wrote from the Central African border on 8 May. 'Still having a great time – Ivory Coast, Benin, Togo and Ghana were one long string of beach camps, good restaurants, cheap booze and barbecued seafood. Cameroon is the place to go for delicious chocolate spread and Nigeria so cheap and friendly. We ate our way through it – Lagos Holiday Inn etc! Hard life is about to start again with the jungles of CAR and Zaire.' A week later, they had the worst disaster of the expedition, as Julie wrote from Bangui: 'A runaway truck hit ours after it had taken down an electricity pylon and two petrol pumps and it crashed into us, which stopped all forty-eight tons of it. Three of our lot ended up in hospital, the worst injury being a broken foot – of the girl I share a tent with, so we spent most of the day in a rather nasty hospital. We got her out that day and I'm playing nursemaid now. Apart from that, and being robbed in CAR, everything's been going fine and I'm having a brilliant time.'

The injured girl was Lucy, who in the rush to escape the runaway truck had leaped to the ground in bare feet and landed badly, fracturing her heel bone. The hospital in Bangui was unwelcoming and demanded payment before taking an X-ray. Julie organized everything and Lucy was put in a cast and told not to stand on the foot for a month. At first, it seemed that Lucy would have to fly home, but Julie refused to allow this and promised to take care of Lucy. 'She did everything for me,' Lucy said. 'She carried a cushion round to put my foot on, always got my supper and tea and everything. She put up my tent and never complained. I think she got real pleasure out of helping people. Nothing was ever too much of a problem for her.' When they passed a river and everyone jumped in for a swim, Julie even conjured a plastic dustbin liner out of her backpack and wrapped it around Lucy's leg so she could bathe.

The rainforests of Zaire, Conrad's heart of darkness, were another highlight of the trip, always full of surprises like Mambo chocolate bars or a little hut restaurant, in the middle of nowhere, which served Julie and Lucy a huge, slap-up break-fast when they had expected only a cup of coffee. At one point, driving along one of the main tracks eastwards through the for-est, they came across a team of workmen laying a pipe. The men had dug a ten-foot hole in the road, so the travellers pitched tents and waited three days until the hole was filled and they could continue. On another occasion, Julie discovered a baby chimpanzee for sale in a village. She spent an hour with the chimp's arms wrapped around her neck, and when it was time to go, both Julie and the baby, which had clearly been starved of affection, were devastated at the prospect of parting. It was with great difficulty that Julie's friends persuaded her that buying the chimp and taking it with them on the truck was not a feasible idea. 'It wouldn't let go of her, it clung to her neck,' Lucy remembered. 'Julie was almost in tears.'

In Zaire, Julie, along with Lucy stumbling through the rainforest in her plaster cast, also went tracking mountain gorillas and spent two magical hours sitting in the middle of a family of the huge, rare apes. 'Arrived in Uganda yesterday after a month in Zaire knee-deep in red mud,' Julie wrote from Entebbe on 18 June. 'It was great fun – a lovely place – but hard work. The highlight was a trek up to see the mountain gorillas. We were very lucky, found them almost straight away and spent two hours with them. At one point three young ones were playing with the big silverback only three feet away. Three and a half films later they had to drag me back to camp. Just spent the day in Kampala, which surprisingly is a really nice and friendly place – we're not lingering, though, and will hit Kenya on Monday. Hope you're all well (I am).' The next day, she sent a last postcard to her workmates at Rowlands before arriving in Kenya. 'Dear Everyone,' she wrote. 'Just to let you know I'm still alive and kicking.'

Julie had been to Nairobi before, but this time she was interested in more than just tourism. After three trips to Africa, she was now completely under the continent's spell and was full of plans to stay in Kenya and start a business. At first, she thought of renting some land near the centre of Nairobi and making a base camp for budget tourists, to compete with the Weld Dixons and the famous Mrs Roche's campsite and hostel. But wandering around Nairobi, Julie saw the exorbitant prices that Kenyan shops were asking for the African art, jewellery and trinkets she had seen on sale for a fraction of the cost by the roadside all across Africa. If this was what tourists were willing to pay in Nairobi, she thought, there was money to be made in buying at origin, in Mali, Ghana, Zaire, Nigeria and the Ivory Coast, all of which had thriving art industries, and selling in Britain or the United States. Julie bought a beautiful coffee-table book about African jewellery, *Africa Adorned*, by Angela Fisher, an Australian who had herself come to Africa as an adult and stayed on. Lucy was also taken with Julie's ideas and the two girls agreed to form a partnership and spent many hours discussing their plans. They also talked to Dave Tree and other old

Africa hands about the best places to buy artefacts and jewellery. 'The idea was to get a couple of Land Rovers. We were going to go on a mechanics course and then drive overland buying things up cheaply. We were dead serious,' said Lucy.

After a week or so, Lucy left Nairobi on an excursion to the coast. Julie had by now become friendly with the Weld Dixons and their dogs and was asked one night to house-sit in Langata. Temporarily in charge of the house and its huge grounds, she had 'six Masai to guard me, complete with spears,' she wrote home. She also took a brief trip to the coast and wrote to her father about the wonderful architecture of the beach hotels. Soon, Julie bought her Suzuki jeep and after a few weeks she decided she couldn't camp out with the Weld Dixons for ever. At first, she moved into the Jacaranda hotel, closer to the centre of town than Langata, and when Lucy returned early from the coast – planning to fly home because her foot was still causing problems – Julie insisted that her friend come and share her room in the hotel. It was, by the standards of the previous few months, a beautiful hotel, with large, clean, airy rooms, a swimming pool, and, to Lucy's amazement, a grand buffet breakfast of eggs, sausages, bacon, potatoes, breads and a huge range of tropical fruit – papaya, mango, water melon, passion fruit. 'Julie paid for everything,' said Lucy. 'That's when I realized she had a bit more money than the rest of us.' Julie also took care of Lucy's problems. 'I was having trouble with my insurance. I called the company in London from the Jacaranda and talked to a horrible lady. She said I was fine and didn't need to come home. I went back to the table practically in tears. Julie was amazing. She called them right back and told the woman she couldn't speak to me like that. She demanded to speak to the boss and arranged for the company to send out a ticket and take me home. I'd never seen her like that. She was obviously so capable.' A couple of days later, Julie took Lucy to the airport and they agreed to meet up in London after a few weeks and work out the details of their new business plans.

The next month was an idyllic time for Julie. She put a notice up in the little shopping centre at Langata, asking for temporary accommodation, and was contacted by Doug Morey, whose cottage had been vacated for a couple of months. Julie moved in immediately. It was a simple one-bedroom cottage set in a grassy garden, but Julie loved it. She made firm friends of Morey's three Rhodesian ridgeback dogs and spent a good deal of time just walking around the garden with them. On one occasion, Morey invited her to lunch with Tony Fitzjohn, a wildlife eccentric, who looked and sometimes behaved like Tarzan, and had worked for many years as an assistant to George Adamson, Joy's husband, raising and releasing lions in the wilds of Kenya. Fitzjohn had also started his own programme with leopards and he captivated Julie with his stories. Although she was still inherently shy, Julie found that in the warm, friendly environment of Nairobi it was as easy to make friends as on the journey itself. She spent a great deal of time with a young family who were lodging in a cottage on the Weld Dixon's land. When 'Master Lawrence', as Julie called the son of the family, had a birthday party, Julie was invited to help. She also met up with her old Australian friends, Beth and Murali, and was introduced to Glen Burns and dozens of other people. She spent much of her time ferrying travellers back and forth from the airport in her jeep. Nairobi was such a small town that everywhere she went, she met people she knew. At the same time, it was the most exciting city in the world for a wildlife fanatic. Apart from the giraffe manor and the snake park, there was, just across the road from the Weld Dixons, the house where Daphne Sheldrick was raising baby elephants, baby rhinos and other animal waifs and strays. And Nairobi itself was still surrounded by wild areas filled with animals, both within the Nairobi National Park and in unprotected bush on the Athi plains and in the Ngong hills. Vervet monkeys swung from the trees in Langata, leopards still lived in the Karen forest and on a still night the roaring of lions could be heard from Morey's house. It made her life in Bury St Edmunds seem like a mere shadow of an existence and by the time she set off on her last safari to the Masai Mara, her plans to return to Kenya were already firmly laid. 'She got caught up in a social whirl and loved it,' said

55

JohnWard. 'Plus the weather and her great love of animals. It was a bit of a Shangri-la for her.'

Julie Ward was by no means the first traveller to find 'Shangri-la' in the grandeur and freedom of Kenya. Early descriptions by the explorers and pioneers of East Africa are peppered with references to paradise and God's own land. 'It seemed to me as if Nature were celebrating,' wrote Johann Rebmann, the pioneering German missionary, in 1848. 'A veritable land of Goshen,' recorded Joseph Thomson in *Through Masailand*, published in 1885. 'Everything,' Karen Blixen said, 'was made for greatness and freedom, and unequalled nobility.' And Elspeth Huxley, who arrived in Kenya in 1913, had this to say of Lord Delamere's first view, in 1897, of what became known as the White Highlands: 'Here indeed, he must have thought, was a promised land, the realization of a Rider Haggard dream of a rich and fertile country hidden beyond impenetrable deserts and mountains. Here was a modern Eldorado, waiting only for recognition.'

The landscape of East Africa still retains a good deal of its majesty, but for the earliest adventurers there were unparalleled glories. The golden-sanded coastline, fringed with palm trees and clear shallow waters, was practically untouched for hundreds of miles. Inland, past the arid scrub of the Taru desert, the plains sounded to the beat of the hooves of countless million animals. The profusion of wild beasts and the possibilities for big game hunting inspired many of the early rhapsodies to Kenya. But it was the land beyond, verdant fields rising into the clouds, that played even more joyful tunes on the imagination of the first visitors. Here, on the Mau escarpment and in the Central Highlands, were millions of acres without people but with limitless potential for farming. The land was green, well watered, temperate and looked, to men who had just struggled through the inhospitable deserts of Somalia and the Taru, like a mythic, prelapsarian England of old. Moreover, the climate was always bearable, neither too hot in the dry season nor as cold as at home in the rains, and the skies suspended over the hills, strung with soft, billowing, pastel clouds, were as high and grand as anything they had ever seen.

More astonishing yet, East Africa still remained to be claimed at a time when the world was already becoming a place for tourists rather than explorers and pioneers. The East African coast was known to European sailors from the fifteenth century: Vasco da Gama recorded stopping at Malindi in 1498, just a few years after Colombus reached America. But for three hundred and fifty years, while explorers carved paths through the Americas, central Asia, India, south-east Asia, China and the rest of Africa, East Africa retained its secrets. America, as far from Southampton as Kenya, had been explored, conquered and settled, had fought for its independence, established its constitution and celebrated the two-hundredth anniversary of its premier university, Harvard, before the first white man even set foot in the East African interior. Beyond the lush coastal strip, maps of the imagination peopled the lands with monsters and dragons, mountains of gold and tribes of unquestionable ferocity, not to mention voracity for human flesh. It was not until 1848, the year that safety matches were invented and scientists proved that Saturn's rings were gaseous, that Johann Rebmann became the first white man to see the snows on the summit of Mount Kilimanjaro, less than two hundred miles from Mombasa. (And even then, there were many who disbelieved him. Desborough Cooley, a respected fellow of the Royal Geographical Society, wrote that Rebmann's claims 'have so little of shape and substance, and appear so severed from realities, that they take quite a spectral character.') And it was not until 1858, two hundred and forty-three years after the discovery of the Great Lakes of north America, that John Hanning Speke reached the shores of Lake Victoria, the source of the White Nile.

The Suez Canal, opened in 1869, finally provided a direct sea route to the East African coast and led to a minor boom in East African expeditions. But by the time the first settlers began to arrive in Kenya to take up grants of farmland, it was already the early years of the twentieth century – the age of automobiles, submarines, airplanes and London's heralded underground railway. In 1901, there were just thirteen settlers in Kenya and the three thousand who sailed in over the next decade were ox-wagon pioneers in the age of the Model T Ford. Today, it takes just forty minutes to drive from the Norfolk hotel to Thika; in 1913, when the young Elspeth Huxley travelled by ox-wagon to her new home amid the flame trees, the journey took three days.

This lateness – almost an afterthought to the great age of colonization – with which Europe had come to East Africa, meant that white Kenya was forged with a unique character that remains even today. Britain in the early 1900s was emerging into the modern world, laying down the foundations of our roads, technology and ideas. The farmers, hunters, traders, prospectors and engineers sailed to Kenya to make their fortune and find adventure, as the Empire builders had done in America, India and southern Africa before them. But Kenya offered something more: the promise of escape from the tentacles of modern life and the prospect of an older, simpler, more liberated existence. As John Gunther, the brilliant American journalist who toured Africa in the early 1950s, wrote, 'They wanted to get away from the red tape and petty restrictions of life in England, with its humdrum patterns, and live in a free, spacious country where, by God, every man saluted the Union Jack at sundown. They were not so much interested in farming itself: they wanted "Africa" – its open spaces, the challenge of a frontier, the isolation and remoteness. They were looking not merely for profits, but for Shangri-la.'

The opportunities to build a new life certainly existed. Kenya alone was two-and-a-half times the size of Britain, but had a population of just two million Africans. Everything was plentiful. Hunting was like chopping down weeds: for every zebra or Thomson's gazelle that was shot, two more seemed to appear. The possibilities for farming (despite the real weeds as well as the crop-raiding animals) appeared almost limitless. 'Maize stalks twice the height of a man, huge flag-like leaves of arrowroot, tobacco ten feet high with eighteen-inch leaves,' wrote Herbert Binks, who arrived in Kenya in 1901. And those shrewd enough to set up services for the farmers and hunters found business opportunities as great as any in the American West. Abraham Block, who arrived in Kenya in 1903 with twenty-three pounds in his pocket, was to buy the Norfolk hotel in 1927 for five hundred pounds and a plot of land and start what is now Kenya's biggest chain of tourist hotels and lodges. Of course there were problems – massive, sometimes overpowering problems. East Africa was never as unhealthy as the sweltering swamps of West Africa, but malaria, bilharzia and various hideous worms, amoebas and sores, not to mention the high, equatorial sun, often made life unpleasant. Even more diseases seemed to afflict the crops and livestock imported on to the farms and Lord Delamere, who laid the groundwork for most other farmers, lost a vast fortune in finding the right cattle and seed for Kenya. On the whole, until the Mau Mau uprising of the 1950s, the African 'natives' took the arrival of the white man and the consequent upheaval of their way of life with equanimity, and there were few frontier problems to equal those in North America or Afghanistan. But settlers had to be particularly careful when dealing with the Masai, the proudest and most warlike East African tribe, who inspired as much awe as the Zulu or the Apache. Every now and again there were incidents when a Masai, usually after a disagreement about cows, drove his spear languidly into a European chest. But the troubles merely sorted out the men from the boys: attracting the individuals, the characters and the eccentrics; and defeating the faint-hearted. As Sir Michael Blundell, a farmer who later became a political leader in Kenya, put it: 'When I first arrived in Kenya in 1925, with two tin boxes, a shotgun and one hundred pounds, I lived in a hut with no window, sleeping on a bed made from a wooden frame with hide ropes thrown across it and using wooden boxes for chairs. Every evening I had to go out and shoot my dinner. Only people who could make their own lives and weren't dependent on society could make it. The settlers who stayed were individualists.'

By the time Kenya became a colony, in 1920, cracks were already appearing in the monolith of Empire. The White Man's Country, as Kenya had come to be known, was never going to last, and for those who hankered after a white domain in Africa, Kenya colony was a fool's paradise. But the country did nonetheless promise – as to a lesser extent, to people like Julie Ward, it still does – a taste of Eden, a chance to dream outlandish dreams, to touch, albeit briefly, a little magic. Kenya drew the adventurers, the eccentrics, the dreamers, the lunatics and the lotus eaters. The romantic life of Karen Blixen, Denys Finch Hatton, Beryl Markham, Lord Erroll and Joy Adamson really did exist, if only for a brief, rapidly closing window in time. The bountiful big game drew the world's grandest people, like Teddy Roosevelt, Ernest Hemingway, the Prince of Wales and Clark Gable. And the lifestyle created a Cannes, a Hollywood, a Shanghai in Africa. 'Nairobi', wrote John Gunther, 'is the focus of an international set, mostly British but with other nationalities represented, that lives on froth and cream, leads playful lives in surpassingly beautiful surroundings, avoids taxation at home and has fun shooting lions and sleeping with one another's wives.'

Ordinary, hard-working white Kenyans still fume at the glamorous but degenerate reputation that Happy Valley and this international set gave to Kenya. But East Africa had never attracted, or let in, the dour working men that built up Rhodesia. Even the ordinary farmers were as likely as not to be from good families – old Etonians, honourables, or at the very least individuals, people in search of something more than simply a better standard of life. 'Gentlemen do not go to the toilet after separating from the ladies,' Gunther noted. 'But walk out on to the lawn and in the equatorial darkness stand in a row, facing a hedge or garden wall, and there relieve themselves, while murmuring a low toast, "To Africa".' Even through Mau Mau, the violent Kikuyu uprising in the 1950s, in which dozens of whites (and thousands of their black servants) were horribly hacked to death, this slightly sun-loosened, do-or-die Kenyan eccentricity remained. 'I saw a Kuke jump off the train as it was pulling into the station this morning. I pulled out my gun and called "Halt!" and damn it all, the fellow halted. I could have bagged him easily,' was a typical dinnertime story. In 1963, when the winds of change gave Kenya its independence, many white Kenyans left for Rhodesia or Australia. But reassured by the wily Jomo Kenyatta, Kenya's first president – 'All of us, white, brown, black, can work together to make this country great' – the best of the white Kenyans, the most rugged and least racist, stayed.

Kenya today is unquestionably an African country. Its population has swollen to more than twenty million, of whom ninety-nine per cent are black. The farms in the White Highlands are now owned and farmed by Africans. Delamere Avenue is now Kenyatta Avenue, Princess Elizabeth Way has become Uhuru (freedom) Highway and Whitehouse Road has been renamed after Ethiopia's Emperor Haile Selassie. Kenya's president, Daniel arap Moi, a former schoolteacher, is a leader very much in the African mould: a chief beyond criticism, ruling by dictate, more comfortable speaking Swahili than English, his photograph hanging in every office and shop. The government's and people's values also differ dramatically from the romantic outlook of the whites. Kenya's population is growing at more than four per cent a year, the fastest rate in the world. The government wants to build more factories, extend the farmland, open more schools and health clinics, lay down new roads and expand the tourist industry. Although the whites do not object to such necessary development – and indeed profit by much of it, working as engineers, hotel managers and farmers – they reflect wistfully on the creation of an expanding African state bringing the inevitable erosion of the land and lifestyle that drew their parents and grandparents to the wide open spaces of East Africa. Shipwrecked sailors, John Heminway called white Africans, in his book *No Man's Land*, their passion for the sea in danger of turning into cynicism.

A few islands of Kenyan 'Society' still remain. The Ngong

races, held on Sunday afternoons during the dry season, still bring out the white ladies and gentlemen, in their hats, blazers and best frocks. The committee of the Muthaiga Club, the settlers meeting place, was composed, when Julie was living in Nairobi, of nine whites, two blacks and one Asian, although, as Sir Charles Markham, chairman of the club, pointed out, the class of member was not what it once was. 'I doubt if three-quarters of the members elected today would have been eligible in 1955. But if you were to expect every member to have been at Eton or Harrow, or in the Cavalry or Guards, it would be unrealistic.' But the majority of whites in Kenya have quietly adapted to life in an African-run country. There are dozens of tribes in Kenya, each with their own language, customs, tradition and beliefs, and the whites have simply become another tribe. They live in areas, such as Karen and Langata in Nairobi, or Kilifi on the coast, that are now almost accepted as white homelands. A phrase like 'Karen boys' is as much a tribal classification as 'Kiambu Kikuyu', defining type, background and outlook. They have their own meeting places – the Karen Club, the Flying Club, Muthaiga – and a friendly, if gossip-filled, social life. Every white Kenyan knows every other white Kenyan and anyone on the edge of this society, like Julie Ward, can quickly become absorbed. The white tribe even has its own dialect, English peppered with Swahili words, like *duka* (shop), *chunga* (look after), *dawa* (medicine), *kali* (hot, wicked, fiery) and *funga* (shut), as in 'funga the door, will you'. The life is on the whole exceptionally comfortable. Although prices are rising, land and houses are far cheaper than in provincial towns in England. When Julie was in Langata, good land a couple of miles away, directly adjoining the national park, with views of giraffe and the occasional lion, could be had for two or three thousand pounds an acre. Plots in Karen and Langata, where ordinary middle-class white families, not particularly wealthy by British standards, have built their houses, are a minimum of five acres. And every house has servants, on wages of thirty or forty pounds a month, cooking, cleaning, washing clothes, gardening, guarding. Kenya's economy is healthy enough that most foreign goods are available in Nairobi, from Marmite to compact-disc players to the *Daily Telegraph*. Attitudes and politics are remarkably coherent within the tribe. Most white Kenyans are firmly conservative, gently prejudiced and in many ways keenly suburban, concerned with manners, hospitality and, while there are hardly enough whites to define this, class.

Equatorial Ealing, as James Cameron put it, is however only one side of white Kenya. For a start, many white Kenyans live not in Nairobi, but alongside airstrips in the bush. Black Kenya is moving steadily into the towns and cities, eyes fixed on apartment buildings, shopping centres, material goods, televisions, videos, telephones, Mercedes Benzes and pop culture. Many whites have therefore found their niche living in the bush, dreaming up projects and taking the jobs that send them in the opposite direction to most blacks: into the wilderness; back to the past. The few remaining white farmers, mostly up around Nanyuki, in the shadow of Mount Kenya, cling to their land and lifestyles. Others have become managers of the huge cattle ranches on Laikipia or Galana, living amid millions of acres of thorn scrub. Whites dominate the flying business in Kenya, usually based in Nairobi, flying out each day into the bush, taking tourists to lodges or tracking elephant herds to protect them from poachers. The great saviour for the whites has been the tourist business and at least a quarter of the three or four thousand white Kenyan families make their living from tourism. The days of the great white hunter, leading his clients by foot on month-long treks in search of that huge tusker or black-maned lion, are over, though a few Kenyans run hunting safaris in Tanzania. But the luxury photographic safari guides are all white naturalists, experts at finding game, identifying birds and catching snakes with their bare hands when they wriggle into camp. The whites run walking safaris, gorilla safaris, bird safaris, even insect safaris. They build and manage lodges. They run private game ranches, protecting rare herds of rhino or bongo. Kenya's tiny white community still has its share of adventurers, geniuses and lunatics. Richard Leakey, based on the shores of Lake Turkana, a stunning but barren land, turned himself into a world-famous palaeontologist by the age of twenty-five. His friend, Alan Root, survivor of bites from a leopard, a puff adder, a gorilla and a hippopotamus, has with productions such as 'Year of the Wildebeest' and 'Castles of Clay', about the secret life of the termite, proven himself to be the best wildlife film-maker in the world. (He is also one of Kenya's best wits: describing being chomped by the hippo, which grabbed him while he was filming in the clear Mzima springs in Tsavo National Park and shook him to within a shake of his life, as like being hit by an 'E-type marshmallow'.) When Julie was in Nairobi, George Adamson, then eighty-two, had just been given two more orphan lions and had started raising them with plans to release them into the wild in Kora reserve, where he had been living, in open wooden shacks, with elephant skulls as toilet seats, for the past two decades. Up in Maralal, west of Kora, Wilfred Thesiger, the last great British explorer and a great critic of Adamson ('Ridiculous idea to release tame lions. Of course they're going to jump on someone. In their nature. Shot more than a hundred myself.'), was living in a mud hut, dressing each morning in tweed jacket, creased trousers and brogues from Jermyn Street. Across Magadi Road from the Weld Dixons' house, when Julie was staying there, Daphne Sheldrick, whose adopted animals made Noah's Ark seem like a second-rate zoo, had finally worked out how to keep the very youngest orphaned elephants alive and was raising two, Oljori and Olmeg, feeding them every four hours, night and day, for their first year.

Life in Britain, controlled by technology, government, strictly enforced laws and a developed culture, springs few surprises. Most people can reasonably expect to live out their three score and ten years. But in Africa, the individual is offered far less protection against the environment. On average, diseases carry off at least one child in every family and often the mother or father as well. Malaria, a foreign horror to most Britons, kills one million Africans every year. Bilharzia affects almost half the continent's population. Practically everyone has worms. The climate is on the whole as predictable as elsewhere, but when it springs surprises they can be catastrophic. Floods and droughts kill thousands of Africans every year. Lightning accounts for a couple of dozen people on the shores of Lake Victoria each rainy season. And all over Kenya, even in Nairobi, people share the land with potentially deadly wild animals. In 1988, a hippo emerged from a sewage tank on the outskirts of Nairobi, where it had been wallowing, and attacked a passing cyclist. A year later, a lion wandered into Harambee housing estate in Nairobi and had to be trapped by the wildlife department. Shortly afterwards, another lion was discovered in a school playground. In Maralal, a hyena came across a secret stash of illegal alcohol, drank it all and then attacked four local people before it was finally shot. Every year, hundreds of people are killed and thousands wounded by lions, leopard, elephant, buffalo, rhino, crocodiles, hippos and snakes. In the last week of January 1990, for instance, the following instances were reported in the *Nation* newspaper alone. On Thursday 25 January 1990, a man on his way home from a funeral in Taita was killed by an elephant. Two days later, one hundred and thirty-two sheep were slaughtered by a leopard. The following Monday, a lion broke into an enclosure in Lamu and slapped and bit fifteen cows to death. The same day, a rogue elephant destroyed a house in Shimba. On the Tuesday, five men were mauled by a leopard they had cornered in Kiambu. And finally, on Wednesday 31 January, a man was gored by a buffalo in Nyaharuru. Many more cases, of children taken by crocodiles, Masai herdsmen mauled by lions, drunks trampled by buffalo and people bitten by puff adders, cobras and mambas, go unreported.

To many Africans, the hardships of nature are a sign that their country has not developed enough and there are regular complaints about lightning, lions and leprosy in parliament. White Kenyans have no love for diseases, but the wildness of the weather and the presence of dangerous animals is part of the pleasure and excitement of living in Africa. Days in Africa are lived more fully, under the high sun, amid the wild animals, than in cold, grey, dreary, concrete England. Many young Kenyans actually collect snakes and sneak away from family picnics to follow lion tracks. The fact that leopards still live in the Karen forest and occasionally take family dogs is a matter of pride. White Kenyans, like the tourists, thrill at the sound of hippos plodding through their campsite at night, or lions roaring in the dark. Life in Kenya is closer to the edge, nearer to danger, and so enjoyed all the more.

Many white Kenyans, in their jobs or simply for pleasure, positively seek out potentially dangerous situations, and most have themselves had a run-in with some kind of wild animal, or at least are related to someone who has. They relish telling stories about being 'chewed on' by a lion or 'hammered' by a buffalo. The recent records of the Flying Doctors, who fly many of the Kenyans and tourists injured or killed by animals back to Nairobi, make sobering reading. The Scandinavian diplomat's wife, attacked by a lion while fishing in the Aberdares. She threw her baby into a bush and was saved only when her husband drove the car straight at her and the lion, which was mauling her legs. The white Kenyan girl, on a walking safari through Tsavo, who dangled her legs into the Galana river and was grabbed by a crocodile. A friend held on to her arms until a ranger could shoot the crocodile, which was pulling from the other end. The seventeen-year-old amateur snake collector who died after being bitten by a puff adder. The retired hunter, protecting an over-eager film-crew from an angry mother rhinoceros, who was tossed, while the film was rolling, ten feet into the air and then trampled on for good measure. When he was in Nairobi hospital, having miraculously survived, the hunter made friends with two injured tourists, one also tossed by a rhino, the other bitten by a hippo. The British army officer, drunk after a party at a lodge in Samburu, who lay down for a nap and woke up with his head and arm in a crocodile's mouth. The lodge manager heard his screams and beat off the crocodile with a torch. The young boy, on a camping safari, bitten repeatedly on the head by a puff adder, dead before help could arrive.

Mark Jenkins, the nephew of Daphne Sheldrick, the woman who ran the elephant orphanage near the Weld Dixons' house on Magadi road, was just two years old when one of George and

Joy Adamson's lions, Boy, nearly killed him. Mark was sitting in a jeep between his two parents when Boy stood up against the car, reached in and grabbed at Mark. Just in time, the little boy raised his arm over his head and the lion's jaws closed over his arm and his head. Only the quick action of Mark's father, Peter Jenkins, the warden of Meru, in gunning the engine and driving away, dragging Boy with them until he let go, saved Mark's life. Even so, Mark was seriously hurt by the sharp teeth of the lion.

4

An Unmurderable Girl

In the days following the discovery of Julie's remains, the blame for her death was laid squarely on the jaws of some roving lion, leopard or pack of hyenas. A few years earlier, two tourists had been gored to death by buffalo in separate incidents in the Masai Mara, one of them while sneaking behind the tent for an illicit rendezvous with another man's wife. Leopard and lions especially had occasionally killed and eaten young Masai herdboys on the outskirts of the reserve. Now, it seemed, the Mara's carnivores had finally notched up their first tourist.

On Friday 16 September, three days after the remains were found, rumours that a British tourist had been killed in the Mara reached the Foreign Press Centre in Nairobi. Journalists calling the Kenyan police were informed that the reports were true and that the young woman must have been caught and eaten by wild animals. On Saturday, Sir John Johnson, the British High Commissioner, told Reuters news agency that the girl, Julie Anne Ward, had been set upon by wild animals after leaving her car to seek help. 'There is really nothing more to the case,' he concluded. The story circulating around the white Kenyan community in Nairobi, spread by the pilots and spotters who had taken part in the search, also portrayed lions or leopard as the villains. The general assumption was that after Julie had left Sand River camp on the Tuesday afternoon, she had taken a diversion off the main road, probably to follow an animal she wanted to photograph. While crossing a small riverbed, her car had sunk into a patch of mud and without its four-wheel drive shaft it had stuck fast. Mud on a jack found in the car and splattered along the sides of the jeep suggested she had tried to free the vehicle. When this failed, she had at first sensibly stayed with the car. After hearing aircraft landing at Keekorok, she had painted SOS on the roof in mud. She had also set some plastic on fire, perhaps as an intended signal. Finally, tired of waiting, she had stuffed various possessions into a shoulder bag and set out to find help. Unfortunately, she had walked in the worst possible direction: away from roads, camps and lodges. By nightfall, she had still not found anyone and had climbed a tree to escape the attentions of wild animals. She had also lit another fire, apparently using some of her clothes and possessions. Alone, frightened and far from habitation, she had huddled in the tree or around the fire until some creature had stumbled across her and savagely killed her.

Some people in Kenya compared Julie's story to the death of a young American woman working at a wildlife research station in Amboseli National Park, south-east of the Masai Mara, fifteen years earlier. Just like Julie Ward, the young woman, Melanie Fuller, had disappeared and her remains, a skull and bits of hair and clothes, had been found some time later, scattered across the bush. At the time of her death, Fuller had been due to go on safari, so the fact that she was absent was not noted for some time. When a search party was finally assembled and her fate was discovered, not enough of her body remained to reveal the cause of her death. Although doubts remained, lions were generally given the blame. Dr Jonah Western, her research supervisor, later told the story as he had seen it: 'One of the rangers found her skull, which was still intact. I was later that week to find her hair, safari clothes, and books. The evidence of scattered books, a few baked tracks and the damage to her clothes [suggested] that she was killed by a lion grasping her neck, but such details are speculation.'

Some of the search party, such as Andy Stepanowich and Sebastian Tham knew, however, that part at least of Julie's body had been severely burned as well as dismembered. While John Ward had sat alone with his bottle of whisky at Keekorok lodge on the Tuesday night after the search, Tham and Stepanowich had mulled over the strange assembly of facts and come up with a possible, though far-fetched, explanation for the charring on the remains. A few days later, both men were interviewed by a Nairobi-based journalist, who wrote up their theories for the *Daily Telegraph*. When it had grown dark and the sounds of the African night had closed in, the article speculated, Julie might have been frightened enough to set fire to her sleeping bag, which she had presumably carried with her, or even her entire backpack. Certainly many of her possessions were found burned in the ashes. 'She was panicked, scared, who knows her emotions,' said Stepanowich. 'If she had lit the sleeping bag and inhaled the fumes, she would have been knocked out in seconds. In air accidents, fumes from the seats are the quickest cause of death.' Alternatively, Julie might have trodden on a snake, possibly a puff adder – a deadly reptile notorious for curling up near the warmth of fires. Either way, she could have toppled unconscious into the fire and been partially burned as she died. The following morning, with the fire cold, hyenas and other scavengers would have moved in, tearing her body apart and scattering the remains over a large area. Julie's death, the *Telegraph* concluded, was a 'story of tragic bad luck'.

Back in Bury St Edmunds, the grieving Ward family read this and other newspaper articles with growing dismay. 'It seemed as though they were writing about someone we didn't know,' Jan Ward said. 'We would read a theory and scream, "She wouldn't do that." She was a sensible girl and she just wouldn't leave her car. You're told to stay with your car and Julie knew that.' Moreover, the Wards were by no means sold on the theory that Julie had been killed by animals. 'Julie was a super kid,' John Ward was to say. 'She was a very kind girl, she had no temper, she never got into arguments, she was always happy. In fact my wife said she was probably the most unmurderable girl in the world. You just can't imagine anyone wanting to kill her.' But that, by now, was exactly what Julie's grieving family were imagining. His daughter, John Ward was convinced, had been brutally murdered.

Sand River campsite

Inset: Julie Ward's Suzuki jeep sitting outside Sebastian Tham's office at Wilson Airport in 1990

David Weston, the balloon pilot, who waved goodbye to Julie from
Serena lodge on the day she disappeared

Paul Weld Dixon, in whose garden Julie camped when she first arrived in Nairobi

Dr Adel Youssef Shaker, the police pathologist

John Ward

Jan Ward

The idea had first begun to crystallize through Ward's tears of grief while he had been collecting his daughter's burned and dismembered remains. 'At first, I had no reason to suspect anything sinister,' Ward recalled. 'But when Police Inspector Othiambo didn't collect the remains I began to think. Their reaction was to kick them, quite literally, under a bush and forget about them.' As he had stood in sorrowing silence in the dying afternoon light in the Masai Mara, nagging questions swirled through Ward's mind. Why, he kept asking himself, had Julie left her map of the Mara and her binoculars – but not a note – in the jeep? Where was her precious camera and telephoto lens? Why would she have walked in the one direction that led her away from help? And, most significantly, how had his daughter's leg come to be burned? Ward had seen the remains of the leg and despite the horror of the situation he had noticed that the charring on the leg was at the surface of the skin and wounds. That surely meant, Ward pondered over the subsequent days, that the burning had taken place after the leg had been severed from the rest of the body. However Julie had died, it was impossible that animals could have torn her apart and then dropped bits of her on to a flaming fire. Of all the creatures in the Masai Mara, only humans would act in such a way.

Before long, John Ward was to have more authoritative evidence to support this premise. On Wednesday 14 September, the day Ward flew back to England, Julie's remains had been driven up from Narok police station to Nairobi. The following day, because John Ward was absent, Paul Weld Dixon was asked to visit the Nairobi city mortuary to make a formal identification of Julie and her possessions. The police pathologist, Dr Adel Youssef Shaker, showed him the leg and the two parts of the lower jaw bone. Weld Dixon also examined various items found in and around the fire – a scrap of towel, sunglasses, a cheap knife and spoon, two charred film cassettes, a tin mug, a metal bowl, some coins, a pair of flip-flops and a chunk of hair. Weld Dixon was unable to identify Julie from such meagre remains, saying only that he thought the leg and flip-flops were about her size. Normally, Weld Dixon would then have been thanked and asked to leave. But on this occasion no objection was made to his staying while Shaker continued to examine the leg and jawbone. Before long, Shaker picked up the leg and said, 'This limb has been severed with a sharp instrument.' He then lifted up the segments of jawbone and said, 'This jawbone has been anatomically dissected.' The wounds were cleanly cut, inflicted almost certainly by a man-made, metal instrument. Finally Shaker turned to Weld Dixon and told him that the only conclusion to draw from the remains in front of them was that it was 'a case of murder'. After leaving the city mortuary, Weld Dixon went straight to the British High Commission to report these extraordinary findings. The next day, Friday 16 September, Ward received a telephone call from a Foreign Office official in London named Nigel Wickes. The initial post mortem findings suggested, Ward was told, that his daughter had indeed been murdered.

By the weekend after the recovery of Julie's remains, Saxonville, the Ward house in Brockley, was being besieged by journalists chasing the story of the mysterious death of a pretty, young woman in the African bush. Photographers tried to sneak into the house and laid ambushes on the road to Saxonville. Jan Ward had to drive around the village a couple of times before the press temporarily withdrew and she managed to reach the safety of her home. The telephone rang almost every minute. 'You can't believe this is happening to your family,' said Jan Ward. 'It was all so unreal, all wrong.' Eventually, John Ward decided to call in a security company to keep out the press and answer the telephone. At the same time, he made up his mind to speak to the journalists. He thought a statement might satisfy them, but he also wanted to make it clear that Julie had been murdered and was 'not just a silly girl who wandered off the track and was eaten by animals'.

Ward began his statement by relating how he had come to hear that his daughter was missing and how he had immediately flown out to Kenya to look for her. 'After an intensive search, her jeep was found abandoned where it had become stuck in a small gully,' he said. 'She had marked a large SOS on the roof and lit several signal fires. Unfortunately, they were not seen. It is not known how long Julie stayed with the vehicle before leaving to walk to find help. I was the first to reach the jeep and it is clear she had taken food and water for the hike to safety. Stories that she was eaten by lions are totally untrue. Her body had been burned and I believe she was murdered. I have no idea who might have done it. There are game poachers in the area but a lot of other people go there as well.' Ward's comments were widely reported in the British press, but despite the findings of the post mortem, the news from Kenya continued to suggest that Julie had been killed by lions. Philip Kilonzo, the Kenyan Commissioner of Police, said several days after the post mortem that it seemed Julie had been killed by wild animals. And even after hearing from Paul Weld Dixon about the pathologist's findings during the initial post mortem, the British High Commission continued to inform journalists that Julie's killer must have been a lion or some such creature. By Tuesday 20 September, John Ward had heard enough and he decided to return to Kenya to find out why both the Kenyan and British authorities were being so unforthcoming about his daughter's murder.

Accompanied by Frank Ribeiro, a director of Butterfly Hotels and a family friend, Ward arrived in Nairobi the following morning, Wednesday 21 September. They were met at the airport by Jenny Jenkins and a security officer from the British High Commission and were taken to the offices of the High Commission in central Nairobi. There, Ward met Sir John Johnson, who now seemed to have been briefed about the post mortem findings, and John Ferguson, the acting First Secretary Consular. The High Commission staff were clearly keen to prevent Julie's death becoming a major diplomatic incident, but it was also obvious that they would not be able to ignore John Ward. By the time Ward arrived at the High Commission, Ferguson had already organized a meeting for later that morning with Dr Shaker, the pathologist. Two days earlier, Ferguson had personally visited the mortuary and handed over Julie's dental records to Dr Shaker. The pathologist had taken just five minutes to identify Julie, comparing the dental records with the teeth still attached to the two pieces of jawbone. He had then reiterated to Ferguson that Julie had not been killed by animals and promised him a copy of the post mortem report. When the meeting at the High Commission finished, Ferguson took Ward and Ribeiro over to the city mortuary. After a few moments, Shaker appeared. An Egyptian Coptic Christian who had left his home country because he felt persecuted by the Moslem authorities, Shaker was a talkative, puppyish man with a wide-cheeked, pock-marked face. He had been in Kenya for only a few months, working as a police pathologist and running his own clinic in the Coptic Centre, just up the Ngong Road, in the evenings. Shaker produced the pieces of jawbone and fitted them neatly together. He said the bone appeared to have been cut cleanly in two. One of the two front teeth was missing, presumably broken off by the blow which had severed the jaw, but its root still remained in the bone. He also said that the jaw and leg had probably been cut by a *panga*, the Kenyan name for a machete. And, moreover, Shaker confirmed Ward's own suspicion that the lower leg had been burned subsequent to the injury. Julie had, it seemed, been chopped up and then tossed on to a fire. All this, Shaker concluded, meant that Julie had been murdered.

Ferguson asked whether they could take a copy of the post mortem, but Shaker said it was not yet ready. He wanted to type it himself and had not yet had time to do so. He promised to complete the report that afternoon and Ferguson said they would return at four to collect it. As they were leaving the mortuary, Ward and his companions saw a man walk up to Shaker and introduce himself as a police officer. They heard the policeman ask for a copy of the post mortem report and saw Shaker hurrying off, promising for a second time to type it up as soon as possible.

From the moment Ward had arrived in Kenya, he had been highly critical of what he had seen of the Kenyan police. For several days now, he had also been harbouring frustrations over the police's apparent refusal to announce a full murder investigation into his daughter's death. Before leaving England, Ward had told Neil Darbyshire of the *Daily Telegraph* that he had not been 'too impressed' by the police search for Julie and voiced his concern that 'this thing is not allowed to slide. Kenya is a country that relies very heavily on tourism and there may be a temptation to look the other way.' He then promised, with the conviction of a successful businessman, that 'if there is a man out there who killed my daughter, I want him.' After leaving the mortuary, Ward returned to the Intercontinental hotel, where he was staying, for lunch, and there spoke briefly with Emma Lee-Potter of the *Evening Standard*. 'I don't know why they are persisting with the claim that Julie was eaten by wild animals,' he told her. That afternoon, Ward would have a chance to find out why. Ferguson had arranged an appointment with Philip Kilonzo, Kenya's Commissioner of Police, and after lunch the three men drove over to police headquarters. With days of anguish and frustration boiling inside him, Ward was ready to confront Philip Kilonzo. It had also been a trying time for the commissioner. Like Ward, Kilonzo was a strong-minded man who disliked being pushed around or told what to think and for the past few days he had been hounded by the forceful British press and had seen numerous British newspaper articles, some of them quoting John Ward, questioning his judgment and the work of his men. Nevertheless, Kilonzo was a well-educated and intelligent man, and had not reached his powerful position without a natural gift for diplomacy. When his visitors entered his office, Kilonzo calmly welcomed them and offered his condolences to John Ward.

Ward lost little time in asking his key question. Why, despite the findings of the police pathologist, had a murder investigation not been launched? In fact, that very day, Kilonzo had appointed a senior detective from the Criminal Investigations Department, Superintendent Muchiri Wanjau, to open an investigation into the suspicious death of Julie Ward and had sent him down to the Masai Mara to take over from the local police. But Kilonzo was cautious – for one thing, he was aware that his words to Ward could well appear the next day in the

British newspapers – and he explained that he would prefer not to announce a murder investigation for fear of sending the perpetrator into hiding. He had, though, already informed the press, some of whose representatives were gathered at that very moment in his waiting room, that murder had not been ruled out. He said that he was aware of the post mortem report and that he intended to talk to the police pathologist later that day. He then reassured Ward that a thorough and meticulous police investigation of all the clues and facts was already taking place. Ward then asked Kilonzo if he was aware that it had been himself, and not the police, who had insisted on collecting Julie's remains at the site where they had been found. Kilonzo replied that he knew nothing of this. Finally, Ward asked the commissioner for permission to return to the Masai Mara to collect the remains of the ashes of Julie's body, which he intended to cremate along with the leg and jawbones. Kilonzo readily agreed to Ward's request. It was all very puzzling, he told Ward. While poachers and bandits occasionally frequented the reserve, such people would have been far more likely to shoot and leave their victims rather than cut them up and burn them. Nevertheless, Kilonzo reassured the worried father, the culprit or culprits would be apprehended. 'The police have a strong track record in solving crimes like these,' the commissioner said.

One hundred years earlier, few people, whether European or African, would have doubted for a moment that the most heinous crimes could have been committed in Masailand. The Masai, whose lands stretched from deep into what is now Tanzania to further north than Nairobi, had a reputation for murder and cruelty to equal the Zulus in southern Africa or the Apache in the American West. Henry Morton Stanley, the journalist-explorer and finder of David Livingstone, who had travelled the entire breadth of Africa, had written: 'I do not know in all my list of travels where you could become martyrs so quickly as in Masai.' For decades, the notorious ferocity of the Masai had persuaded European explorers to avoid their lands, and when one early German adventurer, Dr Gustav Fischer, did venture into Masailand, he was soon attacked and lost several of his men before narrowly escaping with his life. A few years later, a British trader, Andrew Dick, came across the results of a Masai raid on a British food caravan: more than five hundred porters were found speared to death. Indignant, Dick took the case up with the local Masai, and received a fatal spear through the chest for his pains.

In reality, though, such shedding of white blood was rare in East Africa. The British took possession of Kenya, during the latter part of the nineteenth century and the early years of the twentieth, with little resistance from the local people. Unlike the American Indians, who fought back against the white invasion of their lands, the East African tribes gave way to the power of the gun and the inevitability of the changes brought so rapidly to their lands. Even the earliest settlers soon felt as safe, from people if not animals, as they would have done in the English countryside. Young children were allowed to ride horses for miles away from their homes, as long as they were accompanied by syces, or grooms. There was almost an aura of untouchability surrounding the European community and the only notorious murder of a white man in Kenya during the first half of the century was the killing of Lord Erroll, which was almost certainly carried out by another white man.

It was not until the Mau Mau uprising, in the 1950s, that this aura of white invincibility was broken. Mau Mau was the first serious rebellion against white rule in Africa, the first stirring of a brutal violence that was to be repeated later in countries such as the Belgian Congo and Angola. Many thousands of Africans died during Mau Mau, most of them killed for suspected loyalties to white families. But a few dozen Europeans were also brutally chopped to pieces. And while, miraculously, the wounds of Mau Mau were healed during the process of independence, with white and black living on in Kenya in relative peace, the Europeans were never to regain the exaggerated level of respect they had enjoyed for the first half of the century. Even so, when, twenty years after independence, President Moi instituted a drive to replace whites with blacks in government jobs, there was no public backlash against the Europeans (that dishonour was reserved for the Indian population in Kenya). It was rather that, simply, white residents and tourists were now targets for crime like any other wealthy people in a country where the average monthly wage was about the same as the price of a night at a good beach hotel. On the whole, Kenya remained a reasonably safe tourist destination. A tourist was probably less likely to be killed or injured on safari in a Kenyan game park than on a skiing holiday in the French Alps or walking through New York city. But in Kenya in the 1980s there was no discrimination: a white was now just as likely, or unlikely, as a black to end up robbed and, if unlucky, dead.

In the years after independence, one murder in particular demonstrated this. On the evening of 3 January 1980, Joy Adamson, the sixty-nine-year-old author of *Born Free*, failed to return home from her evening walk in Shaba game reserve in Kenya. A colleague drove out to look for her and found her in the beams of his headlights, lying dead in a pool of blood on the road. There were deep wounds on Joy's chest, head and arm, and at first it was assumed that she had been killed by a lion which was known to live in the area. The 5 January edition of the *Daily Telegraph* reported that Joy 'had been watching a lion stalking buffalo at dusk when the lion suddenly turned on her.' A search was started to find the 'killer lion', but before Joy was cremated a post mortem was carried out. One of the doctors to examine Joy was Dr Geoffrey Timms, who had also been involved in the investigation into the death of Lord Erroll. Dr Timms and his colleague soon realized that Joy had not been killed by lions but murdered, almost certainly with a 'simi', a short stabbing knife used by some tribes in Kenya. A few weeks earlier, Joy had fired a young Turkana named Paul Ekai, whom she suspected of stealing money. Ekai had been very unhappy about the loss of his job, and when questioned, he confessed to the murder. He later retracted this confession, but was tried and found guilty of the murder of Joy Adamson, and jailed for life. Joy Adamson's had been a casual murder clearly unaffected by any taboos about killing whites. But at the same time, such incidents were rare.

Eight days after John Ward had found his daughter's remains he was still struggling to come to terms with the tragedy. In normal circumstances, a bereaved family has time after the death to grieve. But from the moment Ward had flown out to Kenya he had scarcely had a peaceful hour to stop and think. A good deal of his anger and energy was directed at the Kenyan authorities. 'Kilonzo doesn't want to commit himself,' he told a small group of journalists later that evening, at the Intercontinental hotel. 'He is still putting around the story that she wandered off the track and was eaten by lions.' Sitting in the bar, a drink in his hand, Ward's conversation was full of wry smiles and acidic comments. He had read all the press reports and reserved particular criticism for each journalist. But from time to time his apparent good humour would be interrupted by moments of anguish and he would slump heavily back in his chair, his face revealing pangs of heart-rending memories. 'I am determined to catch the bastard,' he said at one point. 'Though in some ways perhaps it was better that she was murdered, if she was killed quickly. The thought of her wandering off the track and getting eaten by lions is much worse.' He revealed that Shaker reckoned Julie had died some time on the Monday before her remains were found, after Ward had arrived in the country and begun his search. Perhaps his aircraft flying overhead had even precipitated the killing. 'If I had come over here a bit quicker,' he mused, 'I'd have saved her. But I didn't know.' He then said he was planning to bury Julie's remains in Kenya. 'She was very happy here for the last month of her life and had lots of friends.'

Earlier that evening, Ward had, with Ferguson and Ribeiro, visited Shaker's clinic on the Ngong road to collect the post mortem report. When they arrived, Shaker was sitting behind his table. Ward asked if he had a copy of the report. Shaker replied that he had typed it up that afternoon, as promised, but the original and all the copies had been taken by the policeman.

Ferguson said surely Shaker had kept one file copy. 'No,' Shaker had said, sadly. 'All the copies are gone.' Nevertheless, Ward was determined to release the findings of Shaker's post mortem. He intended to cremate Julie's remains on the Friday and before he left Kenya he wanted to be sure that the police had embarked on a full-scale murder investigation. Media coverage could only help this, he thought, and he therefore decided to hold a press conference. The next morning, at ten-thirty, on Thursday 22 September, several dozen local and foreign journalists arrived at the Intercontinental hotel. Flanked by a severe-looking John Ferguson, who was clearly uncomfortable and refused to talk to the journalists, Ward outlined the evidence which he said proved that his daughter had been murdered. 'The pathologist found sharp cuts on the leg and the jawbone,' Ward said. 'He also found that the leg had been cut and subsequently burned. You can't get more conclusive evidence than that.' Despite his unsatisfactory conversation with Kilonzo, Ward also said that a murder investigation had 'definitely been opened'.

This press conference was to prove essential to Ward's cause, although not quite in the way he had expected. That evening, as Ward and Ribeiro were eating at the Carnivore, a restaurant on the outskirts of Nairobi which serves a variety of exotic meat, such as giraffe, zebra and Thomson's gazelle, they were given some disturbing information. Earlier that day, prompted by Ward's statements, a British reporter had telephoned the city mortuary and spoken to Dr Shaker, who was friendly and helpful on the phone and promised to give the reporter a copy of the post mortem report. At four o'clock, the reporter arrived at the Coptic clinic for his appointment with Shaker. He waited until six o'clock, when the Egyptian finally arrived. In contrast to his mood on the telephone, Shaker was now distinctly unfriendly. He told the reporter that he could say nothing about the case. When pressed, he muttered that what Ward had said at the press conference was not necessarily true. He could not say for sure that the remains had been cut with a sharp instrument – the wounds could have been inflicted by animals. 'More tests need to be done, more evidence is needed,' he said. Ward's suspicions, aroused by the disappearance of Shaker's report, were further fired by this news. Before they had finished their meal, Ward and Ribeiro decided to cancel the next morning's trip to the Masai Mara to collect the rest of Julie's ashes and postpone the cremation, set for the same afternoon. John Ward wanted to find out 'what the hell was going on.'

Early the next morning, Friday 23 September, John Ferguson informed Ward that a copy of the post mortem report would be ready in the afternoon. Ward and Ribeiro waited impatiently until two o'clock, when they walked over to the British High Commission and there read the report. Typed over three pages, its findings were similar to the conclusions Shaker had given by word of mouth to Ward and Ferguson. But there were several crucial differences. Firstly, in the middle of a passage on the second page referring to the leg, the words 'cleanly cut' had been deleted, with each letter typed over with an 'x'. In their place had been typed the word 'torn'. Next, in a passage describing the wounds to the jaw, the words 'cleanly cut' had been replaced by the word 'cracked'. Finally, on the third page, the cause of death had been changed from 'sharp injuries' to 'blunt injuries', although the words 'with subsequent burning' had been left unaltered. Ward, Ferguson and Ribeiro were amazed. The report had obviously – and amateurishly – been changed to suggest that animals rather than humans had been responsible for Julie's death. There was only one thing to do: go and see Shaker. At the mortuary, Shaker seemed, as he had done with the journalist the previous night, a nervous wreck. He had entirely lost the friendly confidence with which he had explained his conclusions to Ward and would now not even look his visitors in the eye. Ward fired questions at him. Why had the report been altered? What about the initial findings? What did 'cracked' and 'torn' mean? What then could be made of the 'subsequent burning'? Sullenly, Shaker refused to answer any of these questions, though he eventually muttered that the alterations had been made by Dr Jason Kaviti, the chief police pathologist, and he suggested that they go to his office at Kenyatta Hospital. Ward and his companions agreed and, dragging Shaker along, they drove over to the hospital and demanded to see Kaviti. Before long, they were shown into the chief pathologist's office. He was a small, well-spoken man with a distinguished face and greying hair. But he too appeared nervous and worried by this intrusion. He had presided over thousands of post mortems, quite a few of them controversial, and never before had the relatives of the deceased stormed into his office. Bristling, Kaviti said that he had chanced upon the report in the typewriter at the mortuary the day before and had read Shaker's conclusions. He explained that as Shaker's English was not perfect, he had realized that the Egyptian had meant blunt injuries, cracks and tears instead of sharp injuries and clean cuts. As a result, he had made the alterations himself. Ward and Ferguson were dumbfounded, but within a few seconds Ward turned towards Kaviti, his face red with anger and his voice heavy with irony.

'Do you make a practice of altering your pathologists' reports?' Ward demanded.

'I am the chief police pathologist and I am entitled to alter any of my subordinates' reports,' Kaviti replied.

'How many other of Shaker's reports have you altered?' Ward said. 'How many post mortems has Shaker carried out?'

Kaviti said nothing, so Ward turned to Shaker and repeated his questions. Shaker said he had performed at least one hundred post mortems and this was the first time one had been altered. At this point, Ferguson quietly intervened. He said that since Kaviti had altered the report he would surely be willing to initial the alterations. To their surprise, Kaviti agreed. He signed and dated the changes and handed the copy of the report back to Ward. Finally, with Ward warning Kaviti that he would be 'taking the matter further', Ward, Ferguson and Ribeiro left.

That afternoon, Ward decided to postpone indefinitely the cremation of Julie's remains. Instead of arranging a funeral, he asked John Lee of Lee Funeral Service to collect, package and send to London his daughter's leg and jawbone. He also booked seats on the flight to Keekorok the following morning. He still wanted to visit the spot where he had found his dead daughter and collect the remains of the ashes from the fire. But now he wanted more than just a funeral: he was finally convinced that a second autopsy was necessary and he wanted to get hold of every scrap of ash – as evidence – that he could. At Keekorok, on the morning of Saturday 24 September, Ward and Ribeiro were met by Superintendent Wanjau, the CID detective in charge of the Julie Ward case. Together, they drove by Land Rover to the site where the remains had been found. There, Ward took photographs of the fire, the tree and the area in general, and collected the ashes in plastic bags he had brought for that purpose. On the way back, they drove to the site where the jeep had been found. It was gone. When the search had ended so tragically, Ward had given the jeep to Sebastian Tham in return for his help. The next day, Tham had returned to remove it. Thrusting a screw driver into the ignition, he had tried to start the jeep, but the battery was dead. He had then tow-started it and driven it to his house at Keekorok. Back at the lodge, Wanjau took advantage of Ward's presence to interview him for an official statement. Wanjau asked Ward about Julie's education and character, questions that only further infuriated Ward. That night Ward slept at Keekorok, just eleven days after he had sat on the porch of the same lodge, contemplating the horrors of the African night.

The next morning, Ward and Ribeiro met Simon Makallah again and he offered to drive them down to the Sand River camp to show them the spot where Julie had camped. With Makallah at the wheel, they followed the winding dirt road for the seven miles to Sand River. About halfway along, Makallah stopped the car and pointed to the track that he said Julie must have taken before her car became stuck in the stream. Later that morning, Ward and Ribeiro took the scheduled flight back from Keekorok to Nairobi. The following morning, while walking through Nairobi, Ward and Ribeiro ran into Shaker on the street. Ward thanked Shaker for helping to arrange papers for the export of Julie's remains.

'When you get the remains to England you will see,' Shaker told them.

'Are you saying that your original findings were correct?' Ward asked.

'Yes, yes,' Shaker replied. 'You will see. You will understand that I could not speak.'

That evening, Ward and Ribeiro flew back to England, with Julie's remains in the cargo hold of the same aircraft.

It had now been two weeks since the discovery of his daughter's remains and for John Ward it was time to take stock. At first, he had been bewildered by the strange reluctance of the authorities in Kenya to accept his daughter's murder for what it was. 'I have found this to be a very law-abiding country,' he had said on his return to Kenya for the second time. 'I can't believe that an attempt is being made to turn it around the other way. I doubt whether I'd have got a meeting with the commissioner of police in England as easily as I did with Kilonzo.' But after his angry confrontation with Jason Kaviti, the chief police pathologist, Ward had rapidly begun to suspect that he was up against more than simply a slow-moving police force. Kaviti, Ward soon decided, was working on orders, prompted by someone who wanted either to protect Kenya's lucrative tourist industry or, more sinisterly, to shield the murderer himself.

Most men in such a situation might have buckled under the huge problems that loomed ahead. Ward had already spent a good deal of money flying out to Kenya twice, staying in hotels and chartering aircraft. The publicity, on top of the tragedy, had strained his family close to breaking point. He had already begun to neglect his new and demanding Butterfly Hotel chain. And now, it seemed, the government of the country in which his daughter had died was unwilling to help him. But John Ward had never been a man to shy at troubles and, in fact, prided himself on thriving under pressure. What was more, he was wealthy enough to stay away from work and spend a good deal more time and money in Kenya. 'If I was the sort of bloke who works in an office, with two weeks holiday a year, we would probably never even have found Julie,' he said. 'But I'm not and what I can't accept is that they are saying she hasn't been murdered and they have tried to lead me around by the nose.' Ward was a stubborn, proud man and, as he put it, 'I don't like being buggered about.' Moreover, his campaign in Kenya had become, in a way, therapeutic; helping him to deal with his sorrow. Through no fault of his own, John Ward had not been there in his daughter's hour of need, but now at least he could do something for her. 'I think I'm more protective to Julie because she was my daughter rather than a son,' he explained in an interview with Caroline Davies of the *Evening Standard*. 'She was my only daughter. It's different with a girl. Boys can look after themselves. She was my daughter and some-one has to look after her. Basically that is still what I'm doing – looking after her.'

Up to this point, Ward's efforts had simply been to persuade the Kenyans to accept their own evidence and start a murder investigation. But after the altering of the post mortem report, Ward decided that he would have to prove actively that his daughter had been murdered. Only then would the Kenyan police start a full murder hunt. The key evidence was the package of Julie's ashes and remains that Lee Funeral Service had sent to England, and Ward's overriding concern was to get a second post mortem report that would show, beyond doubt, what had happened to Julie. As soon as he arrived in Brockley, Ward telephoned the agents who had received Julie's remains and told them to send their package to Professor Austin Gresham at Addenbrookes hospital in Cambridge. John Ward was not a man to do anything by halves, or settle for second best, and Professor Gresham, PhD, MA, FRCP, was one of the most respected pathologists in Britain. Aged sixty-four, Gresham was Professor of Morbid Anatomy at Cambridge University and a Home Office pathologist. Partly bald, bespec-tacled and habitually dressed in a bow tie, Gresham looked like the proverbial absent-minded professor. But he was in fact a sharp and highly articulate man who had turned many a murder trial with his utterly convincing evidence. On Thursday 29 September, John Ward drove over to Cambridge to see how Gresham was getting on with his examination of Julie's remains and to explain what was known of the circumstances of her death. Gresham had only had time for a quick look at the jaw-bone, but he said that it looked as though the bone had been cut by a sharp and probably man-made instrument. Impatient for the results, Ward said he would return to Cambridge the next day. As it turned out, Gresham was ill for the next few days and it was not until Monday 10 October, exactly four weeks after Julie died, that a second meeting between Ward and Gresham took place. Gresham had now had ample time to examine the remains and his conclusions were confident and decisive. Gresham said that the ashes Ward had brought back from the site of the fire contained fragments of bones, some of them finger bones. He then showed Ward the lower leg, which had been packed in preservatives, and said that the portion of the leg before them had been 'separated from the thigh by a clean cut'. This was clear because the kneecap had been divided in two without any crushing of the bone or the cartilage around the joint. The leg had been 'severed with a sharp object', he said, and 'subsequently burned'. He also found, buried in a cut along the calf, a piece of dark cloth, three inches long and half an inch wide – probably material from Julie's trousers. Turning to the two pieces of jawbone, Gresham pointed out that these too had been partially burned after they had been separated from the rest of the skull with a 'sharp object'. There were no marks of animal teeth on any of the items, Gresham said. Several weeks later, on 21 November, Gresham was to receive one more part of Julie's body: her skull, found by rangers and policemen searching near the site of the other remains. The skull was to confirm Gresham's previous conclusions. It was complete, apart from the lower half of the jaw, which he had already seen, and a few other fragments. There were five points at the base of the skull where it had been separated from the lower jaw and the lower cheek bones. All were smooth and symmetrical. 'To produce five symmetrical wounds at the base of the skull is impossible,' Gresham later reported. 'Unless the head was cut off with a single swipe with a sharp, heavy instrument.' Gresham's conclusions almost exactly matched Shaker's original thesis.

Each discovery of new details about Julie's death brought mixed emotions for John Ward: both fresh sorrow and the satisfaction of getting closer to the truth. Gresham's evidence vindicated Ward's campaign, but the professor also gave Ward new and painful food for thought. The basic tenet of the professor's conclusions – that Julie had been chopped up and then burned – was as close to medical fact as a pathologist could get. But Gresham was also willing to speculate, delving into his deep knowledge and long experience, on how the injuries had been inflicted. The leg had been severed at the knee with one strong, expert swipe, Gresham said. He was unable to tell which hand the person had used, but he – and it was almost certainly a man – probably had some basic knowledge of anatomy. 'It was done in a crude way, but required a reasonable level of know-how,' he said. 'A good, strong butcher would be able to do the same thing.' The body, Gresham reckoned, must also have been limp when the cutting occurred. Julie was either dead or unconscious when the stroke that severed her leg, at least, was swung. Later, when he received the skull, Gresham could speculate further. Julie, he reckoned, had been 'decapitated with one stroke from the back'. It seemed likely that she had been lying facing down on the ground and that her killer had pulled her head up and back by the hair and then swung down heavily at the base of the skull. Gresham's examination of the skull did not, however, produce any clues as to how Julie had died. Apart from the decapitation, which probably occurred after death, the skull was flawless. Julie had not, it seemed, been hit on the head. But that still left a thousand possibilities, from a bullet to a knife across the throat.

Gresham also had answers for other questions raised by the position and state of the remains. Shaker's conclusion that Julie had died no more than twenty-four hours before she was found was not unreasonable, Gresham said. Had the leg been out in the sun for much longer than a day, it would probably have been in a greater state of decay. But estimates of the time of death from such little evidence were a risky business, especially when the leg had been partly burned – which meant partly cooked. The most exact measurement of time of death in such a situation would have been made by examining the stage of the life cycle of fly maggots hatched from eggs likely to have been laid in the leg within a few hours of death. Gresham had found a couple of dead maggots in the leg, killed by the formalin Shaker had used to preserve it. But no one in Kenya had the expertise to make judgments using this method, and only one man in England, Dr Zak Erziclioglu, was a real expert. Gresham could, however, explain why the remains had been scattered about and why the jawbone seemed to have been picked clean while the flesh and muscle on the leg were almost untouched. Animals often pick up bones and body pieces without actually eating them, he said, and without leaving teeth marks. A hyena or jackal might have picked up the leg, carried it for a few yards and then, put off by the smell of burning, dropped it again. The leg had clearly avoided any major attack by ants or worms, but the jawbone must have fallen close to some insects. 'Maggots or ants can clean a whole carcass in twenty-four hours,' Gresham said. The jawbone would have taken no more than a few hours. Even if ants or maggots had come across the leg, they might well have avoided it. The leg had been burned for longer than the jaw, and maggots dislike cooked meat.

Finally, Gresham had some clues about the fire. It would have taken between one and two hours to burn most of Julie's body, but once set, the carcass itself would have sustained the fire. 'People are covered in fat and once a body starts to burn it keeps itself going like a candle. It also burns very intensely. There is a layer of fat underneath the skin and it simply melts. It's like putting cooking oil on a fire. The leg probably fell off the side of the fire, because the least burned part was the foot. The most badly burned part was the severed knee joint.' From Gresham's comments a horrific scene could be envisaged: Julie's killers standing over a brightly burning fire, which was fuelled by her melting body, for well over an hour. The chances were that it was dark and that her leg had probably fallen unnoticed from the fire. Perhaps Julie had eaten the can of pilchards Ward had seen, opened in the tree, before she was found and killed. Or perhaps, while her killer or killers had stood over the burning body of their hapless victim, they had helped themselves to a quick snack.

On Sunday 16 October, Ward and Ribeiro flew back to Nairobi to present Gresham's findings to Commissioner Kilonzo. They arrived at Jomo Kenyatta Airport early the next morning, and a few hours later Ward personally delivered a copy of Gresham's report to Kilonzo's office. That evening, John Ward met Glen Burns, the Australian marine biologist who had left his daughter alone in the Masai Mara game reserve, for the first time. Burns had been out of Kenya on both of Ward's previous visits, but several days earlier he had given Wanjau a statement, and was still in Nairobi. 'When I first learned he'd left her there, I wanted to wring his neck,' Ward said. 'But when I met him, I felt sorry for him. He is very clever, more than that even. But he's got no common sense.' Ward knew, though, that Glen Burns had nothing to do with his daughter's death.

The next morning, Ribeiro and Ward returned to police headquarters for their appointment with Kilonzo and Wanjau, who had returned for the meeting from the Masai Mara. John Ferguson was not present at this meeting, but Ward later related the conversation. 'I started by placing Professor Gresham's report on the table and I asked the commissioner if he had read it. He said that he had and that he accepted the contents. He said he had started a new line of inquiry, but he would need more time. He then said that he now treated the matter very seriously, and if there was a murderer in the Masai Mara National Reserve, he wanted him caught before he could do it again. I immediately questioned the commissioner concerning his use of the word 'if', and I asked the commissioner how there could be any doubt, as two pathologists had now quite clearly reported to him that Julie's leg had been severed with a sharp instrument and subsequently burned. Commissioner Kilonzo replied that he certainly did not rule out murder, but wished to wait for the report of his investigating officer, Muchiri Wanjau. Once more I asked the commissioner what else there could possibly be other than foul play. The commissioner stated the same position and I then told Commissioner Kilonzo that I was becoming increasingly concerned at the reluctance of the police authority to accept the obvious evidence which I had presented to them. The meeting with the commissioner ended in an unsatisfactory manner with my request that he now open a full murder inquiry and the commissioner repeating his position that he needed more time for his investigating officer to report.'

Superintendent Wanjau was also present at this meeting and outside Kilonzo's office Ward had a chance to talk to him. From the moment they had met, Ward and Wanjau had taken an instant dislike to each other. Ward had quickly decided that Wanjau was incompetent and obstructive. With his multi-coloured shirts and ties and interest in the ladies, Wanjau was not Ward's idea of a policeman. Wanjau, for his part, had been angered and offended by what he saw as bullying and a lack of respect from the Englishman. As the meeting ended, the two men became increasingly frustrated. Wanjau asked Ward if he had taken Julie's flip-flops from the Mara. Ward said he had not and in turn asked Wanjau if he could produce the pieces of orange towel which had been found in the tree along with Julie's remains. Ward had brought another orange towel from England and wanted to compare the two. But Wanjau said he did not know where the bits of towel were.

Ward left the commissioner's office angry and frustrated. Later that day he drove up to the Coptic clinic to see Shaker once again. Ward gave Shaker a copy of the new post mortem report and the Egyptian was delighted to see his own conclusions matched by those of Professor Gresham. Feeling, like Ward, vindicated, Shaker then confided to his visitors that Kaviti had visited his mortuary on Thursday 22 September, and had briefly looked at Julie's remains, though not at the X-rays that Shaker had taken. It was at this point, Shaker said, that Kaviti had personally altered the report.

The following morning, Ward held another press conference at the Intercontinental hotel. It was almost one month since he had first told the press of Shaker's conclusions. Now, he had a second, more distinguished pathologist firmly stating that Julie had been chopped up with a man-made instrument and then tossed, in bits, on to a fire. The gathered journalists took note. But the Kenyan police, it seemed, were still not convinced.

5

A Father's Obsession

With the publication of Professor Gresham's post mortem findings, there was little more that John Ward could do to prove from the evidence he already possessed that his daughter had been murdered. After the press conference, Ward telephoned Commissioner Kilonzo and offered, not without sarcasm, to organize a third autopsy. But Kilonzo firmly declined. There remained one more option for Ward: to embark on his own investigations, in the hope that he might not only find further evidence of his daughter's demise but possibly even lead the police to the man who had killed her. At this point, Ward had only the vaguest of notions as to who or where the murderer might be. But he did have the beginnings of two potentially valuable leads.

The first was Julie's missing Olympus camera. This was the most valuable possession Julie had taken with her to the Masai Mara and it had still not been found. Perhaps her murderer had kept the camera and sold it: after all, even second hand, it was worth several months' wages to an ordinary African. If the camera could be traced, it might prove a vital clue. A serious attempt to look for the camera would, however, require the kind of leg work for which neither Ward nor the High Commission had time. Ward had therefore arranged a meeting for the afternoon of Wednesday 19 October with Bob Whitford, a British private detective who had settled in Kenya. Whitford was a small, soft-spoken Welshman, married to an African and living on the edge of white Kenyan society. He had been in the Metropolitan police in England before coming out to Kenya when it was still a British colony and joining the CID, Wanjau's outfit. For the

past thirteen years, he had worked as a private detective from
the rather seedy offices of his company, Vigilante Investigations, spending most of his time chasing insurance fraudsters.
'Reliable and trustworthy' was how Whitford seemed to Ward,
and the two men quickly agreed to work together. Whitford's
first job was to start looking for the camera and Ward gave him a
stack of posters offering a reward of thirty thousand shillings for
information leading to the recovery of the Olympus. Ward suggested that Whitford should have them pinned up in camera
shops, auction rooms, lodges in the Mara and other likely
places.

Ward's second lead was more fanciful, but was also, he felt,
promising. It concerned Makari post, the isolated cluster of
rangers huts where Ward had waited for Sebastian Tham and
his helicopter on the day that Julie's remains were found. Ten
days after that fateful afternoon, three journalists – Peter
Godwin of the *Sunday Times* and a reporter and photographer
from *Today* newspaper – had flown down to Keekorok on the
trail of the Julie Ward story. It was the day that Ward himself
had intended to return to the Mara but had changed his plans in
order to confront Shaker, and then Kaviti, with the altered post
mortem report. The journalists were hoping that Ward would
turn up and retrace with them his movements of 13 September.
When he failed to arrive, they decided to set off into the bush
on their own. From the moment the story of Julie's death had
broken, the rangers and the hotel staff at Keekorok had been
warned not to help or talk to the press, and at first the three
journalists were unable to find a vehicle. But Peter Godwin had
grown up in Africa and knew enough Swahili and was ready to
offer enough shillings to persuade the driver of a zebra-striped
minibus to take them for a drive. After a brief stop at Sand River
camp, they turned off the road and drove around the bush for
some time. Eventually, not far from the spot where Julie's car
had been found, they tried to cross the main Sand river. Mid-
way across the river, to their horror, the minibus hit a patch of
thick mud and sank into the mire. For more than an hour, as the
afternoon drew on, they pushed, dug and slipped branches

under the wheels to try and free the vehicle, but to no avail. Then, in Godwin's words, 'the silhouette of a man with a gun appeared above us on the bank and for a split second I wondered, a little nervously, who it could be.' The silhouette then slid down the bank and introduced himself as Peter Kipeen, a ranger based at the nearby Makari post. Armed with an old Lee Enfield bolt-action rifle, Kipeen was patrolling the area. He cheerfully helped with the pushing for a few minutes before suggesting that they walk to the nearby camp of the Swiss camera team and ask for a car to tow them out. Godwin volunteered to go with Kipeen and the two men clambered up the river bank and set off, walking briskly through bush thick with wildebeest and gazelle. Kipeen was, Godwin thought, 'very helpful, very amenable and very nice.' In a mixture of English and Swahili, they talked about life in the reserve and growing up as a Masai. Godwin asked Kipeen about Julie's death and Kipeen said it was a terrible tragedy and suggested that the killers might have been Tanzanian poachers. As they walked, Kipeen pointed out the spot, just around the hill, where Makari post was sited. After a hard forty-five minute walk, they arrived at the Swiss camp. With Godwin apologizing profusely, they were lent a car and a driver, but when they arrived back at the minibus they found that a jeep carrying Simon Makallah had chanced upon the spot before them. The warden was furious with the minibus driver and shouted at him for several mintues before turning to the journalists and abruptly breaking into a smile. Makallah seemed to find considerable humour in the journalists' situation and told them, chuckling, that they were lucky not to have ended up like Julie Ward. Before long, though, the minibus was pulled out of the mud and, with a much subdued driver, the reporters trundled back to Keekorok lodge.

The following Sunday, Peter Godwin's article, titled 'THE FATHER WHO FEARS MISCHIEF IN THE BUSH', appeared in the *Sunday Times*. When John Ward read the story, it immediately raised an intriguing question. If Kipeen had found the journalists' minibus so quickly, why had he not seen Julie's car, which had been stuck in a nearby gully, for several days? Ward's thoughts turned back to the day of the search, when he had been driven to Makari post. Perhaps Kipeen had been one of the rangers he had seen that day. Perhaps Kipeen, or another ranger, had heard or seen Julie's car. Perhaps they had walked down to the Loltukai stream for a look. Perhaps . . . It was almost too painful to consider.

By now Ward's suspicions were beginning to focus on the Mara's rangers. Watson and Burns, two potential suspects, were both hundreds of miles from the reserve at the time of her death and could certainly be discounted. There were many other holidaymakers in the Mara but the evidence hardly pointed in their direction. For a start, tourists seldom visited the parts of the reserve where Julie's car and body were found. And the body had been cut up by someone with experience of dismembering carcasses: unless Julie had run into a vacationing party of surgeons or butchers, tourists apppeared to be innocent. The largest resident group of people in the relevant part of the reserve were the staff at Keekorok lodge. But most of the staff were hired in the cities and would have been afraid to walk in the bush. And all the lodge vehicles were carefully monitored. The local Masai, on the other hand, did occasionally wander around the Mara and could conceivably have stumbled across Julie. So might a gang of bandits or poachers, who also visited the reserve from time to time. But why would Masai or poachers have wanted to hide their deed and so have cut up and burned the body? They would have been more likely to rape, kill, rob and then simply flee. Moreover, apart from her camera, none of Julie's possessions was missing. Some money was even found on the fire. That left just one group: the reserve's wardens, rangers and policemen. These men knew the Masai Mara. They constantly travelled through the bush. They would certainly have wanted to dispose of the body. And if reserve officials had murdered Julie, that might explain why the government was so keen to prove she had been killed by animals.

In fact, although John Ward knew nothing of this at the time, the Masai Mara was suffering from a dramatic increase in indiscipline and bad behaviour by its staff. Despite the huge revenues Kenya collected from tourism, the wildlife system was not treated as a priority by the government. Rangers' wages, at well under fifty pounds a month, were significantly less than those of policemen or soldiers, who faced similar dangers in their jobs. Often, the rangers were paid late. They were seldom given new uniforms and their guns were generally bolt-action, First World War issue. Kenya's parks and reserves, including the Mara, had few working vehicles and were always short of petrol. The roads were appalling. Consequently, morale and discipline within the parks and reserves was very poor.

An incident a year or so before Julie arrived in Kenya served to show the contempt with which the rules of the Masai Mara were treated. Ten years earlier, amid much fanfare, hunting had been banned in Kenya. Yet in March 1987, a senior official of the Wildlife Department and member of parliament brought a party of Arabs, along with some German prostitutes, down to the Mara for a hunting trip. Camping on the edge of the reserve, the Arabs shot some two hundred animals in the space of a few days, including lion and cheetah. The camp was actually outside the reserve, on private Masai land, but the officials hosting the Arabs were brazen enough to drive over to one of the tourist lodges in the reserve one evening and sit at the bar, drinking and boasting of their kills. It was only when the Kenyan *Standard* newspaper uncovered the story that there was a small scandal.

Places like Sekenani gate or Sand River were, in the late 1980s, almost dens of iniquity. The ticket clerks, in league with the rangers, were pocketing the vast proportion of the tourist fees to the reserve. They had false receipt books printed up and would officially record only a small proportion of the vehicles entering the reserve. Enough of the money was paid to the county council administrators to ensure that the number of vehicles entering the park was never checked against the number of tourists at the lodges and campsites. When Bob Whitford had checked the books at Sand River, looking for clues for the Julie Ward case, he had found that only a handful of the hundreds of tourists who had stayed at the campsite in the first two weeks of September were actually registered. By the time Julie visited the Masai Mara, the reserve staff had come to see tourists as targets for money, amusement and even sex. When a car stopped at Sekenani gate to pay the entrance fee, a ranger would often stick his head through the window and ask for a lift or to be given a cassette tape or watch. Until the onset of Aids, the Kenyan coast had been a popular sex location, a sort of mini-Bangkok, particularly among German tourists. Some of this sexual interest by foreigners in Kenyan men and woman had spilled over into the parks and reserves, and the rangers had learned that female tourists were occasionally fair game. The skimpy clothes worn by Western women in the Mara further exacerbated this image.

Life in the reserve could be boring for the rangers, and many of them ended up spending their wages on beer. Just a few weeks after Julie's death, a drunken incident nearly ended in tragedy at the Sand River camp. A ranger and a policeman had become embroiled in a furious argument over a woman. The ranger ended the argument by walking up to Keekorok lodge, where he spent the day drinking beer. In the evening, he returned to Sand River and continued shouting. Eventually, he brought out his gun and fired several shots wildly into the air. All this had taken place in front of a group of tourists, who fled into their tents when the shots were fired. Such was the state of the Masai Mara and Sand River camp when Julie Ward had visited the reserve.

For nearly a month, Ward had mulled over the questions of the possible role of the rangers raised by Peter Godwin's article. On 19 October he finally passed on his suspicions to Wanjau and another detective assigned to his daughter's case, a genial superintendent named Musimi Rudisi. But to Ward's annoyance, the policemen seemed uninterested. Instead, Wanjau asked again where Julie had been to school, infuriating Ward, who refused to answer the question. 'I left them in no doubt as to the frustration I felt at the lack of progress being made by the police and their continual refusal to accept a murder conclusion,' Ward recounted later. As a result, Ward became doubly

determined to fly down to the Mara and return himself to
Makari post. The following day, Thursday 20 October, was a
public holiday, but on the Friday, Ward and Ribeiro,
accompanied by Bob Whitford, took the morning flight to
Keekorok. At the park headquarters, they were told that Simon
Makallah was on leave and none of the rangers present was able
to provide transport for the three men. Eventually, Ward found
Sebastian Tham, who offered to lend them his Range Rover
and his driver, Joseph. Just before they left, Wanjau and James
Sindiyo, an assistant warden in the Masai Mara, appeared and
offered to accompany them.

On the way to Makari post, the group took a detour to the
spot where Julie's remains had been found. Ward quickly
located the blackened circle of soil which marked the site of the
fire, and began to dig out samples of the earth for later testing in
England. There was still, Whitford noted, a 'sickly smell of
burned flesh'. When Ward had finished, the men climbed back
into their vehicles and drove off towards Makari post. Ward
could now clearly see how isolated – as well as scenic – the post
was. Its five huts, painted green, blended in with the surroundings, and four rangers, also in green uniform, were sitting
around on camp chairs. Apart from an old radio, they had little
entertainment and over the years rangers had amused themselves by scratching their names or short sayings in the paint on
the hut walls. Neatly written on one were the words 'Peter M
Kipeen, 13/6/88'. Kipeen himself was present and Ward
showed him and the other rangers a photograph of Julie. The
rangers shook their heads. Ward then showed them Godwin's
article from the *Sunday Times*, which mentioned Kipeen by
name, but again there was little response. Ward asked James
Sindiyo, the assistant warden, what the rangers were supposed
to do at Makari post. He said their job was to patrol the nearby
area, including the spot where Julie's car had been found.
Ward's ears pricked up at this, and soon he had further cause for
suspicion. Wandering around the huts, Ribeiro had found a
tube of Maclean's toothpaste lying in some grass. He picked it
up and showed it to Ward. What was toothpaste doing here?

Did rangers use toothpaste? Ward had seen rangers picking at
their teeth with slivers of wood and assumed that this was how
they cleaned their teeth. Perhaps the toothpaste had been left at
Makari post by someone other than a ranger. Perhaps it had
belonged to Julie.

The following day, Ward and Ribeiro flew back to England.
That weekend, while discussing his trip with his family, Ward
suddenly remembered another item he had found, on his first
visit to Makari post. While he had waited anxiously for Sebastian Tham, he had seen a small battery, of the sort that are used
in cameras, sitting on a coin in the dust. He had wondered what
it was doing there at the time, but had forgotten about it in the
rush of events that followed. Now, however, sitting in
Brockley, Ward put the battery and the toothpaste tube side by
side in his mind. Neither, he reckoned, were normal possessions of rangers in the bush. Together, they suggested one idea:
Julie.

Before long, Ward received more important evidence. The
soil samples from the site of the fire had been analysed at
London Scientific Services and the results showed that an
accelerant, such as petrol, had been used to start the fire. Julie's
body, it seemed, had been smothered in petrol, or a similar substance, and then set alight. Perhaps this also explained why her
leg had not been eaten: animals on the whole dislike the smell
of petrol. Armed with these new leads, Ward and Ribeiro
returned once more to Kenya on Friday 9 November 1988.
Throughout the crisis, the patient Frank Ribeiro had been a foil
to the more tempestuous Ward. Ribeiro was from Portugal, and
with things as they stood, Ward joked, his friend's Portuguese
knowledge of crooked officials might come in handy. On the
day they arrived, Ward and Ribeiro were taken by John
Ferguson to see Commissioner Kilonzo again. Ward produced
the new scientific evidence but Kilonzo was not surprised. His
own laboratories had come to a similar conclusion. Ward was,
however, able to suggest that if the substance was petrol, it
might have come from Julie's plastic jerrycan, which had been
full at Serena lodge and had never been found.

Charming, but firm as ever, Kilonzo assured Ward once again that he was 'determined to get to the bottom of the affair'. But by this stage, Ward had lost all faith in the police chief and he stated his belief that a cover-up had been initiated over Julie's death. Kilonzo emphatically denied this. 'Why then has Kaviti, a most unreliable pathologist, not been charged with perverting the course of justice?' Ward asked. By now, after Wanjau had finally organized a combing operation of the south-east corner of the Masai Mara, Julie's skull had been found. Ward was particularly upset that the skull remained in Kaviti's possession, and he told Kilonzo that he wanted to take the skull himself as soon as possible.

Superintendent Wanjau had also attended the meeting and Ward now gave him the toothpaste tube, telling him that he had found it at Makari post. Ward also informed Wanjau about having seen the battery. Once again, Wanjau showed little interest, so Ward decided to follow up on the lead himself. If he could prove that the tube had been purchased in Langata, where Julie had stayed, it would be strong evidence to suggest that his daughter had been at Makari post. Over the next couple of days, Ward and Ribeiro bought scores of toothpaste tubes in the Langata area, looking for one with a similar serial number to the tube found at Makari. But, to Ward's frustration, they drew a blank. At the same time, Ward was also pressing to receive both a formal death certificate and Julie's skull, which he wanted to send to Professor Gresham. At around seven o'clock on the evening of Friday 11 November, two policemen knocked on the door of Ward's hotel room. They handed him the death certificate, which stated cause of death as 'blunt injuries with subsequent burns', and the skull in a plastic bag. 'I must be the only father who has ever had to spend a night in a hotel room with his daughter's skull,' Ward was later to joke, with characteristically cheerful morbidity.

Ward was now keen to continue his own investigation and the next day, Saturday 12 November, he flew down to Keekorok again, accompanied by Ribeiro, Ferguson and Bob Whitford. The idea was to start from Sand River and try to trace

Julie's route, seeing if any clues lay along the way. Accompanied by Wanjau, they first drove down to Sand River. This was by now familiar ground for the policeman, who had already spent six weeks at Keekorok lodge, and he took them through Julie's movements at the camp. Wanjau had taken a statement from Gerald Karori, a police constable on duty at Sand River in September, who had described seeing Julie arrive at the camp. Karori said that he had been suspicious when Julie began to take down two tents on her own. He had crossed the river to talk to her and had found out that Julie's companion had left by air from Serena. Karori said he had helped Julie pack up the tents. Wanjau then led Ward and his companions to an office, where they met the clerk, David Nchoko, who had been on duty when Julie had left. Nchoko said he had stopped Julie on her way out because she had extra camping fees to pay for the additional days the tents had stood empty on the river bank. Nchoko opened a large register, and pointed to the entry showing that Julie Ward had paid two hundred and sixty shillings at two thirty-seven on the afternoon of Tuesday 6 September 1988. As John Ward peered at the book in the half darkness, Julie's signature suddenly caught his eye. 'I don't think Julie wrote that,' he said, with growing interest. 'I don't think it's her signature.' They took the book out into the light and Ward looked closely at the page, increasingly sure that the signature in front of him was not Julie's, but a forgery. Here was something far more significant than even the camera battery and the toothpaste tube. Trying to hide his suspicions, he laid the book on the ground and photographed the page several times.

The next day, Sunday 13 November, Ward and Ribeiro flew back to England. On the way, Ward discovered that his camera, with the film he had taken at Sand River, was missing, presumably stolen. It could have been a coincidence, but Ward was not convinced. The loss of the camera, sometime after checking in at Nairobi airport, merely added to his certainty that he was facing a far-reaching cover-up. There was nothing to do but return to Kenya and take another batch of photographs. Ward was delayed in England for a time, but eventually he arrived back in Kenya and flew down, yet again, to the Masai Mara. This time, Ward took good care of his film and when he returned to England he sent copies of Julie's signature and the photographed page of the book to two separate handwriting specialists. Both came to the same conclusion. The signature in the clerk's book at Sand River camp had not been written by Julie Ward. 'The whole thing was a forgery,' Ward was to recount later. 'Nchoko was another lying official.'

In the meantime, the Ward family carried out another, more emotional task. On 6 December, almost ten months to the day after they had last seen Julie, they cremated her meagre remains and held a private memorial ceremony at a church in Cambridge. It was a tearful day, but until the murderer was caught and the events of Julie's last days revealed, the family would not be able to complete the process of reconciling themselves to her death.

In the months since Julie's death, the Ward family had reluctantly come to believe that the motive for her murder must have been sexual. The most likely scenario was that she had been abducted, sexually abused and then killed when the search began. It was not an easy idea to accept, and the 'missing week' was soon filled with grotesque and nightmarish imaginations. Julie had probably spent several days in the hands of her captors before she was killed. 'That is what really, really makes me angry,' Ward told Caroline Davies of the *Evening Standard*. 'When I think about the week that bastard held her. For some reason I want to know what she was put through.'

Without a murderer to vent his frustration on, John Ward's anger lay smouldering beneath his usually genial countenance. But in November 1988 he was presented with a perfect alternative target. Early that month, a South African journalist named David Barritt had interviewed Stephen Watson and found out about the night Julie had spent with Watson at Serena lodge. Barritt had also talked to Paul Weld Dixon, asking leading questions about Julie's behaviour, and on 7 November the British

Sunday Mirror published his article under the headline 'LION GIRL'S LAST SEX CRAZED NIGHT'. Even by the standards of tabloid journalism in Britain, this was a particularly unpleasant piece. It pictured Julie Ward as a buxom, scantily clad, sexually overdeveloped nymph who had slept her way through Africa. The implication was that Julie had played with the primitive sexual emotions of Africans and therefore contributed towards her bloody end. The Ward family and their friends were deeply upset. John Ward appeared on television, with Phil Shoard, one of Julie's companions from the Hobo trip, to denounce the article. Later, he asked everyone he could reach who had known Julie to write testaments to her character and received sixty-six replies, which he copied and distributed to journalists. These letters formed a heart-rending document.

> I would describe Julie as a quiet, unassuming, modest girl and one who had a very gentle caring nature. Julie had a natural prettiness and a quiet charm and was without any malice at all. The appalling publication in the *Sunday Mirror* must have shocked anyone who knew Julie. The person described there never existed.

> Naturally of small frame but not quite tall, she could be described accurately as 'thin' and certainly not curvaceous. To suggest Julie to be a 'maneater' in any sense of the word is totally without foundation.

> What can you say about Julie? A string of superlatives could never do her justice. Very rarely in life do you get an opportunity to know someone who embodies the goodness in people so completely. Her generosity, support and selflessness are an indelible memory. The vicious, hateful articles of the *Sunday Mirror* should be treated with total contempt.

> She always lived her life enthusiastically and to a very HIGH MORAL STANDARD.

Julie was one of the nicest people I ever met. She was
thoughtful towards others. I first met her because she
worked for my dad when I was four. I am now twelve.
Because I suffer from asthma and nose problems I was in
and out of hospital a lot. Julie went out of her way to see
me. She would bring me a present to cheer me up. My
mum had to stay in hospital with me once and Julie went
home with my brother and dad to cook them something to
eat. Though she could not cook very well. The most
important thing is that she tried. They may not have ate
much but that did not matter. She was kind and caring.
After her death, I thought to myself why do the nice
people in the world always get killed. She was a good and
sensible person. Julie had a soft spot for cuddly toys.

Before long, John Ward had traced David Barritt to Johannesburg. He quickly decided that he was going to 'go after the
bastard' and he flew out to South Africa. Barritt was an odd
character who had been a political radical when young but had
in recent years turned to gutter journalism, starting up a new
scandal sheet in South Africa and writing about Africa for the
Mirror. Ward hired a private detective and approached one or
two investigative journalists in Johannesburg to dig up whatever information they could on Barritt. 'I know all about the
bastard,' Ward was later to claim, tossing out various allegations. 'I shall make sure that the world's press knows all the dirt
on Barritt. All in the cause of public interest, of course.' Ward
could not himself sue Barritt on Julie's behalf: the dead cannot
be libelled. But he persuaded Stephen Watson to file a suit
against Barritt and promised to bankroll him. 'I am going to sort
Barritt out,' Ward later told Christopher Walker of *The Times*. 'I
have agreed to finance Watson and he will fight the case.'

Barritt, however, was just the beginning. Ward saw the writ
served on Barritt in South Africa as a stepping stone to taking
on the man he considered the real perpetrator of the injustice
against Julie: Robert Maxwell, the *Mirror*'s proprietor. 'I have a
bottle of champagne in my fridge and it's got Robert Maxwell's

name written on it,' he was to say. 'If I ever hear of his demise it will be opened. Maxwell is the boss, the person who sets the policy and gets the profit. I dislike him because he could have put it right and didn't. He doesn't have that suite in the *Mirror* building and the helicopter pad on the roof for nothing. What an absolute egotist that chap is.'

'I am not being obsessive about this,' Ward also said to *The Times*. 'It is perfectly natural to want to defend the name of a loved one who can no longer defend herself.' Ward also dismissed suggestions that his campaign to find his daughter's killers had become an obsession. 'From my point of view it's probably seventy per cent revenge and thirty per cent a combination of factors, including my fear that if the murderer has done it once, he could do it again,' he told another reporter. 'It also comes down to the fact that I don't like being buggered about.' Nevertheless, Ward's quest was taking up not less but more and more of his time and energy. He was flying out to Kenya as often as two or three times a month. He was giving repeated newspaper and magazine interviews and appearing again and again on television, even on the Wogan show. It was only because Ward had set up Butterfly Hotels so efficiently that the company was able to open a third hotel in Peterborough in 1989. 'Opening a hotel is a hefty thing to do, like giving birth to an elephant,' Ward said with his usual grin. 'It's at times like these that you realize you're not indispensable.'

Ward's investigations were also increasingly convincing him that his daughter's murderer was being protected at the highest levels in Kenya. 'Every time I get a new piece of evidence I go to Kilonzo,' he said. 'Here, Mr Kilonzo, is a post mortem report that says my daughter was chopped up then burned. Here, Mr Kilonzo, is proof her handwriting was forged. Here, Mr Kilonzo, is evidence that the men at Sand River lied. What about her skull, Mr Kilonzo, isn't that proof enough? And each time Mr Kilonzo smiles politely and says it is all very interesting but not quite enough proof to require the opening of a murder investigation. Well, what more bloody proof do you need?' He was equally scathing about Jason Kaviti, the police pathologist, whom he saw as a pathetic figure, clinging to the forms but not the substance of his job. But Ward was sure that the conspiracy stretched far above Kilonzo and Kaviti. 'If you get Kilonzo refusing to start a murder investigation all this time and the chief government pathologist changing a post mortem report, it's quite clear that someone told them what to do and that someone has to be more senior than them,' he said. 'I regard Kilonzo and Kaviti as pawns in the game.'

But if anything in Ward's behaviour could be called obsessive, it was his focus on the Sand River camp. For the first few weeks after Julie's death, the assumption that she had rather foolishly driven off the road and stranded her vehicle had disturbed the Ward family. 'She'd just met this dishy young man and arranged to meet him again,' Jan Ward said. 'She had all these business plans. She was coming home soon. She was on a high. Even if a herd of wildebeest had run across the road in front of her I don't think she would have turned off the road. At that stage I don't think she would have bothered to get out her camera for anything.' The forgery at Sand River provided a much more acceptable explanation for the Wards: that Julie had not driven freely from the Sand River camp, but had been abducted from there. David Nchoko, the clerk, had forged Julie's signature. It was a small step to suggest that he was lying when he said she had driven away from the camp that day. Perhaps Nchoko himself had been involved in the abduction. Julie's car could easily have been planted in the gully: that would explain why there was no note in the car and why the map and binoculars were found inside. And it would absolve Julie of making the mistake of leaving the road. 'I think that Julie might have decided to stay at Sand River that night rather than try to reach Nairobi,' John Ward was soon saying. 'She would have felt safe enough. There were people around, it was an organized campsite, there were rangers there. She would have thought the rangers were there to protect her. When she and Glen first arrived, they pitched their tent away from the main site to avoid all the other people. It would have been possible to have been abducted from the camping site even if there had been a hundred people there. The nearest tent was sixty yards away. Certainly far enough for someone to creep into her tent and put a hand over her face.' When Ward had found her car, one of the tents had been neatly rolled and packed away. The other was loosely and untidily folded. If Julie had decided to stay at Sand River, she would probably have taken down Glen's tent and left only her own standing, so that she could leave early the next day. If someone had grabbed her from the camp, he would probably have thrown her tent quickly into the back of the jeep before driving off to some secluded spot. These thoughts led Ward to look again at Julie's tent and sleeping bag, and after close examination he found what looked like a spot of blood near the head of the sleeping bag and another spot on the tent. But when the laboratory in London analysed the stains they found one to be food and the other to be the blood of a squashed mosquito.

Makari post had soon become of secondary importance to the Sand River campsite in John Ward's mind and investigation. On 22 January 1989, Ward flew back to Kenya and a couple of days later met Commissioner Kilonzo once more. Ward revealed his discovery of the forgery to Kilonzo and presented him with all the evidence. The commissioner appeared pleased. He said that he had always considered the investigation to be a partnership between the police and Ward and he was most grateful. 'This is the breakthrough for which I have long hoped,' Kilonzo said. Ward remained sceptical. 'I told Kilonzo icily that we had known all along that a cover-up had been organized, and that it must stop immediately,' Ward wrote later. 'I said that I had no interest in exposing to the world the way in which he and Kaviti had handled the affair: all I wanted was that the man who had killed Julie should be caught.'

By now, though, Ward had already embarked on his own line of inquiry. He was convinced that the secret to Julie's death lay at Sand River and was determined to find out all he could about the lay-out and events of the camp on Tuesday 6 September, the last day his daughter had been seen alive. The receipt book he had photographed had already yielded one suspicious clue. Julie had, according to Nchoko, been issued receipt number B113291, at two thirty-seven on the afternoon of 6 September. But the next receipt, numbered B113292, had been issued to a British tourist named Bower, who according to the camp books had left at nine o'clock on the same morning, five and a half hours before Julie. It all added up, Ward reckoned, to unorthodox bookkeeping. Moreover, the camp records showed that only a couple of dozen people had been at Sand River in the first ten days of September, while Bob Whitford discovered, after laborious checking of tour company records, that the number was actually much higher. Through just one company, Best Camping Tours, which regularly took tourists to Sand River, Whitford found that more than one hundred people had spent the night at the campsite between 1 and 10 September. This included a party of thirty-four French tourists, who had arrived on the same day that Julie had returned to the camp. It promised to be a mammoth, almost impossible task to track down all these people, but Ward decided that he had no choice. Over the following months, he was to fly to Canada, the United States, France, Denmark, Sweden, Switzerland and Finland, and talk to more than fifty people who had stayed at Sand River. Whenever he found a camper he would ask if they remembered seeing Julie and if they had any photographs of the campsite. If they did, he would secure copies. 'Bit by bit,' he said, 'I am trying to piece together a picture of Sand River campsite on 6 September.' At one point, he thought he had found a photograph showing Julie standing by her tent in the camp just before sunset, but when enlarged, the figure turned out to be someone else.

As time passed, Ward and Whitford uncovered further evidence and drew new conclusions that gave substance to their convictions. Julie's jeep had been sitting for months outside Sebastian Tham's house at Keekorok, untouched since it had been driven back from the gully. Eventually, the petrol in the tank was checked. Julie had filled up at Serena lodge and had driven straight from Serena to Sand River. Add on a few miles from Sand River to the gully, and the total would be not much more than forty miles. The tank was only half full. Surely Suzukis could drive more than forty miles on half a tank. What had happened to the missing petrol? Was it possible that the Suzuki had been used to carry Julie, alive or dead, into the depths of the Masai Mara and then been driven back to the gully and planted there? Ward had also begun to doubt that Julie would have written the SOS found on the roof. For one thing, the writing was too square for Julie. And secondly, she would, he reckoned, have been more likely to write 'Help'. Months after Julie's death, Ward also remembered that on an early trip to the Mara he had seen a solitary hut, not far from Makari post. Could this have been the place where she was held and killed? He and Whitford searched for this hut on the ground and by aircraft, but all they could find was a track leading to a flattened, empty patch of grass.

The most important evidence came, however, from the Swiss camera team which had been camped not far from where Julie's car had been found. Ward tracked down Henri Berney, the team's leader, in Switzerland and the two men pored over a map together. The film team had, Berney reckoned, driven past the gully where the car was stuck every day, without seeing the vehicle once. Moreover, the camp was, he calculated, just three or four hundred yards from the gully. 'From such a short distance,' Berney wrote in a statement, 'how could Julie not have heard the noise from our camp: human voices, car engines, radios and most of all, the generator. In my opinion, the vehicle could not have been there, at that point, for more than one night.' Berney's evidence gave emphatic credence to Ward's theory and also threw up a number of other intriguing points. If Julie's murderer had planted the jeep in the gully that night, Monday 12 September, he must have known how to drive. He must also have been sly enough to write SOS on the roof of the jeep. And, Ward reckoned, he must have had an accomplice with another car to carry him at night from the gully to wherever he lived. Together, Bob Whitford and John Ward drew out a profile of the 'qualities and abilities' of the man who had either killed Julie or was the ringleader of her murderers. Ward later gave the results to Christopher Walker of *The Times*, and they made thought-provoking reading. 'He is someone who Julie would have trusted,' the profile read. 'He is intelligent: this is a sophisticated crime. He has freedom of movement in the park. He has transport of his own or access to transport. He has a degree of authority. He is important enough to warrant a cover-up. He must possess an intimate knowledge of the Masai Mara. He probably had an accomplice.'

The profile pointed to a small number of people, notably the Masai Mara's senior rangers and wardens. More narrowly, it almost perfectly fitted one man – Simon Makallah, the chief warden of the reserve. The Masai Mara, Ward felt, was Makallah's kingdom, and he was the man most likely to know and control what took place within the boundaries of the reserve. From the moment Ward had met Makallah, at the site of his daughter's remains, he had taken a dislike to the plump, balding Masai. In an article Ward wrote for the *Daily Telegraph*, he called Makallah 'utterly untrustworthy' and referred to him as 'Safari Suit', because he was the best dressed of the Africans involved in the search. It had been Makallah, Ward had not failed to notice, who claimed to have found footprints leading away from the jeep – a claim that Ward totally disbelieved. And it had been Makallah who after just an hour or two of searching through a huge, dense area of bush had found Julie's jawbone and leg. On top of all this, Simon Makallah seemed to have disappeared from the Masai Mara. In all the recent times Ward had visited the reserve, Makallah had not once been present. He had been 'on holiday', 'on leave', 'away on business'. Ward even heard that Makallah had been suspended for ordering too many vehicle spare parts – a likely story, Ward thought.

Where, Ward wanted to know, was Simon Makallah? He was soon to find out. In July 1989, ten months after his daughter's murder, John Ward's long, wearying and expensive campaign scored its first major victory. The Kenyan government announced, out of the blue, that an inquest would be held in August into the death of Julie Anne Ward. Nchoko, the clerk at

Sand River, Karori, the policeman, Kaviti, the chief pathologist, and Makallah himself – 'liars' the lot of them, in Ward's
book – would all probably be called to testify. 'It's not impossible that little green men came down from the heavens and
killed my daughter,' Ward said. 'But I don't think so. I think I
can say for sure, or perhaps one notch below sure, that I know
within a group who killed her.' The inquest would give Ward a
chance not only to prove to the world that his daughter had
been murdered, but to close in on the group of people among
whom, he was sure, was the man who had carried out the deed.

6

◆◆◆◆◆

The Inquest

As the opening of the inquest drew closer, John Ward was besieged once again by the British press. In the eleven months since his daughter's death, he had shielded his wife and two sons from journalists, but had made himself readily available for reporters and television crews from all over the world (with the notable exception of the *Sunday Mirror*, which had published the 'LION GIRL'S LAST SEX CRAZED NIGHT' article). Shrewd and articulate, Ward felt himself a match for any journalist and relished the thrust and parry of interviews, answering some questions, fending off others and expertly leading reporters in the direction he wished. More than once, interviews or television spots ended with a few drinks or a good meal, paid for by Ward and enjoyed by all. But while Ward clearly savoured the attention of the press, he was also aware that it was by marshalling the media and keeping his campaign alive in the newspapers that he had forced the Kenyan authorities to order an inquest. Even the gentle pressure exerted by the British High Commission in Nairobi had been prompted by the mission's reluctant realization that the Julie Ward case was not simply going to fade away. And now that the inquest was just around the corner, Ward wanted to make sure that the courtroom would be filled with British journalists ready to embarrass the Kenyan authorities the moment there was any sign of cover-up or misdirection of justice.

Throughout Kenya's history, its judiciary has always been somewhat of a cowboy operation. One shady legal judgment in Kenya in 1959, a few years before independence, nearly brought down the British Tory government of the day. Camps had been set up to house thousands of captives during the Mau Mau uprising and in one of these camps, Hola, eleven inmates were beaten to death. At first, the authorities announced that the men had 'died after drinking water from a water cart'. Eventually the truth came out, but after a court inquiry the camp commandant was simply allowed to resign without any charges. *The Times* called it a scandal and a 'grisly affair'. Thirty years later, the reputation of Kenya's judiciary had sunk low once again. The trouble was not so much widespread corruption for personal gain, though there were crooked judges, but a general compromise of the principles of justice to conform with the wishes of the country's politicians. Between 1986 and 1988, a series of controversial trials had been used to break up a political opposition group, Mwakenya. Much of the evidence against the accused was flimsy at best, and lawyers such as Gibson Kamau Kuria, one of Kenya's top criminal experts, who dared to criticize the government, were themselves tossed in prison on even more tenuous charges. Allegations of torture were rife, and during this period there were several deaths of political prisoners in police custody. In 1988, the case of a political detainee killed in suspicious circumstances by the police came in front of Derek Schofield, a British judge who had lived in Kenya since 1974 and was married to an African. The police said they had buried the detainee's body and Schofield ordered that it be exhumed for an autopsy. Dozens of the wrong graves were dug up before Schofield felt forced to threaten a senior policeman with a jail sentence for contempt of court. The result was not a censure for the policeman, but Schofield's removal from the case. He promptly resigned his post, saying: 'I cannot operate in a system where the law is so blatantly contravened by those who are supposed to be its guardians.' In the same year, parliament voted to change Kenya's constitution and abolish guaranteed tenure for judges. The reason was clear: without tenure, judges could be influenced by politicians with the power to appoint – and dismiss – them.

John Ward knew that the inquest would be a tough legal battle and he had taken great care to find the right lawyer:

Byron Georgiadis, a sixty-one-year-old British citizen, born of Greek parents in Tanzania, who had practised in Kenya for most of his life. A white-maned, deep-voiced man, fond of long rhetorical flourishes in court, Georgiadis looked like Anthony Quinn playing Aristotle Onassis. During the inquest, he was to boast to journalists, 'I deal with all the difficult cases here because no one else will handle them. All the sensitive cases going back thirty-eight years.' Georgiadis was in fact the lawyer who had represented the camp commandant in the Hola case and over the years he had indeed handled numerous controversial cases. During the troubled Mau Mau years he had both prosecuted and defended Mau Mau suspects, helping to send more than one hundred men to the gallows and saving another thirty from the same fate. In the years after independence, Georgiadis had travelled the courts of East Africa, from Aden to Dar es Salaam, and the clients he had successfully defended included Kenyan army officers accused of taking part in a coup attempt, a Ugandan newspaper editor charged by Idi Amin's government with sedition and a jilted Greek woman suspected of murdering an Italian count. But these days, Georgiadis preferred an easier life. He lived with his family in a grand, colonial-style home overlooking the Ngong hills and spent more time fishing, shooting and playing golf than practising law. During the 1980s, Georgiadis had on the whole stayed clear of controversial cases, leaving them to a new generation of bright, young, committed African lawyers. But Georgiadis found the idea of the Julie Ward case attractive. It had already drawn enough publicity for him to feel he could safely navigate its potentially troubled course. And he saw in it the chance of a final flourish to his long and distinguished career.

Moreover, by this time, the Julie Ward inquest had taken on an extra significance in Kenya. Julie's death had been the first publicized murder in a game park or reserve since the killing of Joy Adamson, but in the months leading up to the inquest, further attacks on tourists had taken place. In fact, the period between Julie's death and the start of the Julie Ward inquest was the most violent and chaotic in the history of Kenya's parks and reserves. The first incident in the parks had actually preceded Julie's murder by a few days. On Saturday 3 September 1988, while Julie was staying at Serena lodge in the Masai Mara, a group of tourists were attacked by bandits armed with automatic rifles in Meru National Park, in northern Kenya. One male tourist was hit by a bullet in the chest and survived only because a surgeon was immediately flown to Meru by the Flying Doctors. Over the next eleven months there were more armed attacks on tourists in Kenya's wildlife areas than there had been in the previous eleven years. In July 1989 bandits surfaced again in Meru and killed two French tourists, Bertrand Legave and Patricia Coffornic. The French couple had apparently stumbled on a party of armed men feasting on a zebra inside the park and been shot dead. And on three occasions, between April and July 1989, convoys of minibuses had been attacked on the road between Amboseli and Kilaguni lodge in Tsavo National Park, in south-eastern Kenya. During one of these attacks an American tourist was killed and another suffered facial wounds, a bullet carving a deep furrow across his cheek. In both of the other two attacks on the same road, several German tourists were seriously injured. Four British tourists were in one of the minibuses when the first of these attacks took place and while none of them was hurt, one of the men later described the incident to journalists. 'The first we knew was that the first of the three buses suddenly turned around and the driver shouted "Bandits, bandits!" Then the second bus carrying Germans tried to do a three-point turn on the mud track but they had some trouble because it was an old vehicle. Meanwhile, two bandits started firing at the bus. One of the bullets went into the left side of a thirty-five-year-old German woman, blew her left breast away and then went through her leg. She was crouching, and so it came out and pierced the wrist of a German woman sitting next to her. The driver managed to turn round and they sped back in the direction they had come from. Then we saw the bandits running towards us. They were about fifty yards away. My wife shouted, "There! Bandits!" and I said to the driver, "For God's sake, turn the motor round." As we started to turn round, a shot whistled through the cab which seemed to be aimed at the driver. It rushed past my head and past the driver. I pushed him to the floor. Then they fired a second time at the back wheel arch. It went through the wheel and hit the seat support on the floor and went through that. A piece landed in my safari bag. The bullets missed our wives by two inches. The third shot went through the back tyre. We just kept on driving. The driver was kneeling and the two wives were lying flat on the floor in the back. We sped off as fast as we could even though we knew we had a puncture. Just after we had overtaken the other two fleeing vehicles, the tyre came away from the rim and fell off.'

In some ways, it was miraculous that more tourists were not killed or injured during this period. But for the bandits, robbing tourists was just a casual sideline: the major work was poaching elephants for their hugely valuable ivory. For several years, elephant poaching had been worsening in Kenya, as in much of Africa. But in 1988 Kenya's most vulnerable parks, particularly Meru and Tsavo, had virtually been taken over by gangs of Somali poachers, armed with Kalashnikov assault rifles and, in some cases, even rocket-propelled grenades. In the Masai Mara corruption among the wildlife staff manifested itself in ticket fiddles and the occasional poached rhino, but in Tsavo almost the entire staff of the park was directly involved in the killing of elephants and the ivory trade. The warden and his men remained inside the safe castles of the park headquarters while the Somalis, mostly deserters from the Somali army, roamed the parks, shooting elephants, frightening tourists and regularly paying off the men who were supposed to be fighting them. In July 1988 a Kenyan safari guide had come across a gang of men in combat gear, Kalashnikovs slung across their shoulders. 'My first reaction was that they were our own forces,' he later recalled. 'But then I noticed that their fatigues were much darker and they all wore a white sash from shoulder to waist.' So confident were the poachers by this point that the gang barely bothered to turn and look at the safari vehicle, but simply kept walking through the grass. When tourists complained to the park authorities about seeing dead elephants or suspicious activities, their questions were simply shrugged off. One tourist, in despair, wrote to the Kenyan *Standard* newspaper. 'The front of the elephant's face had been sawn off and there were tyre tracks around the carcass, obviously from some large truck,' the letter read. 'When we went to report the matter at park headquarters we saw two rangers curing cheetah skins and the skin of an antelope. When we asked what had happened to the cheetahs, they said, "They died."'

In Tsavo, a vast, arid park the size of Wales, elephant numbers had fallen more than forty thousand in 1960 to a mere five thousand by mid 1988. An aerial survey conducted much against the will of the park authorities counted more dead elephants in much of Tsavo East than live ones. The slaughter was terrible. Tsavo was dotted with putrefying piles of elephant flesh, blackened with the bodies of thousands of fat, shrieking vultures. On 28 May 1988 Patrick Hamilton, a warden based in Nairobi who paid regular visits to Tsavo – where he was treated like an enemy by the park staff – flew over the Taita hills, on the edges of Tsavo, and came across a scattering of twenty-four newly killed elephants, including pregnant mothers and calves without ivory. The entire herd had been shot down in a hail of automatic gunfire. A few weeks later, Hamilton found another pile of twenty-eight carcasses in the same area. 'It was horrible flying then. You never knew. Every morning you'd go up and you had no idea how many new carcasses you were going to see.'

The climax to the killing of elephants and men came in August 1989, at the same time as the inquest. Joy Adamson had been killed ten years earlier, but her husband George, the real lion expert, lived on. By this time George was eighty-three years old, thin and unwell, yet still the charming, mischievous leonine character he had always been. Thirty-three years after he and Joy had acquired Elsa, when George had shot her mother, the old man had just received a new litter of lion cubs to raise. He lived, as he had done for the previous two decades, in a makeshift camp, protected only by a flimsy wire fence, in the

117

remote Kora National Reserve. There, his daily battle was against the Somali herdsmen who invaded the reserve with their goats and cattle. On the morning of his death, George was sitting in camp with a German visitor, Inge Leidertheil, when a light aircraft flew overhead, signalling its intention to land at the nearby airstrip. Inge volunteered to drive the Land Rover to the strip and set out with Bitacha, one of George's staff. Ten minutes later, shots rang through the bush. George and several more staff leaped into another jeep and drove along the track towards the airstrip. By the time they arrived, Bitacha's leg had been broken with an iron bar, and Inge was being pulled into the scrub by a couple of Somalis. George drove straight at the Somalis, who raised automatic weapons and sprayed the car with bullets. George and two of his men, Ongesa and Kiya, were killed almost immediately. With the death of George Adamson, the last of the first great generation of game wardens in Kenya, a marvellous era had finally passed.

On the surface, there was little to connect the death of George Adamson with the probable abduction, rape and murder of Julie Ward. But there was significant common ground. Both George and Julie had been killed in Kenyan game reserves. Both deaths were, in a way, the result of a steady and insidious breakdown in law and order within Kenya's parks and reserves, and within the administration of the wildlife system itself. George had been conducting a single-handed battle, with little help from the warden of Kora, against invading herdsmen. Julie had disappeared from under the eyes of the staff of the Masai Mara. In fact, it seemed distinctly possible that it was the reserve staff themselves who were responsible for her death. Certainly, they had done little to find her when she was missing and still alive. And they had given no worthwhile assistance in the effort to trace her killers.

George Adamson's death added significantly to the bad publicity concerning Kenya's wildlife system. The whole world read of this latest killing and tourists soon began to cancel trips to Kenya. One of the fastest growing tourist industries in the world – and a vital source of foreign exchange to Kenya's economy – was in danger of collapsing because of the shooting incidents. The regular stream of bad news surrounding the Julie Ward case had initiated worries among tourists about Kenya's safety. But the series of incidents in the months and weeks leading up to the inquest had made their worst fears a reality. John Ward knew that the killing of elephants and the shooting of tourists and, eventually, George Adamson, would only make it more difficult for him to force the Kenyans to admit that the mysterious death of his daughter had in fact been yet another murder in one of Kenya's wildlife sanctuaries.

At last, on Wednesday 9 August 1989, eleven months after Julie's remains were found, the inquest into her death opened in the Central Court building in Nairobi. It was the same courtroom in which, in 1941, Jock Broughton had stood trial for the murder of Josslyn Hay, Earl of Erroll. That trial, later to be described in James Fox's book, *White Mischief*, received enough attention to dislodge news of the war from the front pages of British newspapers. The excesses of Happy Valley ('Are you married or do you live in Kenya,' went the music hall joke) revealed in court made the trial the most remarkable in Kenya's history. The Julie Ward inquest, equally revealing in a different way, was to prove scarcely less extraordinary. Indeed, the courtroom had hardly changed in nearly fifty years. The panelled room was dark and dusty and its high ceiling was strung with spider webs. Joseph Mango, the chief magistrate, sat at a long table at the front, beneath a crest of two carved wooden lions. An incisive, cultivated man, with piercing eyes and a goatee beard, Mango's personality, in turn gruff, impatient and humorous was, along with that of the ebullient Georgiadis, to dominate the proceedings. The witness box stood to Mango's right. Behind were the benches where sat the police, Georgiadis and Alex Etyang, the assistant deputy public prosecutor who was charged with presenting the state's case to the magistrate. A middle-aged man with thick glasses and a habit of looking at the ground and scratching the back of his head while thinking,

Etyang was seldom to seem comfortable in court. The next row contained representatives from the British High Commission and two women, Doreen Walford and Christine Radley, whom Ward had hired to take down and type up a complete transcript of the proceedings. John Ward himself was to be called later as a witness, and as such could not yet attend the inquest. Behind the secretaries were several rows of benches dominated by noisy British journalists, who as Ward had hoped had turned up in numbers: all the major British newspapers were represented. The Kenyan reporters generally sat in a press box at the side, and curious members of the public stood behind the benches or squeezed into the public balcony at the back.

The proceedings were opened by Alex Etyang with a brief summary of Julie's arrival in Kenya and her trip to the Mara. On 13 September, Julie's vehicle was found, he said. 'The police officers noticed near the vehicle the remains of a fire, which appeared to have been made from shrubs and plastic materials. It was believed that the fire was made by the deceased, when the night became cold for her. Footprints were noticed heading away from the vehicle, for over one hundred metres. The footprints appeared to suggest that there was only one human being walking away from the vehicle in that direction.' After the body was discovered, Etyang continued, 'The remains were examined by the pathologist to determine the cause of death. We shall put foward evidence of the pathologist who thought death was caused by injuries and subsequent burning. The father of the deceased also carried out investigations, to some extent.' It was not a particularly eloquent opening and Etyang had restrained himself from describing the injuries on Julie's leg and jawbone as cracks and tears. But his intentions were clear. Julie had become stuck in the gully. Julie had walked away from the vehicle alone. Julie, as he was to attempt to show throughout the inquest, had been killed by wild animals. The inquest was to take on the form less of a united effort to establish the true cause of Julie's death than of a trial, a confrontation between Etyang and Georgiadis, between the forces of the Kenyan government and those of John Ward.

120

The first witness called by Etyang was Paul Weld Dixon. A large, genial man, Weld Dixon told of befriending Julie while she was camping in his garden. 'She was a tourist who had fallen in love with Kenya,' he said. 'She wanted to start up a business. What really caused a small friendship between us was two husky dogs, which she owned. I like dogs and have some of my own. This made a bond of friendship.' After Julie had moved out of the Weld Dixons' garden she had returned to visit them in 'typical Kenyan style. She arrived at ten or eleven in the morning and asked for coffee. We liked her.' Weld Dixon told of Julie's decision to visit the Mara, in the Suzuki he described as 'caramel colour. The colour of vomit. A mud colour.' And Etyang slowly led him through the first worrying days after Julie's disappearance, the beginnings of the search and John Ward's arrival. But it was under Georgiadis's cross-examination that Weld Dixon really stirred the court and presented the press with the headlines for the next day's newspapers. Weld Dixon first related how Shaker had told him that Julie's leg and jawbone had been cut with a sharp instrument and had said that 'this makes it a case of murder'. But he then came up with even more dramatic testimony. Shaker had, Weld Dixon said, held up the leg and said: 'Look at the leg. Rigor mortis has set in. The leg has set in the position of someone running. The forepart of this leg is in a straight line; the position when running.' In fact, the position of Julie's foot and lower leg bore no connection to her position or stance at death. As Professor Gresham was later to say, when a human body is thrown on to a fire it curls up like a rasher of bacon in a frying pan. Julie's lower leg had been shaped by the heat of the fire, but the testimony was exactly what the gathered press were waiting for. 'BRITISH GIRL MAY HAVE DIED WHILE FLEEING ATTACKER', read the headline the next morning in the *Daily Telegraph*. Julie appeared to have been 'cut down while fleeing from an attacker'.

The next witness was David Weston, the American balloon pilot at Serena lodge. Weston stood casually in the witness box, his silver-black hair swept high and backwards from his forehead and neat, bespectacled face. His tone was casual, too, and he was quick to point out errors in the ways of others. Glen Burns was 'the jerk who had left her there'. And Julie herself had, in his opinion, been foolish to drive on her own in the Mara. 'I tried to talk her out of going to Nairobi alone,' Weston told the court. 'It's not a good idea for women to be alone in the bush. The car had bald tyres. I was concerned. I offered her money for the air fare. She said no and she left. She said she had been around. It's not a good idea for single women to drive alone in the bush. Poachers, bandits. Someone could be taken advantage of.'

Etyang, however, was more interested in other matters. He had already quizzed Weld Dixon about Julie's friends, asking: 'When she was in the guest house, did you get the impression she was on her own?' And now he pursued the same matter with Weston. Had Julie and Glen Burns had a lovers' tiff? Did Julie book her room at Serena for one person or two? And what about Weston's own evening with Julie?

'Did you escort her to her room?' Etyang asked.

'Yes, I did,' Weston replied.

'Did you go into her room?'

'No, I didn't.'

'That night, did anything strange happen?'

'No, nothing at all.'

The line of questioning was clear: how many men had Julie slept with during her stay in Kenya and her visit to the Masai Mara? Not for the last time, Etyang was trying to put Julie's character on trial. In Africa, a man's character is his fate and, whatever the law says, the killing of a bad man or woman is seldom thought of as murder. If the court could not prove that Julie had died at the teeth of wild animals, then at least it could show that she had asked for whatever it was that befell her.

It had been a lively first day, but the second day, revolving around the testimony of David Nchoko, the clerk who had forged Julie's signature at the Sand River camp, was to prove even more dramatic. Earlier in the year, after Ward had produced evidence from handwriting experts, Nchoko had admitted to the police that he had written Julie's name and details in the visitors book. He had done so, he said, because Julie had forgotten to fill in the book herself. The name and details were necessary for his accounts. He had copied them from another receipt that Julie had filled in with her name and passport number and then signed. A tall, slightly stooping Masai, with missing teeth and the look of a hunted stag in his yellow eyes, Nchoko stood nervously in the witness box. He said he spoke no English and a translator converted his testimony from Swahili. Under Etyang's guidance, he recounted how Julie and Glen Burns had arrived at the Sand River camp in the late afternoon of Friday 2 September. He said they had pitched their tents about two hundred yards from the gate and when he had returned to duty the next morning, the tents were still there but the Suzuki and its drivers had already left. Julie had returned several days later on her own, he said. 'On 6 September I saw the lady. The lady entered at two o'clock with the vehicle. Then she went to the tents. Then later, she came back to the gate where I was. She paid some money to me.' At two thirty-seven that afternoon, she drove off in the direction of Keekorok.

During the lunchbreak, Ward and Whitford, who had talked in person to Nchoko at Sand River camp, told Georgiadis that the clerk could speak English perfectly well. When the proceedings resumed, Georgiadis flew on to the attack.

'Can we establish that you speak English very well,' he demanded.

'No,' said Nchoko.

'You are wasting our time,' Georgiadis roared. 'You gave three statements to the police in English, didn't you? Did you give three statements on three different dates, in English?'

Nchoko stared at the ground, as if he was hoping it would open up and swallow him. Eventually, Mango intervened. 'When you say you don't understand English, are you lying?' the magistrate asked. 'This is serious.'

'It is true that I understand English,' Nchoko reluctantly admitted. 'But I don't speak English well.'

From this point, conducting his examination entirely in English, Georgiadis set about tearing Nchoko's story apart. 'As I understand the position, you are saying that Julie left without entering the visitors book,' he boomed. 'You filled it in innocently from another receipt. When?'

'Half an hour after she left,' Nchoko replied.

'But she had gone off with all the original receipts,' Georgiadis pounced. 'If you look in the visitors book, you had attempted to sign for her in a way that looked like her signature – Julie Ward. Are you telling the court that half an hour after seeing another receipt, you memorized how she signed? And you have maintained, under oath, that this was an innocent act?'

Confused and frightened, Nchoko said nothing. Georgiadis then turned to the question of the Englishman, Bower, who had left before Julie but had been issued with a receipt numbered after Julie's.

'Why was Mr Bower issued with the latter receipt?' he asked. Once again, Nchoko declined to respond. By now, Georgiadis's eloquence, anger and legal trickery had become too much for Nchoko and he had withdrawn into a frightened, sullen silence. Whatever he said, it seemed, only dug him deeper into trouble. From now on, he simply denied everything, trembling so much that Mango told him to keep still. 'Are you an alcoholic?' the magistrate asked impatiently.

Georgiadis raised the subject of the visit by Ward, Whitford and Ferguson to Sand River and asked why Nchoko had not simply told them about forging Julie's signature. 'Why did you lie if it was an innocent mistake?' Georgiadis demanded. 'Why didn't you say straight away?' But Nchoko denied that the meeting had taken place. The three Englishmen were therefore paraded through the court, in an effort to jog Nchoko's memory. When Ward's turn came, he stood just a few feet from the witness box, staring at Nchoko. But the witness still refused to admit he had seen these men.

'The wheels of justice are beginning to turn,' Ward told

reporters later that day. 'The Mafia-style silence is being broken and I'm getting nearer to the people who took my daughter away.' Called as a witness by Etyang, Nchoko had been a godsend to Ward and Georgiadis. His lies about Julie's signature had been compounded by his lies over speaking English and the meeting with Ward, Whitford and Ferguson at Sand River. Rather than demonstrate that Julie had left Sand River camp on her way to Nairobi, Nchoko's testimony had merely focused suspicion on the camp and its staff.

But the most sensational moment of the day was still to come. Reading aloud from Superintendent Wanjau's report of an interview with Nchoko, Georgiadis came across the following entry, made by Wanjau on 7 February 1989: 'I am inquiring,' Wanjau had told Nchoko, 'into a suspected offence of murder, that between 6 and 13 September 1988 you and others still at large murdered Julie Anne Ward. I do have reason to believe that you, David Kandula Nchoko, are either connected with the offence or have such information which may help the inquiry.' For eleven months, the commissioner of police had refused to announce that he had started a murder investigation. But here was Wanjau, the chief police investigator, working on the assumption that Julie had been murdered. And here moreover, standing in the witness box, was one of his prime suspects.

'Game park warden is named as killer of safari girl Julie,' ran the headline in the next morning's *Daily Express*. It scarcely mattered that Nchoko was neither a warden, nor even a ranger, but a clerk, and that he had not been named as a killer, but a suspect. As Norman Luck's story in the *Express* continued: 'Yesterday – to gasps from a packed courtroom – it was revealed that the police had secretly been conducting a murder hunt since February.' By the end of day two of the inquest, the government case was in a shambles while Ward and Georgiadis were jubilant.

The morning of Friday 11 August began with the testimony of Gerald Karori, the police constable at Sand River camp. Under Etyang's examination, Karori spoke in fluent English of seeing

125

Julie arrive at Sand river. 'I saw a lady at the camping site, across the river. She was pulling down a tent. A Suzuki was standing by. It was about two o'clock. She went to the second tent. I crossed the river. There was not much water. I went where she was. I greeted her. I asked her if the second tent was hers. She said it was. I helped her pull it down. I told her I was a police officer, because I was in jungle uniform. I informed her there was an unpaid bill for camping and that she had to report to the revenue clerk. She said she had a problem with the motor vehicle. The vehicle had broken down. Her friend had flown to Nairobi. She was going back to Nairobi. She had to meet him in Nairobi.' A little later, around two forty-five, Karori saw the Suzuki heading up the rise towards Keekorok.

When Etyang finished, Georgiadis took over. From the start, the lawyer made it clear that he objected to Karori's languid style in the witness box. The lawyer was soon at his most aggressive, bellowing at the policeman. 'Brace up and talk!' he shouted at one point. 'Rubbish!' he yelled at another. 'A very literate statement,' he said, when reading Karori's words as taken down by Wanjau. 'How come you give a different impression in the witness box?' Waving the statement in the air, Georgiadis asked why Karori had waited until 25 September, twelve days after Julie's remains were found, before speaking to the police.

'Wouldn't it have been helpful if you had said you had seen the girl and helped her. Wasn't it important? There was a missing person under your care. How come you did all this? Are you hiding something from the beginning?'

Whipped into a frenzy by his own rhetoric, Georgiadis grew louder and redder in the face until finally he burst out: 'Your whole story is a tissue of lies. Why were you hiding the information? You know more about this matter, as does Nchoko, than you are prepared to tell us.'

The court held its breath. What was Georgiadis suggesting? As Karori continued to stare into space, Mango provided the answer. 'Did you kill her?' the magistrate demanded. 'Why don't you say it? Is she haunting you? You and a few others killed the woman. That is what he is saying. What happened to the lady?'

Attacked from all sides, Karori shrunk into the witness box and breathed out a whisper: 'I don't know.'

When Georgiadis had finished with Karori, the inquest broke for lunch. In the afternoon, Sebastian Tham, the balloon pilot from Keekorok, was called. With Etyang questioning him, Tham recounted his version of events from the time when he had first heard that Julie was missing to the discovery of her remains. 'I took an active part,' Tham said, in his clipped military style. 'I inspected the tree and found a can of pilchards and a towel. I examined the fire. In the ashes appeared to be personal belongings – coins, plastic, film cartridges, a piece of hair, bits of molten metal. The hair was next to the fire, on the periphery of the fire. The leg was some distance away. I saw the leg. It took the appearance of a European leg. It probably belonged to the girl in question. It had a blue appearance. It looked like it had been taken off at the knee. It was charred. Some distance away from the leg were two pieces of jaw. They had fillings in them.'

Etyang asked which parts of the leg were burned.

'I'm not used to seeing bits of human beings,' Tham replied.

Georgiadis then took over. Apart from the police and John Ward, who now seemed locked in combat, Sebastian Tham was the only person – and thus the only independent witness – who had seen both the site of the car and the site of Julie's remains on the day of the discovery. Georgiadis took the opportunity to score some points.

GEORG: There may be evidence about a set of footprints moving away from the vehicle. Did you see any, moving away from the vehicle?

THAM: No. No sign. No tracks. There appeared to have been some rain. There were no real car tracks either.

GEORG: Two things. The vehicle was meant to be carrying a

127

plastic jerrycan full of petrol. Did you see any plastic can?

THAM: No.

GEORG: If a girl, like that girl, was going off across country because, say, she was stuck or lost, do you think she would have carried a plastic jerrycan with petrol?

THAM: I doubt it.

GEORG: If someone had set off and was lost or stuck, and set off across country, would you expect them to leave binoculars and a map behind?

THAM: No.

GEORG: You found flip-flops at the fire?

THAM: Yes.

GEORG: Would you expect someone to take off across country in flip-flops?

THAM: I would use flip-flops if I had nothing else to wear.

It had been another disastrous day for Etyang. His own witnesses had already torn gaping holes in his case. Desperately in need of time to consolidate his position, the assistant deputy public prosecutor asked for a temporary postponement, and to the frustration of Ward and Georgiadis, Mango agreed to adjourn the inquest for three weeks. 'It's very disappointing,' Ward told the *Sunday Times*. 'I'm afraid the case will lose momentum. You would have thought that after eleven months they would have got themselves organized. I suppose I should be grateful. At least they are holding an inquest and it does give me the chance to follow up new lines of inquiry.' A few days later, he took yet another trip down to the Masai Mara and visited the Sand River camp. There, on the spot where Julie had camped, he found a bunch of fresh flowers neatly encased in cellophane. The nearest flower shop was a hundred miles away. 'This,' he said, 'is a bloody funny country.'

The inquest resumed on Monday 4 September, with Alex Etyang immediately returning to the subject of Julie's morals.

With Doug Morey, Julie's landlord, in the witness box, Etyang probed for any hint of Julie's love life. 'What was Julie doing while she stayed in the guest house?' he asked Morey. 'Do you know if Dr Burns visited her? Did Dr Burns stay with her? If he had moved in, would you have seen him?' Morey answered these questions emphatically. Julie had friends but, as far as he knew, no boyfriends. She had had no 'overnight guests'.

The rest of the week was to be dominated by the testimony of one man, Simon Makallah, the chief warden of the Masai Mara at the time of Julie's death. This was the man who had found Julie's remains, who had control over the reserve and whom Georgiadis liked to refer to as a 'king' in his 'kingdom'. At the very least, Ward and Georgiadis were sure, Makallah must have known what had happened to Julie. Etyang's examination of Makallah lasted just a few hours, but Georgiadis was to keep the warden on the stand for three days. Whenever Makallah stumbled or contradicted himself, Georgiadis pounced. He asked whether Makallah knew what SOS meant. He quizzed Makallah about the issue of machetes, such as might have been used to cut up Julie's body, to his rangers and to himself. And he established, to Makallah's annoyance, that the warden had been on enforced leave from just a few weeks after Julie's death. But it was over two issues that Georgiadis went for the warden's throat. The first was the question of Makallah and cars. On his first day in the witness box, Makallah had told the court that he did not possess a driving licence and was always driven around the Masai Mara by official drivers. But Ward remembered that on one occasion Makallah had personally driven him and Frank Ribeiro to Sand River.

GEORG: You said yesterday that you do not drive.
MAK: Yes.
GEORG: Do you recollect on 25 September you drove Mr Ward and Frank Ribeiro from Keekorok to the Sand River camp?
MAK: What date?
GEORG: 25 September.

MAK: No, I never.

GEORG: And if Ward comes in and tells the court that you drove him and Mr Ribeiro would that be untrue?

MAK: No, because I am saying what I can from my recollection.

GEORG: Please answer the question. Would that be untrue?

MAK: It would be untrue.

GEORG: Why did you ask just now, when I put the question, about the date?

MAK: Because I was not sure and I did not get your question correctly.

GEORG: I suggest to you that you were off guard at that moment and would recollect driving on 25 September.

MAK: No.

Georgiadis was convinced that Makallah was feigning ignorance of driving in an attempt to divert attention from the possibility that he had driven Julie's car to the gully where it was found. Later, James Sindiyo, Makallah's own assistant warden, was to testify that he had seen Makallah drive on numerous occasions and even recounted an incident where Makallah had crashed a vehicle. When asked what he thought of Makallah's denial that he drove, Sindiyo replied, 'I think it's strange.' Georgiadis had also noticed that during his earlier testimony the warden had remarked that the Suzuki would have been able to navigate the gully if it had been equipped with four-wheel drive. This, Georgiadis felt, was another potentially damning statement.

GEORG: How do you know that this vehicle was not a four-wheel-drive vehicle?

MAK: Generally Suzukis are four-wheel drive so I did not mean that particular jeep.

GEORG: How did you know that this vehicle did not have four-wheel drive?

MAK: I did not know.

GEORG: Please tell the court. How did you know that this particular Suzuki did not have four-wheel drive?

MAK: I did not know.

GEORG: I will ask you again. Your answer can only come from knowledge if you have driven that vehicle before and were aware of its lack of four-wheel drive.

MAK: My answer came from what I saw.

GEORG: Is it magic that you knew it had no four-wheel drive? I suggest you know all about that vehicle and that you had driven it before into that Sand river tributary.

The second key point of contention between Georgiadis and Makallah concerned vultures. Makallah said he had been guided to Julie's remains by vultures rising from the ground and sitting in a nearby tree. But Georgiadis knew from the pathologists' reports that neither the leg nor the jawbone bore any signs of claw or beak marks.

GEORG: You found her remains at four forty-five approximately? When you saw vultures on the ground?

MAK: Vultures in a tree.

GEORG: And when you got right close to the tree, they took off and some more took off from the ground as you got closer. Then you saw a trampled area which was about, you think, ten kilometres or more from the Suzuki?

MAK: Yes.

GEORG: You have seen many kills in the Mara over the last fourteen years?

MAK: Yes.

GEORG: Have you seen many remains stripped bare by vultures?

MAK: Yes.

GEORG: (Handing over a photograph of Julie's lower leg) Look at this. Does the leg bear any signs of strips taken off by vultures in any way? Can you see flesh torn by vultures?

MAK: The leg is torn, I don't know by what.

GEORG: I'm asking specifically. You have expertise about vultures. I'll make my point clear. If this girl had been lying in this area for many hours am I right she would have been stripped to the bone?

MAK: You are not right. I can't tell when the vultures arrived unless I was one of them myself.

GEORG: May I suggest to you that the only reason you mentioned vultures at all, in this matter, was because you had to give a reason why you went in that direction.

MAK: Your suggestion is wrong.

GEORG: What I am saying is that you put the vultures there. You did it to give you a reason for finding the remains. To show cause and reason for finding the remains.

MAK: Vultures are free, wild birds. I can't take them from a zoo and put them there.

The battle of wits between Simon Makallah and Byron Georgiadis ended in stalemate shortly before lunch on Thursday 7 September, the seventh day of the inquest. Up to this point, the evidence had been concerned primarily with Julie's character, her last days in the Masai Mara and the search of 13 September 1988. The next ten days would see a dozen police officers and scientists called by Alex Etyang to give evidence on their investigation into Julie's death. To the amazement of many Kenyans, this testimony was to prove a unique opportunity to scrutinize the workings of the Kenyan police force. By the late 1980s, the police in Kenya were a feared and deeply disliked organization. Despite the good intentions of some senior officers, petty corruption was almost universal in the lower ranks of the force. Crimes were as likely to be committed as prevented by many policemen. And brutality was commonplace: suspected criminals were routinely beaten until they confessed to crimes they may or may not have committed. Very occasionally, articles such as one entitled 'Too much force by the Force', published on 26 August 1988, in the *Weekly Review*,

Kenya's most daring publication, would accuse the police of 'negligence, indiscipline and sheer thuggery'. But on the whole, the police were untouchable. Yet as Etyang called police officer after police officer, Georgiadis set out to demonstrate that the 'alleged investigation', as he liked to call it, into the death of Julie Ward had been a fiasco from start to finish. Witnesses such as Superintendent Wanjau and Jason Kaviti, the chief pathologist, walked into the court smiling and left with deep scowls on their faces. Under Georgiadis's aggressive, bullying examinations, it was almost as though Kenya's police force was in the dock.

In fact, the investigation was not quite as bad as Georgiadis tried to make out. Despite a lack of manpower and equipment, some good work had been carried out, particularly by the 'scene-of-crime' expert from Nairobi, Superintendent Musimi Rudisi. Both the gully where the car was found and the site of Julie's remains were, eventually, thoroughly combed, and bags full of ashes, pieces of cloth, cigarette butts, orange juice cartons, chunks of hair and other potential evidence were collected and taken back to Nairobi for examination. Julie's skull was found several weeks after her death, nearly a mile away from the rest of her remains. A tiny plant growing in the ashes of the fire was uprooted and examined by a scientist at the National Museum of Kenya, who concluded that it had germinated between 10 and 12 September. The police had even carried out rather amateurish acoustic tests to see if screams at the site where the remains were found could be heard at the Masai village, a mile away: they could, faintly. But some of the policemen and experts involved in the investigation were clearly incompetent, and as Georgiadis was to emphasize, a series of crucial errors and suspicious omissions had been made.

Georgiadis soon caused a good deal of amusement among the foreign press, if not the locals, when he prompted Inspector Othiambo, the senior policeman in the Masai Mara, to admit that the Mara river post possessed no vehicle. 'So what hope do you have,' Georgiadis asked, 'as an inspector in charge of the whole Mara, to check anyone poaching or nastily inclined towards anyone else, unless you stumble on them in broad day-light?' But he soon turned to more pertinent matters. Julie's Suzuki, he revealed, had been left by the police in the gully and only remembered after it had been removed by Sebastian Tham and washed. Even then, no attempt was made to dust it for fingerprints. Nor was the can of pilchards found in the tree near Julie's remains fingerprinted. No photographs were taken of the footprints across the Sand river, and Julie's flip-flops were themselves lost. The remains of her brassiere, found in the fire, were burned to a cinder in a 'flammability test'. Eventually, with heavy sarcasm, Georgiadis asked one of the police experts, 'You don't do all your inquests like this?' Bemused, the policeman replied: 'Yes, your honour.'

The most disastrous police witness was a man Georgiadis was later to compare to Inspector Clouseau: Superintendent Muchiri Wanjau, the Criminal Investigations detective assigned from Nairobi to lead the Julie Ward investigation. With well-groomed sideburns and a broad, colourful tie, Wanjau stepped grinning into the witness box. The smile did not last long. 'To shoot oneself in the foot happens in the best-regulated circles,' Georgiadis was to say about Wanjau. 'But to shoot oneself repeatedly in the foot until the gun is empty is a little unusual.' The policeman had spent more than three months based at Keekorok and a further three on the Julie Ward case in Nairobi. He had seen all the post mortem reports. He was presented with the forensic evidence showing that the fire in which Julie had been burned had been started with a man-made accelerant. He had been well aware of the forgery at Sand River and had himself accused Nchoko of murdering Julie. And he had been told about all the other evidence John Ward had collected. Yet in his final report, on 6 April 1989, all he could come up with was that 'the remains were found burned and eaten and after extensive investigation no evidence of foul play came to light. If anything, the deceased committed suicide.'

When his turn came to question Wanjau, Georgiadis was like a bull pawing at the dust. By this stage of the inquest, Mango

Bryon Georgiadis,
Ward's lawyer
at the inquest

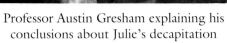

Professor Austin Gresham explaining his
conclusions about Julie's decapitation

Chief Magistrate Joseph Mango

David Nchoko,
clerk at Sand River campsite

Simon Makallah,
chief warden of
the Masai Mara

Above left: Detective Inspector David Shipperlee; *Above right:* Detective Superintendent Graham Searle

Superintendent Muchiri Wanjau

A ranger patrolling Makari post

Peter Kipeen walking
to find help for the
journalists stranded in
the Sand river

had shown his willingness to allow a good deal of latitude to the lawyers and Georgiadis lost no opportunity to insult and degrade the policeman. 'I am surprised you are still in office,' Georgiadis soon said to Wanjau. 'I think a long refresher course is needed.' When Wanjau denied hearing a discussion in the police commissioner's office, Georgiadis said he must have been wearing ear plugs. And on more than one occasion the lawyer glared at Wanjau and said, 'You are just making this up as you go along.' Before long, Georgiadis had also drawn out the extraordinary admission from Wanjau that in six months of investigation he had not bothered to take down the names of any of the rangers in the Masai Mara, let alone interview them.

'Can you even give the names of the rangers posted at Makari post during the period 6 September 1988 to 13 September 1988?' Georgiadis asked.

'I did not take any names of the rangers,' Wanjau replied. 'They had been involved in the search for the lady and therefore from the beginning had not been taken as suspects.'

'That,' said Georgiadis, 'is funny.'

Wanjau soon told the court that he had kept no record of the investigation, other than a handful of statements. He had not only failed to interrogate Simon Makallah but had actually used him as a translator on one occasion. He had made no attempt to talk to the Swiss camera team, when they were still in the Masai Mara, though he did check with Makallah that they had 'permits' to camp in the reserve. Similarly, he entirely failed to seek out any of the tour guides who had brought tourists down to camp at Sand River during the period Julie had stayed at the camp. And when asked whether he had attempted to find out if the rangers in the reserve were issued with machetes, such as might have been used to cut up Julie's body, he replied: 'It was not relevant.'

Wanjau had been particularly dismissive of the evidence turned up by John Ward. The Swiss camp which he had never visited was, he insisted, not three hundred yards from Julie's car but nearly three miles. He insisted that Ward had never told him about the camera battery found at Makari post. And he had thrown away the toothpaste tube Frank Ribeiro had picked up behind one of the huts at Makari. 'It was not found at Makari post,' he explained.

'Mr Ward was helping you, was he not?' Georgiadis asked.

'No,' Wanjau replied.

'What do you think he was doing?'

'I did not ask him.'

Wanjau also dismissed the possibility that Julie had been abducted and held before being murdered during the missing week in the Mara, prompting Georgiadis to ask: 'So what did you think she did for a whole week from 6 September until the thirteenth, when her remains were found?'

'She was a lady who would go out with any man in the park,' replied Wanjau.

On questioning, Wanjau admitted that his only evidence for this suggestion was the article published in the *Sunday Mirror*.

'Let me suggest,' Georgiadis eventually said, 'that you were not in the least bit interested in doing a proper investigation in this case.'

'I was interested,' Wanjau protested.

'That you suspected that the revenue clerk and Karori knew a great deal about this matter.'

'Yes.'

'And that they were probably the key to unlocking the door to this investigation.'

'No, that is not true.'

'And that you stopped short of finding out who really could have been involved in this murder.'

'No.'

'I suggest to you that far from doing an investigation in the accepted sense of the word you did nothing of the sort,' Georgiadis proclaimed. 'You went through the motions of asking a few people and recording a few statements, but unless you were pushed by Mr Ward you did nothing. I am beginning to think that you did not go there to investigate but to conduct a cover-up.'

*

The 'cover-up' was a corner-stone of John Ward's theories and had become a war cry for Georgiadis in court. Yet Superintendent Wanjau's police work smelled less of cover-up than gross incompetence and negligence, as Etyang himself was later to admit. ('Inefficiency and incompetence,' as Etyang put it, in his one criticism of Kenyan officialdom.) Wanjau had achieved almost nothing in his investigations because, quite simply, he did not know where to start. But when the inquest turned to the testimony of the pathologist who had examined Julie's remains, clearer evidence of diversionary tactics by the Kenyan authorities soon began to emerge.

Dr Shaker, the Egyptian pathologist who had carried out the initial post mortem, was as nervous in the witness box as he had been with John Ward after the alteration of his initial report. The cause of death, he said, was – as described in the altered report – 'blunt injuries with subsequent burning'. Etyang asked Shaker if he was sure. 'It could have happened,' the doctor replied uncertainly. Georgiadis was less patient with Shaker's indecision. 'If you are going to get difficult and guarded, I can be twice as difficult,' he warned. And before long, Shaker admitted to telling Weld Dixon that Julie's remains had been 'cut with a sharp instrument'. Why, then, had Dr Jason Kaviti, the chief police pathologist, altered the report to suggest the bones were cracked, not cut?

'We re-examined the leg together and he convinced me that the edges were uneven,' Shaker said.

'This is not your original report?'

'Only two words are different,' Shaker defended.

'These two words,' Georgiadis thundered, 'make the difference between heaven and hell.'

When Dr Kaviti took the stand, he explained under Etyang's lead the reasons for the alterations. Shaker, he said, wanted a second opinion on the remains. Kaviti had examined the leg and had seen 'no evidence of cutting by a sharp instrument. Instead of a cut I saw a tear. This indicated a blunt object. The two pieces of jaw had been cracked, not cut. The wound on the leg was lacerated.' Kaviti also said that he had warned Dr Shaker not to jump to conclusions as to the cause of death. 'This was because it was not certain that the person to whom the leg belonged was dead,' he explained. In conclusion, Kaviti said, the injuries were probably caused by a 'blunt object like the teeth of a carnivorous animal'.

Once Etyang had finished with the witness, Georgiadis embarked on a cross-examination that was to stretch across three days. Much of this time was taken up with extensive discussions of technical aspects of pathology, but there was one particular point on which Georgiadis was able to force Kaviti into a corner. When altering the original post mortem report, the chief pathologist had crucially omitted to change the phrase 'with subsequent burning' in the conclusion. The changes from 'cut' to 'torn' were hardly relevant if Julie's leg had been burned after it had been dismembered.

'Whether it was a "blunt instrument" or a "sharp instrument", do the words "with subsequent burning" not mean human intervention?' Georgiadis demanded.

'Not necessarily,' Kaviti answered.

'Can you explain the words "not necessarily"?' Georgiadis asked. 'The leg could have been flung into the fire by animals, just for a little barbecue?'

'When they were tearing and gnawing the bones some pieces could get into the fire, something they were fighting over.'

'Come on, you know and we know that carnivores do not like fires and they go nowhere near them. Does it occur to you how the fire was lit?'

'It must have been human,' Kaviti said.

'And you know from your evidence the use of an accelerator, probably petrol? Animals do not go around lighting petrol.'

'I have not heard of it.'

'Do you agree with me that it is surely unlikely that any innocent, itinerant Masai finding a dead caucasian in the bush, would just dismember it and then burn it just to tidy up the veld?'

'Masai don't usually go near dead human beings.'

'So if it was dismembered and burned as appears to be the

138

case, it would appear that someone was trying to hide the body, make it disappear?' Georgiadis asked.

'It could be,' Kaviti finally agreed.

By the end of the third day of Kaviti's testimony, enough doubt had been entered in the court to question both the chief pathologist's conclusions over the death of Julie Ward and his own integrity. When Professor Gresham, the British patholo- gist, took the stand, his evidence was to confirm these doubts. With a precision and authority that had been lacking in every witness so far called into the courtroom, Gresham laid out the facts which showed that Julie Ward's remains had been force- fully and expertly dismembered by a human being with a heavy, sharp instrument. The wounds in the skin, muscle, ligaments and bones all pointed to such a conclusion. Gresham described the beheading of Julie's body in graphic detail. 'You may have seen pictures of goats' heads being amputated with a sharp instrument,' he told the court. 'That is the sort of force, although it depends how sharp the instrument is. Such injuries must have been, and only have been, produced by one single swipe with a sharp instrument. That is my conclusion.' Prompted by Georgiadis, Gresham also said that when two pathologists disagreed over findings, they produced two sepa- rate reports.

'Is that standard and recognized practice?' Georgiadis asked.

'Absolutely,' Gresham replied.

Gresham's evidence ended on Wednesday 20 September, the sixteenth day of the inquest. The time had finally come for John Ward to take the stand. For the previous month, he had been forced to pace around Nairobi every day waiting for his two secretaries to type up the transcript of the evidence. Each after- noon, he would be standing outside the courtroom, asking journalists, 'How did it go, do you think we're getting any- where?' But now he was taking centre stage. He stood in the witness box, his large hands clenched against the wooden edges, and painstakingly began to tell his story. He took the courtroom through his recollections of hearing that his daughter was missing, flying out to Kenya, organizing the search, finding his daughter's grisly remains and battling for months and months with the Kenyan authorities. It was a moving tale and he avoided no detail, however terrible: 'I was shown the bottom part of a left leg, lying in the grass. The leg had been burned at the top end. There were also insect bites on the foot and a long, vertical cut on the calf. Some ten to fifteen feet away there was a jawbone; the bottom of a jawbone which was in two halves . . . I went through the ashes of the fire with my fingers to see if I could find anything else . . . There was a large tree and on one of the lower branches a tin of fish. The label had come off the tin and someone had written the word "pilchards". I believed the writing to be that of Julie . . . I noticed a lock of hair at the back of the fire. I knew her hair, I thought it was probably hers.'

Ward's evidence outlined the lengths to which he had gone to search out the man who had killed his daughter. And it emphasized his own suspicions – about Makari post and particularly the Sand River camp. But that weekend, Ward received a disturbing telephone call. It was from a young man named Paul Molinaro, a twenty-year-old Italian who had grown up in Kenya. Molinaro had just returned from the United States and had read about the inquest in the newspapers. The reports reminded him that he had seen Julie on several occasions on her last Tuesday, on 6 September 1988. He was certain, he told Ward, that she had driven away from the Sand River camp that afternoon. Ward immediately arranged to meet Molinaro with Bob Whitford and Georgiadis. Molinaro told them that he and three friends had driven down to the Mara for a few days in his father's Land Rover. They had spent their first two nights at a camping site on the banks of the Mara river and were heading, on the morning of 6 September, for Sand River. On their way, they stopped at Serena lodge for some drinks. The three friends entered the lodge while Molinaro stayed outside to fix a rattling exhaust pipe on his jeep. In the car park, his eye was caught by a white girl standing over the open bonnet of a Suzuki jeep. She was young, blonde and pretty, and she seemed to be on her own. But he made no effort to talk to her and walked into the lodge, where he had a few drinks and swam in the pool. After an hour or so, the four friends left Serena lodge and drove, quite quickly, to Keekorok, where they stopped again. Here, they had a few more drinks and some food and then proceeded on to Sand River. About halfway between Keekorok and Sand River, Molinaro saw the Suzuki, bumping slowly down the road ahead of them. As he overtook the Suzuki, two of his wheels climbed up on to the grass at the side of the road, and he slowed down, waving and glancing into the car. The woman smiled and Molinaro said he caught sight of a camera with a long lens on the seat beside her. A few minutes later, Molinaro pulled into Sand River. He and his friends proceeded to unload their tents and lazily started erecting them. While they were doing this, Molinaro looked up and saw the woman arrive and begin to dismantle two tents on the other side of the river. He wondered why one woman was taking down two tents and a few minutes later looked over again. This time the tents were gone and the car was heading towards the gate. Then he watched it climb up and over the rise on the road towards Keekorok. Two weeks later, when Julie's death was revealed in the press, Molinaro saw her photograph in the *Standard* newspaper and realized that the woman he had seen was Julie Ward.

John Ward was deeply suspicious of Molinaro's story. Why would Nchoko have forged her signature if Julie had indeed left Sand River that afternoon? Ward had put in weeks and weeks of work tracking down campers at Sand River and trying to establish that Julie had not left the camp of her own accord. 'Why did Molinaro come along now, out of the blue?' Ward was to say later. 'We had Nchoko and Karori in a corner and suddenly here was Molinaro saying he had seen Julie drive away. This allowed Etyang to make a big play, saying OK, Nchoko and Karori may have lied, but Julie was nonetheless seen driving away alive from Sand River. It all seemed very pat and we immediately began to suspect Molinaro was a plant.' Molinaro was young and rather bohemian in appearance by white Kenyan standards. Ward also stressed that Molinaro's father ran a casino in Nairobi. The proceedings of the inquest had only deepened Ward's suspicion that forces in Kenya were still intent on covering up Julie's murder.

Ward mulled all this over in his mind and decided to check up on Molinaro's story. One of Molinaro's friends from the safari, Rupert Smith, was English and lived in Oakham, near Leicester, and Ward sent a visitor to Smith to see if he could corroborate Molinaro's story. Smith was a vague, sleepy young man, and while he happily talked about the trip to the Mara, he scarcely remembered seeing Julie. Later, Ward was to fly to Los Angeles and Helsinki to talk to Molinaro's two other companions, but neither was able to erase Ward's doubts. Ward was also suspicious about Molinaro's statement that he had seen Julie's camera on the seat beside her. He and Whitford took a Suzuki and a Land Rover out for a drive to test if it would have been possible for Molinaro to have looked down on the passenger seat of the Suzuki as he was passing. Ward decided Molinaro could not possibly have seen the camera. 'He may have made up the bit about the camera to add authenticity,' Ward said, 'perhaps to collect the thousand pounds reward for information about the camera. But it certainly wasn't true.'

At the time, however, there was little Ward could do. He and Georgiadis realized they had to call Molinaro to testify, or they could have been charged with withholding evidence. But at least Molinaro's evidence could have shown that Nchoko and Karori were lying about the time Julie had left. Molinaro was unsure of the exact time he had seen the Suzuki driving away from Sand River, but he thought it was around mid-afternoon. Whitford quizzed the young man again and again. What was the position of the sun? Was it getting cooler? Darker? Under Whitford's guidance, Molinaro eventually testified in court that it was after four o'clock when Julie had driven away. 'If you saw her and the Suzuki leave the camp site at four, could she have possibly reached Narok before dark?' Georgiadis asked Molinaro at the inquest. 'She could not,' Molinaro replied.

Narok was the first proper town between the Mara and Nairobi and it was unlikely that Julie would have left the reserve without being sure she could make it to Narok, at least, by dark. Where then would she have been going at four in the afternoon? Molinaro's evidence had certainly been a boon to Nchoko and Karori, but Georgiadis had sown enough doubts in his evidence to leave questions hanging in court. One important omission was that Molinaro had not seen Julie at the wheel of the car when it had driven away. Was Julie alone? And, anyway, was Molinaro telling the truth?

On Thursday 28 September, after the testimony of Paul Molinaro, the inquest drew to an uncertain pause. Throughout the proceedings, Etyang had been waiting for Glen Burns and Stephen Watson to arrive in Kenya and give evidence. Both had been contacted by Interpol, in Australia and England respectively, and Etyang asked for another postponement to give the two young men time to fly out to Nairobi. Georgiadis voiced his objection. 'Both men were questioned at great length by Superintendent Wanjau, who checked their movements and released both of them a very long time ago,' the lawyer said. 'Watson has been requested to come here in order to be belaboured in connection with a publication like the *Sunday Mirror* as to whether he did or did not spend the night with Julie Ward. I cannot see any relevance in that regard other than besmirching the name and reputation of the deceased. If there had been any suggestion that either man was involved in Miss Ward's death, extradition proceedings could have been instituted for their return to Kenya ten months ago.' By now, Mango was also impatient to finish with the Julie Ward case and was becoming increasingly grumpy. 'I am warning you for the last time,' he had snapped at Georgiadis a couple of days earlier. 'If you abuse people in court you deserve to be abused yourself.' Indignantly, Georgiadis had denied he abused people in court. 'Where do you abuse them then?' Mango had replied. 'In your home? We are trying to finish this inquest otherwise it will go on until next January.' Nonetheless, Mango agreed to adjourn the inquest for one more week.

As it turned out, both Watson and Burns declined the invitation to testify. Watson was already involved in one court case over Julie Ward – suing David Barritt of the *Sunday Mirror*. Ward was worried that Watson's presence in Kenya could damage that suit and he advised the young man to stay away. Watson, already deeply upset by the public airing of his private life, readily concurred. Glen Burns also saw little reason to attend the inquest and he explained his feelings in no uncertain terms to an Australian radio reporter who called him by phone in Port Douglas, Queensland. 'I'm pretty angry,' Burns said. 'I'm in a mood just to thump somebody. The story I got is that I've been avoiding an inquest in Nairobi which is so far from the truth that it makes me really upset and angry. It's a dreadful thing and I just wish there was something I could do and then you read that you are an absolute arsehole and you won't go to the inquest because you're scared. What I know is probably not going to help them convict anybody. I wouldn't put my faith in the Kenyan police at all. There's nothing I could really do for Julie.'

By Wednesday 4 October it had become clear that neither Watson nor Burns had any intention of attending the inquest. An attempt by Georgiadis to recall Simon Makallah to answer further questions about his statements on driving, had also failed, and it was now time for the final submissions from the two lawyers. Throughout the inquest, Etyang had failed to present a coherent line of argument to explain the events of Julie's death. Instead, he had simply tried to deny or dismiss the claims made by Georgiadis. One of his key defences was that Julie had died because she was a woman of little education and loose character. In his summary, Etyang returned to the same allegation. 'She left school at the age of seventeen years,' Etyang said. 'This might be considered a relatively young age for a girl to leave school.' Julie's time in Kenya, Etyang suggested, was spent moving from one man to another. Julie was taken to the Weld Dixons by 'a man called David Tree, we never heard of Mr Tree.' During June, he said, 'Mr Dixon could not tell the court what Julie really did in Kenya.' She then met Glen Burns: 'I cannot tell how Julie met Dr Burns.' Later, she met David Weston, the balloon pilot, 'who fancied her, got her into conversation, bought her a beer or so, had cocktails with her, escorted her to her room and that was that. But he had invited her into his room, listened to music and he took her to her room.' And finally, there was Stephen Watson, 'the man who slept with Julie at the Masai Mara'. This then, Etyang concluded, 'was Julie – a twenty-eight-year-old, adventurous woman, with three men in her life at the Masai Mara, who were close friends'. (Originally, Etyang's own typed notes showed, the state lawyer was planning here to say not 'were close friends' but 'loved her'.) 'What could possibly have happened to Julie after 4 p.m. on 6 September 1988? We shall never know because I do not think we shall ever know who Julie really was.'

Etyang's entire submission was a web of similarly contradictory and ultimately unconvincing arguments. On the central subject of the wounds on Julie's remains, Etyang skirted around the controversy over Kaviti's alteration of Shaker's report and represented Kaviti and Shaker as having reached a single conclusion: that Julie had been torn and cracked apart. Professor Gresham, he argued, must have been mistaken. 'Whereas Professor Gresham examined preserved remains, whose condition had considerably changed, both Dr Shaker and Dr Kaviti examined them when they were fresh – raw – and observed the uneven ragged edges on the lower leg. These were no longer noticeable when Professor Gresham received the remains. The skin had shrunk. Professor Gresham may be an eminent pathologist in the UK, but he is human. Could he have made a mistake? He cut this leg with a knife. Where did he cut? Who was with him? Just because he is a professor of medicine in Cambridge doesn't make his reports and findings unquestionable.' Moreover, Etyang questioned whether the leg and jawbone examined by Gresham were actually the originals. The remains were 'taken to the airport by people we don't know, received in London by people we don't know and taken to

Professor Gresham in a state we don't know. No photographs are taken of the leg. Are we talking about the same remains?'

The most logical conclusion, Etyang suggested, was that 'no offence was committed by anybody. What is the motive in this case? I don't see any. The other possible verdict is that this was death by misadventure.' Nevertheless, having established his belief that Julie had not been murdered Etyang then waved aside logic and started suggesting that Glen Burns and Stephen Watson should be suspected of murder. 'Did Julie meet Mr Watson after she left Sand River gate?' Etyang asked, ignoring the evidence that Watson was by this stage in Naivasha with a party of twenty tourists. 'We shall never know because Julie is dead and Watson will not be coming to testify. If they had met and Julie told him that she had to get to Nairobi to see Dr Burns, was Watson happy about it? What was his reaction? In my submission this court cannot exonerate Dr Burns and Mr Watson.'

From the opening of the inquest, Etyang had been in a difficult position. All the evidence suggested that Julie had been murdered, that the police investigation had been at best incompetent and that government officials had attempted to divert the blame for her death on to wild animals. Indeed, Etyang's own stand had long prompted Ward and Georgiadis to assume that the assistant deputy public prosecutor had himself been instructed to lead the inquest away from a verdict of murder. Georgiadis, on the other hand, had a far easier task. Most of the evidence lay in his favour and while his final submission was no masterpiece, Georgiadis clearly won the debate, in his inimitable, no-holds-barred fashion. The state's argument was, Georgiadis said, 'as bizarre and unlikely a tale as ever to emanate from our inventive and imaginative police force'. The police alleged that Julie had left 'the security and warmth of the Suzuki car, which contained food and beer, and leaving her two maps, binoculars and gym shoes, but carrying tins of food, a bag, sunglasses, a camera, cassettes, knife, mug and spoon plus twenty litres of petrol, flip-flopped across the Mara wilderness between 6 and 12 September, clanking like a Christmas tree, and then on the night of 12 September, after consuming half a tin of pilchards, decided life was not worth living and hacked off her left leg with a non-existent sharp instrument like a panga, then lopped off her head and finally decided to douse her mortal remains with petrol and set fire to herself, thus committing suttee after she had committed suicide'. Despite its flipness, Georgiadis's speech put most of the arguments advanced by Etyang into their true perspective. To all but the state witnesses it now seemed obvious that Julie had been brutally murdered. The real question was why all this fuss had been necessary. Why, Georgiadis asked, had the police not simply said, 'We are sorry, this was a very nasty murder, we do not have a monopoly on murders, they occur in any country, and we shall do our very best to find out the culprit or culprits and bring them to justice'? The efforts to cover up rather than investigate Julie's murder had brought far more trouble to Kenya, and to those individuals involved, than a straightforward investigation would have done. Kaviti's alterations of the initial post mortem report had only damaged his own reputation. 'In the light of the evidence, can one possibly accept any of his evidence?' Georgiadis asked. 'I submit not. If he said his name was Jason Kaviti I would want to see his original birth certificate and I may even be constrained to check with the registrar of births.'

It was all marvellous copy for the journalists gathered in force in the courtroom. But Georgiadis was not satisfied with merely establishing proof of the murder and the cover-up. He had not yet finished with Simon Makallah. 'A charmed life,' he said of the warden. 'He, of all persons, had the mobility, the intimate knowledge of his kingdom over which he reigned for over four years, and the authority.' Makallah's claim that he had followed a single set of footprints from the car and then been guided by vultures was 'unbelievable'. Makallah, 'our resourceful Mr Makallah', as Georgiadis had taken to calling him, 'chose the one direction which he single-mindedly followed for ten kilometres and found what remained of her. What a coincidence.'

Confident that he had beaten Etyang, Georgiadis wanted to end what was likely to be his last great appearance in court with a flourish. Not only was he sure that he had proved that Julie Ward had been murdered, but here he was, his voice ablaze, delivering the murderer to the court. 'As a cynical old lawyer,' he boomed, 'I don't believe in fairy tales. Mr Makallah knew where her remains were. Mr Makallah knows a good deal more about this sad affair than he admitted to the inquest court.' Makallah, he clearly seemed to be saying. There's your man.

7

❖❖❖❖❖

Closing In

The final statements of Alex Etyang and Byron Georgiadis brought the inquest into the death of Julie Ward to a close on the afternoon of Thursday 5 October. Chief Magistrate Mango announced that after three weeks of consideration, he would deliver his verdict on 27 October. In the interim, John Ward flew back to spend a few days with his family in Brockley, and when he returned to Nairobi it was his fourteenth trip to Kenya in as many months. For most of that period, the lion's share of Ward's energies had been devoted to forcing the Kenyan authorities to accept that Julie had been murdered. The decision now lay in Mango's hands. Ward had done everything in his powers to make it impossible for Mango to deliver any verdict other than murder, but in the days leading up to 27 October he took care to keep his hopes in perspective. 'I hope the inquest comes up with a murder verdict,' he told journalists. 'But I have grave doubts about whether the Kenyans will be brave enough to come to that conclusion. A murder verdict means they have to accept that their chief government pathologist falsified a post mortem report. They have to accept that their investigating officer made a complete bungle of the investigation and they have to admit that there has been a colossal cover-up.'

When the day finally arrived, John Ward soon began to worry that his fears had been justified. Mango walked solemnly into the crowded courtroom and with little fuss settled down and began, slowly and solemnly, to read his statement. Despite the pitiful performance, both in the field and in the witness box, of Superintendent Wanjau, the policeman who had headed the Julie Ward investigation, Mango dismissed criticism of the Kenyan police force. 'Some very good investigations were carried out,' the magistrate said. Indeed, he added, if anyone was to be castigated then it should be John Ward himself. 'It is quite clear that Mr Ward refused to give the police time to breathe.' Mango also passed, without comment, over Dr Kaviti's alteration of the original post mortem report, though Dr Shaker, as an Egyptian, could be safely rebuked as 'completely unsatisfactory'. And while the magistrate accepted that there were reasons for Ward to have suspected Simon Makallah, he himself rejected them as without any real substance. The explanation for Nchoko's forgery was, he concluded, 'implausible', and enough to cast suspicion on the clerk, 'but only suspicion'. And as far as the rangers in general were concerned, he gave little substance to the belief put forward by Georgiadis that Julie had been killed by reserve staff. 'Why would some poor ranger want to kill and carve up a lone caucasian woman? Rape? This is speculative without anything to support it.' Sitting in the hot courtroom, the tension on John Ward's face told of the emotions coursing through his mind. 'I was confused by what Mango was saying,' he recounted later. 'I thought several times that the end product was going to be that he couldn't decide.'

But Ward, along with the foreign journalists in the courtroom, had underestimated both Mango's skill and his desire to retain his integrity. His statement was to prove a masterful piece of navigation, not just between the rocks of truth and falsehood, but between the razor-sharp reefs and crags of political pressures. His strongest criticisms were reserved for those who, like Shaker, were powerless to harm him in return. Once he had dealt dismissively with the Egyptian, Mango turned his attention to the two most 'obvious suspects': Glen Burns and Stephen Watson. 'The judiciary was paying their tickets so that they could come and testify,' Mango said. 'They flatly refused. What a way to treat a friend.' But as he drew to his conclusion, Mango returned from such speculation to the narrow role of the inquest: to decide the cause of Julie Ward's death. The key evidence had been that of Professor Gresham. 'The animals,' he said, 'are innocent. If they are guilty at all, it may be of eating what they found which had already been killed.' The court-room held its breath. 'I agree,' Mango continued, 'with Mr Georgiadis. There is ample and circumstantial evidence to show tht Julie Ward died as a result of foul play by a person or persons unknown.'

A collective gasp of relief rose up from the court. Georgiadis had won. The verdict had gone the Ward family's way.

For those who had battled away in the Ward camp, the initial reaction to Mango's statement was elation. 'Everyone I speak to is delighted with the result,' Bob Whitford, the private detective, said. 'It says a lot for Kenya that this has had such a public airing. It certainly would have been different in other East African countries. They most probably wouldn't have allowed John Ward into the country after he started digging.' But John Ward himself was more circumspect. 'No one can be happy to have confirmation that his daughter was murdered,' he said. 'But under the circumstances I am relieved at the result.' The previous fourteen months had been 'quite traumatic' and Ward had little doubt that further hurdles and anguish lay ahead. Mango's decision, he felt, was not the result of Kenyan concern for justice or a change of heart by the authorities, but simply a necessary and pragmatic reaction to the presence of so many predatory British journalists in the courtroom. 'The Kenyan authorities have gone to enormous lengths to stop this murder being openly declared and I would love to know exactly why,' he told the journalists. 'I am sure that if no further questions were asked, not much else would happen about this. I don't believe there is currently a convoy of police cars heading down to the Masai Mara.'

The next morning's newspapers merely confirmed John Ward's scepticism. The state-owned Nairobi daily, the *Kenya Times*, which represented the voice of the government, came up with a revealing interpretation of the magistrate's conclusions.

JULIE'S DEATH, NONE TO BLAME ran the headline across the front page. 'Nobody may be held responsible for the death of a British girl, a Nairobi court ruled yesterday.' Continuing, in eccentric style as well as content, the article noted: 'The court blamed the Wards' family lawyer, Mr Byron Georgiadis, for keeping at bay obvious suspects whom the lawyer did not even want their names mentioned.' Ward was even quoted in the article as saying: 'I praise the Kenyan police for this.' Not once did the article mention that Mango had reached a verdict of foul play.

Nevertheless, John Ward was revitalized by his victory and he was soon making it clear that whatever the Kenyans decided to do, he had no intention of giving up his own investigations. 'This is a solvable crime,' he said. 'At the end of the day, some-one murdered my daughter and I don't want him to get away with it.' In Ward's eyes, the testimony given in court had simply strengthened the case against men such as David Nchoko, Simon Makallah and Jason Kaviti, all of whom, he was con-vinced, were involved in either the murder of his daughter or subsequent attempts to cover it up. Ward was also all the more certain that the key to uncovering the mystery of her murder lay at the Sand River camp in the Masai Mara. Now that the inquest was over, he was willing to admit that one of the points over which Georgiadis had grilled Nchoko – the question of the Englishman Bower's receipts – had been a red herring. Nchoko had wound himself into knots trying to explain how Bower had signed out from the camp before Julie, yet had been given a receipt numbered after hers. As Ward had known before the inquest had even started, the explanation was simple: Bower had just written the wrong date in the camp book. He had left the camp on the morning of 7 September, the day after Julie's alleged departure, but had mistakenly logged the date as 6 September. Ward knew the question of Bower was irrelevant. But his insistence on the importance of Nchoko's forgery of Julie's signature remained as strong as ever. 'The only place he can have obtained the details to carry out the forgery was from the register that she signed on 2 September when she first entered the reserve,' Ward told Christopher Walker of *The Times*. 'We are still hopeful that eventually Nchoko can be persuaded to explain who instructed him to forge the signature and why.'

The inquest, which had interrupted John Ward's investigation for more than two months, was now over, and within days, his momentum restored by the verdict, Ward was back on the trail of the tourists who had stayed at Sand River on the night of 6 September. 'I am sure I shall find the truth before I finish,' he said a few weeks later. 'Right now there's more information coming in than ever before.' The media coverage of the inquest itself had helped: firstly, in widely publicizing Ward's hunt for tourists who had camped at Sand River; and secondly, apparently, in bringing new clues to light. The first of these clues came in the shape of an anonymous letter Ward received from Kenya. It informed Ward of a location where, it said, some of Julie's missing possessions, including her camera, were being kept. And it hinted at the identity of her killers. But when Ward returned to Kenya and investigated the information in this letter, he soon realized that the trail was a false one. A few weeks later, a second and more convincing set of clues arrived in Bury St Edmunds, brought in person by a Kenyan who was visiting England on business. 'He was a well-dressed guy,' Ward later recalled. 'He was wearing a Crombie overcoat. He had the whole story: who killed her, why, how and where. It involved two men, one of them a ranger, and a couple of things that hadn't been revealed at the inquest.' It took Ward the best part of a month, including a trip to Kenya, to convince himself that these claims were also false. The story involved drug-dealing and the man certainly knew a lot about drugs. 'He was either a dealer or a policeman,' Ward said. 'Take your pick: either he was after the reward money or he was a policeman carrying out diversionary tactics. It was certainly a bizarre episode. Both attempts were very plausible but in the end they were just attempts to cheat me of the reward money.'

By this time, though, Ward had new food for thought. In early December, less than five weeks after Mango's verdict,

Kenya's President, Daniel arap Moi, met Douglas Hurd, Britain's Foreign Secretary, at an official function. Among the subjects was the Julie Ward case and Moi expressed his desire to conclude the case, the publicity from which was continuing to damage Kenya's tourist industry. Perhaps, he asked Hurd, a team of British detectives could visit Kenya and take up the Julie Ward investigation. In the years before and after independence, Scotland Yard detectives had regularly helped out in difficult or controversial cases in Kenya and other British colonies. More recently, this tradition had almost died, but a few days after the meeting between Moi and Hurd, it was announced that Scotland Yard had accepted the offer and that a senior detective would shortly be flying out to Kenya for a reconnaissance visit. John Ward's initial reaction was cautious. 'If they have requested a couple of finger-print men, or people who just want to be shown around Kenya, they won't find anything,' he told the *Daily Telegraph*. 'It needs a couple of good, down-to-earth detectives, prepared to get stuck in. I am a little sceptical. It could simply be a cosmetic exercise by the Kenyan authorities.' Ward's worries were soon placated. On 1 January 1990, Detective Chief Superintendent Ken Thompson of Scotland Yard's International and Organized Crime branch, flew out to Kenya. A large, genial man with a handshake like iron, Thompson was as down to earth and as experienced in international crime as any policeman in Britain. In his years with the police, he had run Britain's branch of Interpol and had travelled around the world. Only a couple of years earlier, Thompson had spent several weeks in Uganda investigating the murder of a former Ugandan cabinet minister. He was in fact just three months away from early retirement, looking forward to the prospect of his new job as head of security for one of Britain's national high street banks, and a trip to Kenya to help sort out the Julie Ward case seemed like the perfect end to a distinguished career.

Thompson arrived in Nairobi in the midst of the equatorial summer and the high tourist season. Although tour companies were complaining that the safari business had suffered from the

publicity over the Julie Ward inquest and the other attacks on
tourists in 1989, Nairobi was still full of Americans, Germans,
Italians and Britons. It was flowering time for the yellow cassia
trees and pink bombax, as well as the various bright blossoms of
the bougainvillea bushes, and Nairobi glistened colourfully in
the sun. Thompson was immediately introduced to Superintendent Wanjau, who was still in charge of what was left of
the Julie Ward investigation, and to Commissioner Kilonzo.
Thompson's visit finally prompted Kilonzo to announce a
reward for information leading to Julie's killer, although he
omitted to inform the public that the ten thousand pounds had
been put up by John Ward and that it had been on offer for
more than a year. 'Kenya Police Appeal for Public Assistance in
Connection with the Death in Masai Mara of JULIE ANNE
WARD,' ran the text of the reward poster finally provided by the
Kenyan police. 'An English tourist who had come to see
Kenya's flora and fauna. SUBSTANTIAL CASH REWARDS for any
information that will assist police inquiries into this tragic case.'
Thompson lost no time in visiting the Masai Mara and speaking
to a number of key witnesses in the case and it was soon clear to
him that there was ample scope for some of his own officers to
embark on a full investigation. Just four days after arriving in
Kenya, Thompson flew back to Britain and a week later sent his
conclusions to the Kenyan authorities. The diplomatic tone of
Thompson's report, which praised the Kenyan police for their
role in the investigation, struck just the right note. The
attorney general, Matthew Muli, responded favourably to the
report and readily agreed that a team of Scotland Yard
detectives should visit Kenya and carry out a new investigation.
By now, John Ward had also come round to appreciating the
arrival of Scotland Yard on the scene. 'I am still working on the
investigation but things seem to have come to a bit of a stand-
still,' he said. 'I am delighted Scotland Yard have become
involved because I am convinced that some good, professional
detective work could soon crack this case, even after all this
time.' Ward was particularly keen for Scotland Yard to use
Interpol to help him track down the remaining tourists who

had been camping at Sand River. And before long he was handing over to the police a copy of his massive dossier of information, photographs and statements collected from Kenya and all around the world.

Before the Julie Ward case was re-opened, however, a second much-publicized murder took place in Kenya. This too was soon to involve Scotland Yard and to have a bearing on the progress of the Julie Ward investigation. On 13 February 1990 Robert Ouko, Kenya's urbane and experienced Foreign Minister, went missing from his farm in western Kenya. Three days later, the minister's body was found in wasteland about four miles from his home. His body was crumpled, with both arms and legs and other bones broken, and seriously burned. The first official announcement, based on testimony from none other than Jason Kaviti, Kenya's chief police pathologist, suggested that Ouko had committed suicide. The announcement was widely dismissed, especially by the Luo, the large and vociferous tribe to which Ouko belonged. Brandishing posters demanding 'No cover-up', the Luos took to the streets of Nairobi and Kisumu, rioting and looting. Eventually, President Moi was forced to concede that Ouko appeared to have been murdered and, for the second time in a couple of months, Scotland Yard was asked to send detectives to Kenya to investigate a murder.

Towards the end of February, the two British teams flew out to Nairobi. The Ouko team, as befitted the murder of a cabinet minister, was the larger, with four men, including a forensic scientist, led by Detective Superintendent John Troon. The Julie Ward team consisted of two men, Detective Superintendent Graham Searle and Detective Inspector David Shipperlee. Graham Searle, the senior officer, was a thick-set, dark-haired man of medium height, whose abilities as a detective were rivalled only by his skills on the bowling green. David Shipperlee was taller and always quick with a joke. It was on these two men's broad shoulders that the responsibilities for finding Julie Ward's killers now lay. In Nairobi, the detectives set up shop in the Intercontinental hotel, where John Ward had also stayed on earlier visits to Kenya. They soon had a direct line installed to Shipperlee's room, which became their office, and announced that anyone with any information pertaining to the Julie Ward case could call them directly. Searle and Shipperlee were also assigned to work with Superintendent Wanjau. Despite Wanjau's abject failure in his own lengthy investigation, he was still the Kenyan officer who knew most about the case, and, official requirements apart, Searle and Shipperlee needed a local man to translate and organize. It was never to be an easy relationship. Wanjau's attitude was relaxed even by Kenyan standards while the two Scotland Yard men were on instructions to complete their inquiries as efficiently and quickly as possible. Understandably, Wanjau resented his new foreign senior officers and his displeasure only increased when Searle began to demand both hard work and hard information from the Kenyan. During their first two weeks in Kenya, Searle and Shipperlee were to talk to scores of people. They went back to most of the witnesses who had given evidence at the inquest, including Sebastian Tham, Paul Weld Dixon, Doug Morey, Simon Makallah, David Nchoko, Gerald Karori and the various policemen involved in the investigation. Before arriving in Kenya, both had also read through John Ward's considerable store of information and talked to Ken Thompson, and they had soon begun to form their own ideas of what might have happened. Like Ward's, the policemen's suspicions increasingly focused on the reserve staff. Only rangers or wardens would really have had the contact, means and know-how to have abducted, held, murdered, chopped up and burned Julie. Wanjau, as he had been forced to admit at the inquest, had paid little attention to the reserve rangers and had failed even to collect the names of the rangers at Sand River camp and Makari post, where the greatest suspicion had fallen. When Searle asked him to provide the names and postings, at the time of Julie's death, of all the rangers in eastern parts of the Masai Mara, Wanjau said at first that this was impossible. But with persuasion he produced Narok County Council records that told the detectives everything they needed to know.

Simon Makallah was still on enforced leave from the Masai Mara, but Michael Koikai, the new chief warden, provided Searle with an office at Keekorok in which to interview the rangers. For two days, Searle, Shipperlee and Wanjau sat in the office and painstakingly went through a long, varying list of questions with more than thirty rangers, who came in one by one. Some of the questions were merely probes for clues. Others were more direct: Where were you in the first half of September 1988? Who else was there? When did you first hear of the search for the missing girl? Were you involved? Did you ever meet Julie Ward? When did you hear about her death? Did you kill her? The detectives' chances of uncovering anything in this way seemed slim. The murder had taken place eighteen months earlier. Most of the rangers did not speak fluent English or insisted upon talking in Swahili. There had been ample time to confuse the trail and leave Searle and Shipperlee groping in the dust. But on the morning of Wednesday 14 March 1990 the *Daily Mail* in England revealed that the two detectives had made a breakthrough. Two rangers, the newspaper said, had been arrested on suspicion of involvement in the murder of Julie Ward. It was more than eighteen months since Julie's death, and Searle and Shipperlee had been in Kenya for just nineteen days.

That morning, suddenly back in the news again, John Ward played host to television crews and reporters at his Butterfly hotel in Bury St Edmunds. Smiling and joking with the journalists, Ward gave interviews to the camera for both the BBC and then ITV. 'It's been quite productive,' he said of the Scotland Yard investigation. 'We are getting closer to a conviction. We get closer and closer all the time. I didn't expect it to come so quickly, but I am very pleased. All the things the Scotland Yard detectives have achieved in the past nineteen days could have been achieved in the first nineteen days after the murder.' But Ward was firmly convinced that the arrest of the two rangers would not be the end of the investigation. 'I am sure that this is just the beginning,' he said. 'These two arrests will lead to other arrests. The Kenyans will be shown to have covered up the murder deliberately, to quite a high level. Too many lies have been told. It is hard to accept that the Kenyan authorities mounted such an elaborate cover-up merely to save the skins of two lowly park employees.'

In fact, though, John Ward had little idea of what was going on in Kenya. The previous night he had spoken briefly to Graham Searle, who had simply said that two unnamed rangers had been arrested and detained in Nairobi for questioning. Ward concluded by telling the journalists that he was planning to fly out to Kenya at the weekend to talk to Searle and Shipperlee. 'The Scotland Yard men are just the sort of people needed for the job,' he was now saying. 'Some good, down-to-earth coppers. I was able to meet them for some time before they went to Kenya and to identify some areas which needed looking at. We are moving now in the right direction.'

In Kenya, besieged by telephone calls and visits from journalists, Graham Searle decided to hold a press conference. Sitting between Shipperlee and Wanjau, Searle said that the two men, whom he declined to name, were among thirty rangers interviewed in the Masai Mara. They had been called back for more talks and 'as a result of these interviews both men have been detained by the Kenyan police here in Nairobi and are assisting with inquiries into the disappearance and death of Julie Ward. Everybody has to be arrested or detained prior to charging and at that stage they are assisting police with their inquiries.' Articulate and confident, Searle told the gathered journalists that he and Shipperlee had 'made progress. Much will depend on the next seventy-two hours.'

Searle also had other comments to make. With a daughter of his own in her twenties, the policeman was sensitive to the suffering caused to the Ward family by the uncertainty surrounding Julie's behaviour in Kenya. He was critical of her for travelling alone through the Masai Mara: 'Now we've done the same drive, from the Masai Mara to Nairobi, I can only say it was very foolish of Julie to try to do it alone. I know she was very single-minded and confident, and had been in Africa for several months, but it was far too dangerous for a woman to attempt unaccompanied.' But he was equally insistent that Julie had not brought her death upon herself by her sexual behaviour. 'Can I say,' he told the gathered journalists, 'that during my investigations I have obtained statements from several people in Kenya and England that Julie Ward was not promiscuous in any way. It's rubbish to suggest that she was popping in and out of bed with people. She was a normal, twenty-eight-year-old woman, who from time to time had regular boyfriends, and enjoyed life to the full.' For John Ward, Searle had nothing but praise. 'His determination has been an inspiration. The information he was able to give us has been vital. If it had happened to my daughter I would love to have had the determination and resources that John Ward did to be able to follow it up.'

For most of the press conference, Superintendent Wanjau sat saying nothing at Searle's side. But eventually, one of the British journalists asked him why none of the rangers, including the two now in detention, had been interviewed during his investigations. 'They were,' Wanjau said, blatantly lying. Neither the journalist who had asked the question nor his colleagues knew quite how to respond.

That weekend, John and Jan Ward arrived in Nairobi. It was John Ward's seventeenth trip to Kenya, but the first on which he was accompanied by his wife. For more than a year and a half Jan Ward had taken no part in the quest to find Julie's murderer, but she had finally decided to come out to Kenya to see the land where Julie had lived her life at its fullest and then been killed. For John Ward, none of the beauty of Kenya had ever really emerged from behind the horror with which the country had confronted him on his first visit. But Jan, who shared Julie's interest in wildlife, quickly saw the magic the country must have held for her daughter. For both Wards, though, it was to be a difficult weekend. Soon after arriving, John Ward met up with Graham Searle and David Shipperlee. Much had been done since he had last talked to them. In less than three weeks, Searle and Shipperlee had uncovered a good deal of new evidence, as well as examining the old clues with fresh, experienced eyes, and they had come to rather different conclusions from John Ward. Unlike Ward, who had been forced to battle for information at every stage with the Kenyan officials, Searle had the authority to demand any document he wished. At Sand River he was given the entire collection of receipt books and registers, which Ward had been denied. In the main register he saw where the clerk, David Nchoko, had written in his own hand the details of Julie's name, home address and passport number, and then forged her signature. From where, Georgiadis had demanded at the inquest, had Nchoko got these details? From where had he copied Julie's signature? The only source, Ward and Georgiadis reckoned, could have been the Sekenani gate office, where Julie and Glen Burns had entered the park. If that was the case, then the forgery was more than simply a piece of straightforward bookkeeping, as Nchoko had claimed. But looking through the receipt books, Searle found one that Ward had not seen. Here was a carbon copy of a receipt with all the details found in the register and, apparently, signed by Julie Ward. The writing appeared to be Julie's. If she had filled in one receipt but omitted to fill in the register, then Nchoko could easily have copied the details from one book to the other, and then signed an approximation of Julie's signature. This, in fact, was what the frightened Nchoko had originally told Wanjau, but at the inquest he had not been given the chance to offer this simple and acceptable explanation. 'Nchoko is innocent,' Searle concluded. 'I am convinced he only did it to complete his record because Julie had forgotten to sign.'

This information was a surprise to John Ward. For many months he had been concentrating his energies on tracking down and talking to dozens of tourists who had camped at Sand River. He had grown increasingly sure that Julie had not left Sand River of her own free will and that her nightmare had started at the Sand River camp. Yet here was a simple piece of evidence that suggested Nchoko had not lied and that Julie may well have simply driven away from the camp, as had originally been thought. Later, back in England, David Shipperlee was to go and interview Paul Molinaro, who in the spring of 1990 was living in London. Ward's suspicion that Molinaro had been planted as a witness by the Kenyans had always been rather tenuous. In fact, Molinaro had told his friends in Kenya about seeing Julie at the time of her murder, a year before coming forward at the inquest. One of the friends was the daughter of Sarah Elderkin, managing editor of the *Weekly Review*, Kenya's only political magazine, and because of this Sarah Elderkin had completely discounted Ward's suspicions from the start. When Shipperlee went to see Molinaro, he found him to be a perfectly good witness. The young white Kenyan clearly remembered seeing Julie on several occasions on 6 September and, crucially, reckoned that it was probably early to mid-afternoon when she had driven away from Sand River. At the inquest he had agreed with Byron Georgiadis that she could have left in the late afternoon; but that had been after considerable prompting from Bob Whitford. In retrospect, he recalled that it was probably earlier, at around three o'clock.

Having talked to Nchoko, Searle and Shipperlee were convinced that Julie had driven away from the Sand River camp safely and alone on the afternoon of 6 September. Moreover, while Ward was convinced that Julie's Suzuki had been planted in the gully where it was found, Searle was equally certain that Julie had driven it there herself. For a start, the jeep was facing away from the road between Sand River and Keekorok, which was the direction in which Julie would have been travelling. It was clearly stuck, rather than just abandoned. Mud was splashed all over the back of the vehicle, as though the driver had churned the wheels in the mud trying to free the jeep. The jack, found inside, was also covered in mud, suggesting that the driver had attempted to jack the wheels out of the mud. There was also evidence that someone had spent some time in the gully: an orange juice carton, a cigarette butt and the burned square of plastic, as well as the open food packets and bottles found in the jeep. Moreover, it was locked and SOS had been written on the roof. 'If these people had just killed, chopped up and burned a girl, and were driving away from the scene of the crime, in the dark, and they got stuck, they wouldn't have taken the time to lock the jeep and write SOS on the roof,' Searle hypothesized. 'They would have legged it away as fast as they could, leaving all the doors open.' John Ward's conviction that the jeep had been planted had in large part stemmed from the evidence of Henri Berney, the leader of the Swiss camera team, camped nearby, who had said his camp had been just three to four hundred yards from the jeep. Berney had told Ward that the jeep could not possibly have been in the gully for more than one night. But when Berney was contacted by Scotland Yard, his evidence turned out to be less than convincing. Berney, the police concluded, must have mistaken the exact location of his camp in relation to the gully. Moreover, more precise information was available from another source: Andy Stepanowich, the survey pilot who had first found the jeep. While flying over the gully, Stepanowich had, to direct the other planes and cars to the site, measured the exact distance, as a Cessna flies, between the Swiss camp and the jeep. Stepanowich was a trained Canadian survey pilot. He was using global navigation equipment. And he noted down the distance. It was 0.8 of a nautical mile: just over 0.9 of a statute land mile. By air, Julie's jeep was nearly one mile from the Swiss camp. By land, it would have been a mile and a half. With thick vegetation all around, there was every reason to believe that Julie could have spent a couple of nights by her jeep without hearing or seeing the Swiss camp. And if Berney could be so far wrong about the distance between the jeep and his camp, his insistence that his team had driven daily past the gully was also open to doubt. It was the two detectives' theory that Julie had been found at her jeep by the man who had eventually killed her. She had been led from the jeep to the spot where she had been held and murdered.

Listening to Searle's careful explanation of the conclusions of his investigation, Ward was not totally convinced. If just two rangers were involved, why the massive cover-up? And what about Simon Makallah's lies? There was no doubt, Ward felt, that the warden was involved. Searle and Shipperlee disagreed.

In a more relaxed environment than the courtroom, Searle and Shipperlee had interviewed both Simon Makallah and Police Inspector George Othiambo, who had led the search for Julie's remains. They had also talked to several rangers involved in the hunt. From this, they had built up a detailed picture of the events in the Masai Mara on 13 September 1988. The logic which had led Makallah and Othiambo to drive south-east was the same as that which had prompted Tham and Stepanowich to fly their helicopter in the same direction on the same day: if Julie had walked in any other direction she would have found civilization. The search party had not arrived immediately at Julie's remains, but had first driven, turning back and forth, in a southerly direction, to the Tanzanian border. Finding nothing along the way, they had then driven eastwards, parallel to the border, until just as they were about to turn back, they had spotted vultures and driven over to investigate. This explanation did not satisfy all the doubts that had been raised at the inquest. The discovery was still a chance in a hundred. And why, as Georgiadis had asked, did Julie's remaining flesh and bones show no signs of vultures' beaks or claws? It was, in truth, possible that the vultures had come to look at the leg yet been put off touching it by the smell of petrol. Perhaps they had picked up other scraps of Julie's body and eaten those. As far as Searle and Shipperlee were concerned, such questions were irrelevant: they were satisfied that the search had been genuine.

Moreover, they had come to the conclusion that Simon Makallah was innocent of any involvement in either the murder or the cover-up. His main lie during the inquest had been to claim that he could not drive, when Ward and others had seen him do so. The explanation, slightly bizarre from a Western point of view, made complete sense in Kenya. In the months before Julie's arrival in the Masai Mara, Makallah's own position as warden of the reserve had come under threat. Opponents within the Narok County Council were trying to manipulate his dismissal and were looking for any way to discredit him. It was the charge of over-ordering spare car parts – a possible scam for making money – that had in fact led to his suspension from duties shortly after Julie's death. If Makallah had admitted driving county vehicles without a licence and without permission, he would have been liable to dismissal. If Makallah was innocent of any involvement in Julie's death, why should he have risked his position in the Mara by admitting to unlawful behaviour? Searle and Shipperlee, career policemen, well understood the importance of appearing to stick to regulations. During their questioning of Simon Makallah, Searle and Shipperlee also found that he had actually been out of the reserve for much of the time Julie was missing. He had attended a conference in Narok from Wednesday 7 September until Friday 9 September, the period during which Julie was almost certainly abducted. Hotel records in Narok confirmed these dates. Makallah was back in the Mara by the weekend, and there would still have been time for Makallah to have discovered Julie dead or alive at the spot where she was being held and to have helped to dispose of her, but Searle and Shipperlee were inclined to believe that this was not the case. 'There is,' Searle said, 'not a shred of evidence against Simon Makallah.'

In fact, the Scotland Yard explanation for Julie's death took much of the wind out of John Ward's firm belief that the attempts to obscure the events surrounding Julie's murder were part of a far-reaching conspiracy. It could not be denied that Dr Jason Kaviti, the chief police pathologist, had altered the original post mortem report in order to suggest that animals and not men had been the killers. But who had told him to do so? Ward suspected high-ranking members of the government. Yet once Kaviti had learned that his department was dealing with what appeared to be a murder in a tourist reserve, he would almost certainly have contacted a middle-ranking civil servant. Someone in the Home Ministry, perhaps. Or a senior police officer. What, Kaviti might have asked, should he do? Bureaucrats all over the world are masters at avoiding inconveniences. The answer could well have come back: better make it appear she was killed by animals. Don't want the tourists thinking there are murderers running around the Masai Mara. After all, the girl was dead. The killers, probably poachers, would have been long gone. So Kaviti would simply have changed a few words in his report. A small piece of bad publicity averted. A job, from a bureaucrat's perspective, well done. And if Julie's father had been anyone other than John Ward, the deed would probably never have been discovered.

Once John Ward did, to Kaviti's horror, appear and challenge him, it would then have been impossible for the pathologist to have admitted the reason for his actions. Accepting blame is a very unKenyan action. In Swahili, the national language, a man does not fall off a ladder. He is thrown off one. And Kenyans are, like most Africans, intensely proud. It is not hard to imagine that within minutes of John Ward storming into his office, Kaviti would have forgotten his own unethical behaviour. The important fact was that this rude, loud Englishman was insulting him in his own office. This was the crime. Here was the real wrong. From this moment, Kaviti would stand up against anything John Ward could throw at him. Ward's dealings with Kilonzo, Wanjau, Makallah and other Kenyan officials appear to have followed a similar pattern. In Kenyan culture, a man who storms and rages and makes threats never wins his way. He may be treated politely, but he will not be helped. Commissioner Kilonzo's attitude towards John Ward suggested that the police chief believed the case of a single foreign girl to be of little importance and that he objected to Ward's demanding manner. As for Wanjau, as even Alex Etyang was forced to admit at the end of the inquest, here was a man whose incompetence and bumbling inability at police work left little room for sinister conspiracies. Inspector Clouseau, as Georgiadis had called Wanjau. The Kenyan police force contained some good officers, though initiative was usually stifled by fear of upsetting the order of things. But Muchiri Wanjau was certainly not one of the stars of the CID.

The mere fact that the Julie Ward case had come to an inquest suggested that some hands within the Kenyan government were honestly stumbling after the truth. And while Etyang, the government's man, was doing his best to argue a case he could scarcely have believed, Mango, another whose future lay in the hands of his political masters, still delivered the verdict that refired the case. Indeed, Mango had spoken well. Several months after the inquest he was promoted to the position of High Court judge. The unhelpful, detached and at times infuriatingly obstructive attitude of many Kenyan officials over the Julie Ward case had never really looked like a well-orchestrated conspiracy. It had the appearance more of a typical Kenyan political confusion, with some parties moving in one direction and others wandering in another. Certainly, the Kenyans seemed at first to hope that somehow animals might get the blame, but before long other matters were clouding the issue: the longing to show John Ward that the days of empire were over and that white people could no longer bully their way around Kenya; a suspicion, particularly in Wanjau's mind, that Ward was producing false evidence to discredit the Kenyan police; and a general desire to blame everyone – first lions, then Tanzanian poachers and finally Glen Burns and Stephen Watson – but their own. Personally, men like Kaviti and Wanjau saw little reason to help John Ward. But even in Kenya the wheels of justice do, sometimes, turn. It had not been easy, but John Ward had forced an inquest. The verdict had gone his way. Scotland Yard had been called in. And now, given the necessary information by the Kenyan authorities, Searle and Shipperlee seemed, at last, to be closing in on the killers of Julie Ward.

All this was a great deal for John Ward to take in – and accept. There were still, he reckoned, questions that remained un-answered. He was still loath to believe that Julie herself had been foolish enough to have driven alone down a faint path and into a muddy gully. He found it hard to accept that all his great efforts had been directed simply at uncovering two lowly rangers. Nevertheless, it seemed that the investigation was finally unearthing the events surrounding Julie's death. It was, for John Ward, a sobering and saddening experience and over the next two or three months he was to maintain an uncharacteristic silence. Since the arrival on the scene of Scot-land Yard, Ward's own investigations had come to a halt. Now, he began to devote more time to his hotel business. His appearances in the press and on television fell almost to nought. And he started spending more time at home.

When Searle and Shipperlee had given their press conference on 17 March 1990 they had been hoping that, under intense interrogation, the rangers they had arrested would crack. Yet by the end of the rangers' first week in custody, neither of them had admitted anything. Searle still felt that his notebooks contained enough evidence for a strong prosecution case against the two rangers, but before making any rash recommendation, he decided to return to London and take his time in writing up a report. The rangers could only be held for a limited time without being charged, and on 21 March Searle ordered that they be released on police bail. A day later Searle and Shipperlee flew back to London. For three weeks, Searle and Shipperlee sifted through their notes until, in mid-April, just after Easter, they completed their report and sent it through the Foreign Office to Kenya. Outlining in detail what the two Scotland Yard detectives believed had happened to Julie Ward, the report concluded with the recommendation that regarding the two rangers arrested and questioned 'there is clear evidence for a prosecution' for the murder of Julie Anne Ward.

A few days later, it was confirmed that the report had reached the attorney general's office in Nairobi. But as the weeks passed, neither the British High Commission in Nairobi nor Scotland Yard received any reply. Scotland Yard's recommendation that two men be arrested and charged with the murder of Julie Ward was soon revealed in the British press and subsequently repeated in the Kenyan newspapers, although the names of the two men had still not been released.

Meanwhile, new troubles had emerged in Kenya that were sweeping away any concern for the effects of the Julie Ward scandal. In early April two leading politicians, Kenneth Matiba and Charles Rubia, held a press conference at the Hilton hotel in Nairobi and declared that it was time for Kenya to open its political system to a multi-party democracy. Matiba and Rubia were both Kikuyu, the largest and once most powerful tribe in Kenya, whose members had slowly been side-lined during the presidency of Daniel arap Moi, who belonged to another, smaller tribe. Following the extraordinary events enacted a few months earlier in Eastern Europe, Matiba's and Rubia's statements quickly became a rallying call for both Kikuyus and other Kenyans hoping for greater political freedom and a change of government. Just as Luos had taken to the street following the death of Robert Ouko, so Kikuyus now began to parade and riot in Nakuru, Nyeri and Nairobi. Two fingers held aloft, in the fashion of Winston Churchill, became a symbol of support for multi-party democracy in a state which had been run unchallenged by the ruling Kenyan African National Union for the entire twenty-seven years since independence. KANU leaders, holding their own rallies, threatened to cut off the fingers of any who made the democracy symbol. Shops in the centre of Nairobi were looted and for several days the streets in town were empty. The clashes soon led to greater violence and over several days in mid-July, dozens of people were shot dead by riot police. Roadblocks were set up, mostly by the army but also by thugs claiming to support democracy. Cars were stopped, overturned, set on fire and their passengers beaten up. Matiba and Rubia were both arrested and held in political detention, alongside several leading lawyers. One human rights lawyer, Gibson Kamau Kuria, who had already spent several months in detention, fled to the United States embassy and then to America. The American ambassador, who brought the message from Washington that aid money might soon be linked to political reform, was told by President Moi to stop interfering. For a few days, Moi's government seemed on the edge of collapse and even when the rioting stopped his position had been profoundly weakened.

It was at this sensitive moment that Scotland Yard's other Kenyan murder investigation hit the news again. Parts of the lengthy report compiled by John Troon and his colleagues from several months' work in Kenya were leaked to the *Sunday*

Correspondent and published in London on 22 July 1990. According to the newspaper, the Ouko report insinuated that cabinet ministers were implicated in Ouko's death. The motive was anger at Ouko's anti-corruption campaigns. Ouko, the newspaper claimed, had been taken away in a police car and shot through the head. The body had been dumped from a helicopter. Scotland Yard immediately denied that the leak had come from them – although the contents of the article were not disputed. But the newspaper report caused a furore in Kenya. Once again, Moi's leadership was called into question. And, in the lashing out for someone to blame, criticism fell on Scotland Yard. 'We highly regret this completely unethical behaviour of Scotland Yard,' Commissioner Kilonzo complained.

Ironically, though, the breaking of the Ouko report may well have rescued the Julie Ward case from its forgotten position under growing layers of dust. It gave the Kenyans a chance to hit back at Scotland Yard. Within hours the first, highly critical Kenyan comments on the Julie Ward report emerged. Matthew Muli, the attorney general, who had been so pleased with Ken Thompson's diplomatic recommendations six months earlier, was clearly not so enamoured with Searle's more detailed paper. On 24 July, the day after the Ouko report broke in the Kenyan press, Muli announced that more work still needed to be done in the Julie Ward investigation. 'The report has been studied carefully and in view of certain vital information which is lacking in the report, the attorney general has requested the same Scotland Yard detectives jointly with the Kenyan police to further cover by investigation the areas which are lacking before the final decision by the government can be made.' In particular, Muli pinpointed the need for further statements from witnesses: meaning, though he did not say it, Glen Burns, who was in Australia and had not yet been interviewed by Scotland Yard. As a result, Muli said, 'There will be a further delay in reaching the final decision on this tragic and mysterious death.' He asked that 'all concerned bear with us for a little longer period which is necessary to obtain further necessary information in the matter'.

*

170

It was now more than twenty-two months since Julie's death, but John Ward was hardly surprised by the new delay. 'There is no doubt in my mind that this is another delaying tactic by the Kenyan authorities,' he told the *Daily Telegraph*. At the same time, Ward himself was not averse to further investigations. As time had progressed, he had grown increasingly sure that Searle and Shipperlee had failed to uncover all the facts. 'I welcome Scotland Yard's return because I feel there is more to be done,' he said. 'I would hope that they take their own forensic man with them this time.'

Sitting in the shade on the porch of his Butterfly hotel, in Bury St Edmunds, on 1 August 1990, dressed in casual shirt and slacks, his large face tanned, his wispy silver-black hair showing distinct signs of thinning, John Ward's confidence was soaring again. 'I'm certain that the Yard guys have got it a bit wrong,' he said. 'I start at the same point as Scotland Yard and then we immediately diverge. We cross again at another point. Their investigation then stops while mine goes on a couple of stages further.' Despite Searle's explanation for the forgery at Sand River, Ward was still working on the assumption that Julie had not left the camp under her own steam. 'I never have thought that she left Sand River. The point is, how did the jeep get in the gully? In order for the police theory to be credible, Julie must have driven her jeep across the bush and got stuck. Perhaps I have an advantage in knowing her and knowing that she wouldn't have done that. It's possible that Julie drove across the bush. It's also possible that when Graham Searle and David Shipperlee arrived at Sand River they climbed on to the gatehouse and did a jig. Everything's possible, yes. But probable? Zilch. That leaves us back at Sand River.' The receipt book found by Searle and Shipperlee contained only a carbon copy and, Ward said, while the writing appeared to be Julie's, handwriting tests had not been conclusive. 'I've learned not to make any assumptions in Kenya,' Ward said.

Ward was also still deeply suspicious of Molinaro's evidence and uninterested in anything that threw doubts on the Swiss camera team's statement that they had been camping just three hundred yards from Julie's car. He accepted the involvement of the two rangers, but saw them as simply 'minor players'. 'Why did Kaviti bother to go to all that trouble and expose himself just for a couple of rangers?' Ward asked, once more. 'I believe there are other people and bigger fish involved. And I am also totally sceptical about Simon Makallah.'

Ward's initial enthusiasm for Searle and Shipperlee had also declined and he spoke freely about his disagreements with them. 'The police are human,' he said. 'Once they've made up their minds about a theory, they stick to it and ignore evidence if it doesn't fit into their theory.' He spoke of a woman who had been in contact with him whose daughter had been found dead at the bottom of a block of flats. The police assumed the death was suicide, but the mother insisted it was murder. 'The police hadn't even tried to contact the taxi driver who saw her last,' Ward said. 'One problem is that Searle and Shipperlee credit the Kenyans with absolute stupidity, when actually they ain't that stupid. Look at Nchoko's handwriting: you're not talking about a moron.

'It's rather a pity that Scotland Yard came on the scene just when they did,' Ward continued. 'I had momentum going. I've done little fieldwork since they started and I rather wish I hadn't stopped, though it's never too late. I didn't go to Kenya, I didn't want to get in their way, get under their feet. But I am going to get involved again.' But with the threat of political instability still looming, Ward was not overjoyed at the idea of returning to Kenya. 'I'll take a good weather check on the violence. I don't want to end up as another statistic. It would be very easy now. I will be very, very careful.'

8

❖❖❖

The Murder

In the corridors of Scotland Yard, the Kenyan attorney general's statements on the Julie Ward case were received with some surprise. The International and Organized Crime branch, for which Graham Searle and David Shipperlee worked, was already in some disarray over the leaking of the Robert Ouko report, and Muli's comments on the subject of Julie Ward arrived out of the blue. On 25 July a spokesman for the Yard told a reporter from the Kenyan *Daily Nation* newspaper that Searle and Shipperlee had 'completed their investigation and we do not expect them to return to Kenya'. Over the next few days, however, messages passed back and forth between Scotland Yard and Kenya, through the British Foreign Office, and on 30 July the Yard issued a new statement announcing that new lines of inquiry were being followed at Muli's request. 'Recently the Kenyan attorney general requested that further inquiries as suggested in the interim report be completed and this is being done,' the statement said. 'The results will in due course be communicated to the Kenyan government. At no time have New Scotland Yard stated that they do not intend to send detectives back to Kenya.'

Neither Searle nor Shipperlee was convinced that further inquiries were necessary: they had no doubt that they had found the right men. But they also knew that without confessions, and with only circumstantial evidence, their case remained less than watertight, and they were keen to stay on the right side of the attorney general. Like all policemen who have put time and effort into an investigation, they very much wanted the case to go to trial. The detectives could also see the advantage of returning to Kenya in the weeks ahead. On their earlier trip to Kenya the Masai Mara had been waterlogged and they had been able to reach key locations, such as the spot where Julie's body was found, only by helicopter. If they returned in September, at the time of year that Julie had been in the reserve, they would get a far clearer picture on the ground of the eastern corner of the Masai Mara. In a case such as this, which relied on the evidence of location and circumstance, the investigating officers could not spend enough time examining the scene of the crime. Before returning to Kenya, though, Graham Searle had another task to perform to satisfy Muli. At the end of the inquest, Chief Magistrate Mango had pinpointed Stephen Watson and Glen Burns as vital witnesses and while the Yard had taken a statement from Watson, they had yet to speak to Glen Burns, who was still in Australia. Burns had left the Masai Mara two days before Julie disappeared and had not returned to Kenya until weeks after her death, and Searle doubted that he would have much of relevance to say. But as it turned out, Burns's evidence was to give the investigation one of its final twists.

Far from Kenya, in Port Douglas, Queensland, Glen Burns had managed to put the death of Julie Ward behind him. Contacted from time to time by journalists, he eventually refused to talk about the case. But when Scotland Yard approached him, he readily agreed to meet Graham Searle. As the detective had expected, the interview was mostly routine. Burns and Julie had just been friends. The Suzuki had broken down. Glen had needed to get back to Nairobi. He had not heard about her death until weeks later. But when, in reconstructing the days Julie had spent in the Masai Mara, Searle showed Burns an aerial photograph of the Sand River camp, the Australian came up with a surprise. Wanjau had told Searle and Shipperlee that, according to David Nchoko, the clerk, and Gerald Karori, the police constable, Julie and Glen had camped not far from the gate, within sight of the police post. Looking at the photograph, Burns pointed towards an entirely different spot, two hundred yards from the gate, on the far side of the river. Suddenly interested, Searle asked again if Burns was sure. The Australian was positive: there had been a lot of tourists at the camp that night and he and Julie had not wanted to pitch their tents in the middle of a massive tour group. Why then, if Julie and Glen had camped in one spot, had Nchoko and Karori told Wanjau that the camp was in another spot? The next day, his work in Australia over, Searle flew back to London and before long passed on the news to John Ward, who received it triumphantly. Ward had claimed all along that Nchoko and Karori were involved in Julie's disappearance and that his daughter had been abducted from Sand River camp. Here at last was evidence that would sway Scotland Yard towards his own theories: proof that Nchoko and Karori were lying, further indication that Julie had not left the Sand River camp that afternoon. A few days later, without revealing the details of the new information, Ward was confidently saying that his theories would soon be vindicated. 'Just wait and see,' he said with a wink.

On 2 September 1990, exactly two years after Julie and Glen Burns had driven out of Nairobi on their way to the Masai Mara, Searle and Shipperlee flew out once more to Kenya. Reunited with Superintendent Wanjau, the detectives soon flew down to the Masai Mara for a rendezvous with Nchoko and Karori. In the five months since they had last visited the reserve, it had undergone a transformation. Back in March, during the rainy season, the Mara had been wet and covered in long grass. The skies had been overcast and the wildlife scarce. Now, under white, puffball clouds drifting across a blue sky and burning September sun, the grass was short and brown and the reserve was crammed from hillock to stream with a million grazing wildebeest and zebra. The migration that had drawn Julie and Glen Burns to the Mara two years earlier was in full flow once more. Following the rains, the wildebeest had moved up in great numbers from Tanzania to the lush grazing on the Kenyan side of the border. With them had come the predators: hyena, cheetah and especially lion. Michael Koikai, the new warden of the Masai Mara, acted as the detectives' guide and on one occasion he stopped not far from a pride of lions on a kill. When the men climbed out of the jeep and walked to within two hundred yards of the feeding lions, the cats stood up and slunk back into the grass. Almost immediately, Searle noticed, a group of vultures which had been perched up in branches a safe distance from the carcass, hopped down and over to the meat. When the men turned and started walking back to the car, the lions padded back to their meal and the vultures flapped up into the trees again.

Soon after arriving in the Mara, Searle and Shipperlee drove the few miles down from Keekorok to Sand River to meet David Nchoko. The detectives took him out to the banks of the river and asked him where Julie and Glen Burns had camped. Unworried by the question, Nchoko turned and pointed out the spot. It was two hundred yards down the river, on the far side of the bank: exactly where Burns had put it. Gerald Karori had not turned up at Sand River, but later when Searle and Shipperlee showed him photographs of the camp, he picked out the same site as Nchoko and Glen Burns had. Where, then, had Wanjau got the idea that the tents had been pitched just below the gate? Wanjau shrugged at the question. Nearly two years earlier, when Wanjau had interviewed Glen Burns, he had neglected to ask about the position of the tents. Burns's statement as recorded by Wanjau said, simply: 'At the camp site we pitched our two tents and spent the night there.' It was hard to believe, but it seemed Wanjau had also failed to ask the same question of Nchoko and Karori. When Searle and Shipperlee had first visited Sand River, Wanjau must simply have picked a spot at random. The investigation arising from Searle's new clue, gleaned from a journey halfway around the world and back, had turned into a farce. Nevertheless, the charade at Sand River had served at least to confirm one point: that Nchoko and Karori were telling the truth. As far as Searle and Shipperlee were concerned, these two men were now finally and completely eliminated from suspicion.

The detectives spent another three days in the Mara and the visit proved to be far from useless. For the first time they were able to drive freely around the corner of the Mara where Julie had died. They visited the gully where the Suzuki had been found and drove from there to the site of the Swiss camp. The distance between the two was, as the pilot Andy Stepanowich had said, about a mile as the crow flies. There was, moreover, a large hill on the south side of the Swiss camp that would have muffled noises from the camp and its generator and hidden the lights from cars and a fire. Julie could easily have spent a night or two in the gully without hearing or seeing the Swiss camp. The detectives also drove along the track they suspected Julie had followed, alone, on the afternoon of 6 September 1988: between the gully and the Sand River–Keekorok road. It was not a good track, but it would certainly have been passable, even for Julie's old Suzuki. Finally, the detectives drove out to the corner of the bush in which Julie's sad remains had been found. They had flown there by helicopter before, but this was their first opportunity to drive all the way through the bush. It was as remote a spot as any in the Masai Mara. There were no tracks to follow and the jeep rocked and crashed through the dense vegetation. Someone driving a car would have been unlikely to have come this way unless they had no other choice. Someone walking, and wanting to get away from tourist tracks, might easily have ended up here.

After three days at Keekorok lodge, Searle and Shipperlee returned to Nairobi. All in all, the trip to the Masai Mara had been worthwhile and the detectives were now even more convinced that they had found the right men. They had not come across a single piece of evidence to suggest that David Nchoko or Gerald Karori were in any way incriminated in Julie's death: in fact, quite the opposite – whenever their evidence could be corroborated, Nchoko and Karori turned out to have been telling the truth. A couple of days later, Searle and Shipperlee drove down to Tsavo West National Park, to talk to another man at whom fingers of suspicion had been pointed during the inquest: Simon Makallah. The former warden of the Masai Mara had finally gone back to work, appointed to the prestigious post of warden of Tsavo West. Makallah welcomed the two detectives and happily chatted for a while, eager to answer any questions and help clear up a point or two. Byron Georgiadis had picked out Simon Makallah at the inquest as a key figure in Julie's death. Searle's and Shipperlee's investigations quickly and comprehensively cleared his name.

On the evening of 13 September 1990, two years to the day since Julie Ward's remains were found in the Masai Mara, Graham Searle and David Shipperlee went out for a good, rich curry at the Minar Indian restaurant on Banda Street in Nairobi. The pleasure of a good meal was mixed with feelings of satisfaction at a job well done.

'It's been a very interesting case,' Searle said, sitting back in his chair and sipping at a Coca-Cola. 'It was frustrating to pick it up so late. The most important thing to us is the scene, and this scene was eighteen months old when we arrived. But we were at least given complete freedom by the Kenyan authorities to do what was necessary.

'We've lived and breathed this investigation,' he continued. 'I had an operation on my sinuses over the summer and was laid up in hospital after coming back from Australia. But there was no way I wasn't going to see this case through. I was determined to come. The registrar at St Thomas's didn't give me the go-ahead until the Friday and we flew out on the Sunday. Mind you, I've brought a little chemist's shop with me.'

The Scotland Yard investigation into the death of Julie Ward had straddled six months. Searle and Shipperlee had spent more than a month and a half in Kenya. Interviews had been conducted on three different continents. They had taken statements from several dozen people and filled more then five hundred statement sheets. Finally, on Monday 17 September the two policemen, along with Superintendent Wanjau, were called to meet the Kenyan attorney general, Matthew Muli. The attorney general listened carefully to what they had to say and asked a series of questions. He seemed impressed, but he told them that he was not yet prepared to commit himself to a prosecution. First, Searle and Shipperlee would have to return to England and complete their second report. In it they would describe once again how they believed Julie Anne Ward had arrived at her death.

There was no question that, on the morning of Tuesday 6 September, Julie had left the Serena lodge to drive towards Sand River. David Weston, the balloon pilot, had waved her off. Driving at her usual steady pace, she had retraced the route she had taken with Glen Burns three days earlier, heading first for Keekorok and then turning south towards Sand River. A few miles before the camp, she was overtaken by the young Italian Kenyan, Paul Molinaro, and his friends in their Land Rover. As Molinaro drew level with the Suzuki, the right hand wheel of the Land Rover climbed the bank at the edge of the road and the vehicle tipped towards Julie's jeep. Molinaro waved and Julie smiled back. He also saw a camera on the seat beside her, ready in case Julie should spot a lion, rhino or elephant by the side of the road.

A little later, after he had arrived at the Sand River camp, Molinaro looked up from where he and his friends had parked to see Julie's brown Suzuki roll into camp and draw up beside two tents. Wasting no time, Julie proceeded to take down the first tent. As she was doing so, Gerald Karori, the police constable, dressed in green fatigues, waded across the river towards her. Karori was notorious at Sand River for his interest in female foreign tourists and immediately tried to engage Julie in conversation. He told her that he was a policeman, even though he was wearing 'jungle uniform'. Karori and David Nchoko the clerk had noticed that the two tents had stood, apparently empty, for several days and Karori was interested to find out why. Julie explained that her car had broken down and that her companion had flown back to Nairobi. Hurriedly, Julie finished packing the tents in the car and then drove up to the gate, where she was stopped by David Nchoko. The clerk told her she would have to pay two hundred and sixty shillings for the two extra nights the tents had stood empty on the river bank. Julie handed over the money and wrote her name and passport number in a receipt book and then signed it. While doing so, Julie told Nchoko that she was in a hurry because she wanted to get back to Nairobi that night. Then she climbed back into her car and drove up the road away from the gate. Looking up again, Molinaro saw the Suzuki climb over the ridge and disappear down the other side. After she had gone, Nchoko realized that she had failed to sign the main register. He copied the details from the receipt that Julie had filled in and then made a rough replica of her signature.

The most direct way to return from Sand River to Nairobi was to head directly north out of the Mara, past Keekorok and Sekenani gate and on to the tarmac road towards Narok. This was the route Julie and Glen had taken on their way down to the reserve. However, halfway between Sand River and Keekorok, Julie turned off the main road and on to a smaller dirt track. Her reason for doing this will probably never be known. It may have been that she saw an animal, such as a leopard, which was exciting enough for her to decide to make a quick diversion. It was more likely, though, that she was following her map. When John Ward first found the empty Suzuki, he discovered Julie's map of the Masai Mara still in the jeep. It was a simple, glossy fold-out with a photograph of a cheetah on the front. Although Julie was probably unaware of it, the road system marked on the map was out of date. The map showed a 'road' (superior, on the map, to a 'motorable track') leading eastwards from halfway between Sand River and Keekorok, crossing the Loltukai stream just where Julie's Suzuki was found, and carrying on from there towards Ololaimutiek gate. There was even an 'interpretive point', a viewing spot with a hut and information, marked on this road. From Ololaimutiek, the map showed a road heading 'To Narok', the main town on the road between the Mara and Nairobi. There was no indication on the map that this was a far slower route to Narok than the road past Sekenani gate, which Julie had taken on her way to the Mara. Nevertheless, even on this road Julie would probably have made it to Narok by dark. From there, she would have had perhaps three hours' driving on a well-used, tarmac road to reach Nairobi.

Alternatively, Julie may have decided to try to stay at one of the lodges in the Mara for the night. Rather than sleep alone in her tent at Sand River, she may have been looking for a lodge room. She may have stopped in at Keekorok on the way back from Serena and been told that Keekorok was full. The staff may have recommended Sopa lodge, at Ololaimutiek gate, which almost always had rooms. The road Julie's car was found on was, on her map, clearly the most direct route between Sand River and Sopa. Much later, the staff at Keekorok were interviewed and did not remember Julie: but one quick question from a tourist at a reception desk always crowded with foreigners could easily have been forgotten. Whatever the case, Julie must soon have discovered that the track was not the wide, graded road that the map promised. In fact, since Makari post had been set up, this track had been abandoned by the reserve staff. Now, they entered this region by another track heading south from the Keekorok–Ololaimutiek road to Makari post. The interpretive point no longer existed. Rattling along the track, Julie would eventually have come to the Loltukai gully. Cars did occasionally pass this way. In fact, a week later Derek Dames, a Ker & Downey safari guide, was to cross the stream just a few yards from where John Ward and Sebastian Tham were standing by the Suzuki. But, without four-wheel drive, the Suzuki slid down to the bottom of the gully, slewed in the wet earth and came to a halt, one wheel buried in mud and another hanging free in the air.

It is not hard to imagine the frustration and sudden worry that must have run through Julie's head as she realized she was stuck. The mud on the sides of the car showed that she had tried to gun the car out of its hole, but it had not moved. When the car was found, the battery was dead, so she may have gunned and revved until the battery gave out. She must have tried to shift the car with the jack, but this also had not worked. By now, it was already mid- to late afternoon and Julie would have been loath to stray from the car, her only security against the wild animals. It seems almost certain that she spent the night in the gully, sleeping uncomfortably in the Suzuki. It may be that she lit the piece of plastic, which was found later, that first night to keep animals away or to try to attract attention. There are few more desolate experiences than spending a night alone in the African wilderness, beneath the huge dark sky, listening to the howls of hyenas and the grunts of lions drifting through the stillness. It must have been a huge relief for Julie to see the first gentle rays of dawn creeping up over the shoulder of Ololoitikoishi hill.

On the morning of Wednesday 7 September it seems likely that Julie heard the sound of aircraft landing a few miles away at Keekorok airstrip. She scraped mud up from the floor of the gully and carefully painted the letters SOS on the roof. At some point, being a cigarette smoker, she may have dropped the butt that was later found. She may also have, without thinking, let fall an empty orange juice carton. This would have been an aberration. Despite her predicament, Julie carefully stored most of the rubbish in the car. She may have been stuck, but there was no need to drop litter in the Masai Mara. Although she cannot have known it, Julie was stranded less than a mile away from the camp of a Swiss camera crew. Had she climbed the hill in front of her, she would have seen this camp lying just on the other side.

In their report, Searle and Shipperlee had suggested that Julie spent at least one and possibly two nights on her own in the Suzuki. On either Wednesday 7 September or the following day what must have seemed like help finally arrived. Someone had seen or heard Julie in the gully and had come to investigate. Whoever it was arrived on foot: there were no other car tracks when the Suzuki was found. He or they also seem to have appeared friendly to Julie. The evidence suggests that Julie had no inkling at this point of what lay ahead. She must have been extremely relieved and grabbed her most valuable possessions, including her passport, money and camera, and thrown them into her shoulder bag, along with other bits and pieces. She didn't even bother to change into the tennis shoes in the car, but kept on her flip-flops. But she felt secure and calm enough to lock the car before leaving. Then she was led off into the bush.

To the events of the next few days, the two detectives could bring only educated speculation. Many months earlier, the Ward family had come to accept that the motive for Julie's death must have been sexual, and Searle and Shipperlee had come to the same conclusion. Although her camera was missing and still not recovered, some money had been found in the fire in which her body had been burned. Robbery, it seemed, had been at best an afterthought. To the men who were to kill her, Julie's body must have been her most attractive possession. It may have been that Julie's killers had initially intended to rescue her, and that at some point temptation had simply grown stronger than common sense. But the inevitable conclusion, whatever else may have happened, was that Julie's rescuers had turned into her assailants and raped her. Far from help, in a remote corner of Africa, Julie was pitched into a terrible nightmare, a heart of darkness. It was hardly surprising that, following his own speculation, John Ward had become possessed of such fury at the thought of what had happened to his daughter.

For several days, Julie must have been held and perhaps further abused, while her abductors had grown increasingly worried about what to do with her. From her reaction, it must have been obvious to them that they could not release her without landing themselves in serious trouble. They knew, also, that her car would sooner or later be found and that a search would almost certainly follow. When Sunday 11 September came they may have heard Perez Olindo flying an unusual route along the Sand river, searching for a sign of Julie. The next day another plane carrying John Ward flew back and forth across the eastern side of the reserve. At this point, perhaps, panic set in and they may then have decided to silence their victim. How they did it, only the murderers know. Not enough of Julie's body was ever found to reveal the means of her death. It seems probable that she was killed either with the machete that was later used to cut up her body, or perhaps strangled by the bare hands of her abductors. What is certain is that by the afternoon of Monday 12 September 1988 Julie Ward was dead.

That evening, some five miles away, Julie's dismembered

body was burned on a fire. The chances are that the body was cut up at the spot where she was killed rather than at the site of the fire. A lifeless human body, a dead weight, would have been heavy to carry, and in Africa hunters usually cut up their prey where it falls and carry the parts home. With a sharp, heavy machete, the killers would have methodically cut Julie into small pieces. Professor Gresham had found that the leg and the skull had been cut with one sharp, expert blow each. The men who did the job knew how to dismember a carcass, and it would not have taken long. Once in pieces, the body would have been easier to carry. Perhaps her parts were placed in one or more bags and slung over the shoulders of her killers. Then, they would have walked the five miles into the remotest corner of the bush, to dispose of her body. Under ordinary circumstances, it would have been more likely that her body would simply have been left in the bush for the hyenas and vultures to eat. But Julie's murderers needed to destroy both Julie's body and her possessions as quickly as possible. At some point, one of the murderers must have visited the Suzuki to pick up Julie's jerry can full of petrol. He may also have collected the tin of pilchards from the jeep. Deep in the bush, they had dumped Julie and her possessions in a pile, covered her with petrol, and set her alight. The slight singeing on the flip-flops suggested that they were used to fan the fire. The murderers probably stood over the flames for some time, waiting for the fat in Julie's body to inflame and destroy the rest of her remains. Evidence found by the Kenyan police suggested that one of them had defecated near the fire. At some point, probably before the fire had burned down, it grew dark. This would explain how her skull and leg escaped the worst of the fire: they would have fallen off unnoticed into the dark. While waiting, the murderers seemed to have eaten some of the pilchards from Julie's jeep and left the tin, opened and half empty, in a nearby tree. It was an act of extraordinary callousness.

Eventually, under cover of darkness, Julie's killers would have crept away, leaving the remains to be discovered the next day. They had clearly acted in panic and their attempts to dispose of the body had been crude and slapdash. But if John Ward had not acted so promptly, flying out to Kenya and hiring aircraft to search for her, the crime may never have been discovered. Julie's car would have eventually been found, locked and abandoned, like an earthbound *Marie Celeste*.

On Wednesday 19 September 1990 Graham Searle and David Shipperlee flew back to London. As far as they were concerned, they had left no stone unturned in their investigations. There was no possible alternative theory. Their report would repeat their belief that the two rangers who had been arrested and released six months earlier had murdered, dismembered and burned Julie Anne Ward.

During their second trip to Kenya, the detectives had decided not to interview the two men again. But they had, by chance, come across one of them. Driving back from the spot where Julie's remains had been found, they had, just short of Keekorok lodge, passed a truck carrying a group of rangers. Several men peered down at the detectives, curious but unconcerned. However, one pair of eyes, the balls yellow, burned down at them. It was John Magiroi, one of the rangers whom they had arrested and were now recommending should be charged with murder. Two years earlier, Magiroi had been based at Makari post, in the eastern corner of the Masai Mara, along with the other man whom the Yard detectives believed was responsible for Julie's death, Peter Kipeen. Neither ranger had yet been charged with any crime and both were still working freely in the Masai Mara. Magiroi was based at Keekorok, where one of his jobs was to accompany tourists who requested a ranger guide. Kipeen had been posted to Ololaimutiek gate, on the eastern edge of the reserve.

The detectives' attention had been drawn to Makari post early on in their investigations. This was the isolated ranger post where John Ward had stopped to call for a helicopter after Julie's jeep had been found and while he was trying to reach the site of her remains. And Peter Kipeen was the ranger who had found the journalists from the *Sunday Times* and *Today* stuck in the middle of the Sand river, no more than a mile down the river from where Julie's own Suzuki had been found. A quick glance at a map of the Mara was enough to suggest the possible importance of Makari post. On the map, the south-eastern corner of the Masai Mara could be seen as a rough square. To the west was the road from Sand River camp to Keekorok. Along the north lay the road from Keekorok to the Ololaimutiek gate. The eastern edge of the square was formed by the eastern boundary of the park. And the base of the square, to the south, was the border with Tanzania. The Sand River gate, Keekorok lodge and Ololaimutiek gate, all inhabited by a sizeable number of people, made up three of the corners of this box. Inside the box lay forty square miles of rough bush. It was deep in the heart of this square that Julie's Suzuki and her remains had both been found. And within this square there was just one permanent place of habitation: Makari post.

In fact, during the week that Julie had been missing there were also two temporary campsites set up within the square. One of these camps, just a mile from Julie's Suzuki, up the Loltukai stream, was inhabited by the dozen members of the Swiss wildlife film crew, two of whom were women. Each one of these members was eventually interviewed by David Shipperlee and a Scotland Yard sergeant in Switzerland and nothing suspicious was discovered. As Searle and Shipperlee well knew, it would have been almost impossible for a dozen people to have managed to keep up the same lies without tipping off an experienced policeman. The other camp was set up several days after Julie first went missing by the Ker & Downey guide Derek Dames, who had passed Julie's jeep on the day it was discovered by her father. Dames had several Kenyan staff and an American family on safari with him. This group, too, was interviewed and for similar reasons eliminated from suspicion.

It was during John Ward's own investigation that an interest was first taken in Makari post. When Ward had read the article in the *Sunday Times* by Peter Godwin, describing the rescue from the Sand river by Peter Kipeen, he had wondered why the journalists had been found by the rangers from Makari post, while Julie and her car had not been seen. Searle and Shipperlee asked the same question. When in the Mara, the two detectives drove from the gully where the Suzuki was found to Makari post. The distance was less than one and a half miles, no further than from Makari post to the spot in the Sand river where Kipeen had found the journalists. The banks of the river, within a mile and a half of Makari post, were, from the evidence given by the journalists, clearly within the patrolling range of Makari post. Yet, apparently, Julie's Suzuki had sat in a gully just a few yards north of the Sand river for a full week without being seen.

Moreover, Makari post lay not much more than five miles from the spot where Julie's body had been found. During John Ward's investigations, it had been assumed that Julie's body must have been taken to this place by car. But in Masailand boys grew up walking long distances through animal-infested bush with scarcely a worry. A young Masai boy would think nothing of walking five mile to school, or to find a stray cow, every day. To Masai rangers such as those employed in the Masai Mara, a five-mile walk through the reserve would constitute not much more than an hour's easy stroll.

Although most of Ward's efforts had been directed at investigating Sand River – on the trail of David Nchoko's forgery – he had initially uncovered a couple of interesting clues at Makari post. The first was the button battery for a camera which he had discovered on his first visit to Makari post. The second was the toothpaste tube found by Frank Ribeiro a few weeks later. When Searle and Shipperlee had conducted their interviews of the rangers in the Masai Mara they had asked a series of questions designed to find out the likelihood of a battery or a toothpaste tube being in a ranger post for innocent reasons. How do you wash? What do you use? Do you clean your teeth? With what? Do you have any photographs of yourself? Does anyone have a camera? They quickly realized that some of the rangers did use toothpaste and, when questioned, they mentioned several brands, including the one found at Makari post.

But not one of the rangers possessed or knew anyone else who possessed a camera which took the sort of battery John Ward had seen at the post. And Julie's camera, which did take such batteries, was still missing. Unfortunately, Ward had not kept the battery once he had picked it up, but it was still a worthwhile clue.

From the list of rangers' names supplied eventually by Wanjau from the Narok County Council records, Searle and Shipperlee had worked out that there had been three rangers present at Makari post during the period that Julie had been missing: Peter Kipeen, John Magiroi and Francis Liaram. A fourth ranger was posted at the station, but had been on long leave for the entire period. However, when the detectives interviewed Liaram, they found that he had been expected back by the second week of September, but had been late and did not arrive until 14 September, the day after Julie's body had been found. Searle and Shipperlee checked this information and other sources confirmed it was true. Liaram had been posted at Makari but had not been present at the time of the murder. Consequently, his evidence was extremely important. He gave the detectives a clear idea of the duties carried out at Makari post: watching out for poachers, helping any stranded tourists, keeping an eye on any elephants and rhinos in their area, and patrolling a wide area around the post. Did this area include the banks of the Sand river? the detectives asked. Liaram replied that it did. In discussions with Simon Makallah and Michael Koikai, the new warden of the Mara, Searle and Shipperlee double checked this information. There was no doubt that the spot where Julie's vehicle had become stuck in the mud was within patrolling range of the rangers at Makari post.

Eventually, the time had come to interview John Magiroi and Peter Kipeen, the two men who had been staying on their own at Makari post for the entire period that Julie Ward had been missing. Peter Kipeen, the younger of the two at around twenty-three years old, was recently married, to a plump, teenage Masai girl. Like many young Masai men, Kipeen's life so far had straddled two worlds. He had been born into a primitive, cattle-herding existence. His father was a Masai elder who had only ever worn the traditional Masai garb of red toga, leather belt and sandals, and who had always carried a spear. The family's boma, or ring of low, dark huts built of sticks, mud and cowdung, was located in an isolated part of Masailand between the villages of Aitong and Lemek, not far from the rough track that leads from the western side of the Masai Mara to the main Nairobi road. It was a poor boma even by Masai standards and Kipeen had spent much of his youth helping to herd cattle. The name Peter was given to him when, as a boy, he had started attending Lemek primary school. Over the years, his education had been combined with periods at home herding the cattle, and it was not until he was almost twenty that he had finally finished primary school. Not long after that, he secured a job as a ranger for the Narok County Council, which administered the Masai Mara. He was a neat, good-looking young man, with an open, honest face. Unlike many Masai, his ears had not been pierced and he had no gaping holes through his lobes. He wore his green uniform and heavy boots well and was generally liked by his fellow rangers. John Magiroi, Kipeen's companion at Makari post, came from a similar Masai background. Most tribes in Kenya have embraced modern ways: seeking education, moving to the cities, working for money. But the Masai, supremely proud of their own existence and their cattle, which they believe were a gift from god, have resisted Westernization longer than most. At around twenty-seven, Magiroi was slightly older than Kipeen. He was also a little taller and heavier in build. His teeth were brown and crooked, and the whites of his eyes were tinged with yellow. He was also married, with one child and another on the way.

Both men had been posted at Makari for several months prior to Julie's death. Theirs was the most isolated job in the reserve. Tourists seldom drove past the huts where they lived. They had little communication with Keekorok other than by radio, which worked only now and again. They seldom saw their wives and had no form of recreation at the post. Their huts were basic, uncomfortable and often leaked. A few weeks after Julie's remains had been found, on 27 October, James Sindiyo, the assistant warden in the Masai Mara, jotted down a few notes on what could be done to improve life at Makari post: '1 Change of unihuts to better house. 2 Recheck the radio system. 3 Sports facilities, e.g. darts.'

In their report, Searle and Shipperlee were to write that on the whole the rangers they had interviewed at Keekorok had been transparently honest. Kipeen and Magiroi, on the other hand, had stood out like a pair of sore thumbs. When presented with a photograph, taken by the *Today* photographer, showing him standing with the journalists in the Sand river, Kipeen had readily agreed that he had found the journalists. But at the same time both he and Magiroi said that they could not have found Julie's car, that they did not patrol that area, that the rules meant they had to stay in the camp. Though one of them denied it, the other admitted that they had on at least one occasion used their official guns to shoot a game animal, which they had cut up and eaten. But much of the time, the two rangers simply muttered 'Sijui', Swahili for 'I don't know', when asked questions. There were, Searle and Shipperlee felt, too many inconsistencies and lies in the replies of Kipeen and Magiroi. And one of the first rules of police work is that people seldom lie without some reason.

A few days after interviewing Kipeen and Magiroi, Graham Searle contacted John Troon, the Scotland Yard detective in charge of the Robert Ouko investigation. Troon's larger team contained a forensic scientist, David 'Sandy' Sanderson, and Searle wanted to borrow him. Before long, Sanderson was brought down to Keekorok and taken over to Makari post. It was now more than eighteen months since Julie had died, but if she had been held at Makari post then it was not impossible that some trace of her presence might remain. Sanderson's job was to try to find it. From each of Makari's five huts, Sanderson collected bags full of dust, hair and cigarette butts, as well as scrapings from the walls and floors. Every time he came across a possible blood stain, he rubbed a piece of test paper over the stain and handed it to David Shipperlee, who dipped it in chemicals. If the test read positive, Sanderson collected a scraping. When he had finished, not a stray hair or stain was left in the huts. It was the best cleaning Makari post had ever had. For a couple of days, the bags of possible evidence from Makari post had sat in Shipperlee's hotel room in Nairobi, attracting the attention of journalists who visited the two policemen in the hope of clues about how the investigation was going. But eventually the bags were sent to London for examination by a police scientist named Phil Toates at the Forensic Science Laboratories. In Kenya, another piece of forensic work was also carried out. Julie's Suzuki, now in the hands of Sebastian Tham, was still sitting outside the balloon company office at Wilson airport in Nairobi, where Tham had driven it a few weeks after Julie's death. Because it had been washed before they had access to it, the Kenyan forensic scientists had not bothered to search it for fingerprints. A year and a half later, Sanderson dusted the inside of the vehicle and came up with a single, faded print. In the end, the print proved unhelpful, but it showed that even after all that time forensic work could turn up evidence which might just prove useful.

In the following weeks, John Ward, his wife Jan and their two sons Robert and Tim had given blood samples to Scotland Yard's forensic men. Julie's blood type was unknown and her remains had been cremated more than a year earlier. But somewhere in the mass of dust and rubbish taken from the Makari huts it was possible that there was a stray blonde hair or a piece of congealed blood or skin that could be matched to the DNA or blood of one of Julie's family. Sorting through and examining the evidence from Makari post was a mammoth task for Phil Toates and his assistant at the Forensic Science Laboratories. The dust inside each bag was like the contents of an industrial vacuum cleaner, and every speck had to be examined under a microscope. Eventually, after months of work, Toates was forced to admit that he had been beaten. To the intense frustration of Searle and Shipperlee, there was nothing from Makari that could be identified with Julie Ward. The forensic work had begun eighteen months after Julie's death, but the police had hoped that, by miracle, some sign might have remained to prove that she had been held in the post. Without any forensic evidence, the detectives were going to have to rely on circumstantial evidence.

As Searle and Shipperlee saw it, Kipeen and Magiroi had certainly had the opportunity to kill Julie. Makari post was the only fixed habitation in the region where the Suzuki and Julie's remains had been found. It was the most isolated post in the reserve, and the only one where fewer than a dozen men were present at any time. There was no doubt that Julie could have been held at Makari for several days and then killed and dismembered without anyone other than the two rangers knowing about it. Had Julie been held at the Swiss camp, or at Keekorok, Sand River or Ololaimutiek gate, a score or more rangers, camp followers and policemen would have had to have known what was going on. A conspiracy involving ten or twenty people is hard to keep quiet, but over a period of two years no one had spoken out about the murder. Two men would have found it far easier to hold their tongues. Searle and Shipperlee had also discovered that, during the week Julie was missing, the radio set at Makari post had been only intermittently working. This piece of information fitted neatly into their supposition that whoever had found Julie in the gully had not initially intended to attack her but had given way to temptation when night had fallen. If Julie had been taken to Makari post, then the rangers would probably not have been able to call Keekorok for help. Julie would have had to stay the night.

At the same time, Magiroi and Kipeen had had the means to kill and dispose of Julie and the expertise to dismember her body with the skill that Professor Gresham, the pathologist, had described. One of them had admitted that while at Makari post they had shot game, cut it up with a machete and eaten it. The same machete and the same expertise at cutting up game could have been used on Julie. As far as Searle and Shipperlee were concerned, John Magiroi and Peter Kipeen, and these two men alone, were responsible for the murder of Julie Ward.

*

In early October 1990, a couple of weeks after Graham Searle and David Shipperlee had returned from Kenya, John Ward paced around the outside of his Butterfly hotel in Bury St Edmunds. Despite the economic recession, business was good. Plans for a new Butterfly hotel in Colchester, the fourth in the chain, were well under way. A sign at the entrance to the Bury hotel apologized for any inconvenience to guests from the construction that was taking place: twenty new rooms were being built. The new wing was almost finished, and John Ward peered up at it and then looked at a roof tile in his hand. 'This is the sample tile they sent me,' he said. 'This tile matches the tiles on the old buildings. The tiles they are actually using on the new building are not the same colour as this tile. And they are not the same colour as the old tiles. They're trying to feed me a lot of rubbish about the kilns and clays, and how with a little weathering it will all be fine, but I don't buy that. I don't care how they do it, but I want all the tiles looking the same.'

A few days earlier, John Ward had driven down to London to spend several hours with Graham Searle and David Shipperlee at Scotland Yard. Together, they had painstakingly gone through all the details of the Yard investigation. Over the previous few weeks, Searle and Shipperlee had grown somewhat frustrated at Ward's public criticism of their work, and they were keen to show him the logic of their conclusions. But Ward would have none of it. He agreed with Searle and Shipperlee to a certain point. He, too, was convinced that Makari post had played a vital part in his daughter's murder. And he saw no reason to argue with Searle's recommendation that Kipeen and Magiroi be arrested and charged with murder. But he was still absolutely certain that the two policemen had uncovered only part of the story, and that the Sand River campsite had played a part in Julie's abduction and death.

Central to his argument was his insight into his daughter's behaviour. He disagreed with suggestions that Julie's seven months in Africa might have made her more adventurous or careless. 'I think they've misjudged her character,' he said, sitting down to lunch at his favourite table in the corner of the hotel restaurant. 'Take the question of Glen Burns. I think he is a bit of a loner, and tends as such to put number one first. It's quite possible that when the opportunity to drive down to the Masai Mara with a girl arose he fancied his chances a bit. I think his nose was put out of joint when it turned out to be just a photographic trip. There is evidence that when the jeep broke down, he was not in a good humour. At this stage Julie would have felt responsible, it was her jeep that was broken down. I don't think Glen's leaving was a sign of Julie being brave or adventurous, she was just being generous. I think she was very concerned about being alone. She wouldn't have driven off the road.'

Graham Searle had made it clear at the meeting in London that, barring the emergence of unexpected new evidence, the Scotland Yard investigation had come to a close. Yet John Ward was not worried. He had started his investigations before the arrival on the scene of Scotland Yard and he could continue after they were gone. *Reader's Digest* had just published a story on the case, and Ward was furious that in the British edition they had failed to voice his specific request for information from anyone who had camped at Sand River. 'They've sworn to put it into all the other editions,' he said. 'Including the Chinese one.' Ward also had plans to return to Kenya. There was a clerk at Keekorok lodge he had not yet talked to. The man had retired, and Ward had plans to track him down. It was difficult, Ward said, to trust evidence that he had not collected himself. So many people in Kenya had an angle on the case. He was, he said, particularly sceptical about the evidence given to Scotland Yard by Andy Stepanowich, the Canadian survey pilot who had first found Julie's Suzuki. Stepanowich, who worked for the Kenyan government, said the Suzuki was almost a mile from the Swiss film camp. Henri Berney, the Swiss cameraman whom Ward himself had tracked down, claimed the camp had been just three or four hundred yards from the car. If Stepanowich was to be believed, Julie could have driven the Suzuki into the gully. Berney's evidence made this extremely unlikely: she would undoubtedly have heard and seen a camp just a few hundred yards away. 'While I keep an open mind, if I had to make a choice, I'd go for the people who were totally independent rather than the man who works for the Kenyan government,' he said. 'I talked to Henri Berney after he had spoken to the Yard. He told me the police kept saying to him, "You could have been wrong, couldn't you?"' John Ward smiled and shrugged. 'I am aware that in Kenya I shall start getting rubbished now. They will say, here's this guy, he's a fanatic. He won't accept the facts even when they come from the British police. It's sure to come.'

But after all this time, John Ward was not to be ruffled. In fact, he had even launched a suit against the Kenyan government to recover some of the money he had spent. Under Kenyan law, the police only need to request an inquest when there is some doubt as to the cause of a death. As far as Ward was concerned, Commissioner Philip Kilonzo had 'absolute proof' in his possession long before the inquest that Julie had been murdered. There was no doubt. 'The inquest put me to a lot of unnecessary expense,' he said. 'That's why I'm suing.'

The words came out between mouthfuls of cake and custard. When he had finished eating, he ordered a coffee from one of the waitresses who buzzed around his table. He sipped at the hot coffee and spoke once more. He had no regrets about the campaign which had come to dominate his life. 'It was the only thing I could do, unless I had just turned away. It's a strange, strange story. I shall be glad when it's over. In a way, I wouldn't mind if the clues dried up and I had to give up. But while they keep coming in, I shall continue. I will be going back to Kenya soon. There's more work to be done.'

Epilogue

On the morning of Tuesday 20 September 1988, exactly two weeks after Julie Ward had gone missing and one week after her Suzuki and remains had been found, Dr Peter Southwell, a British tourist, drove away from the Hotel Boulevard in Nairobi for a week's safari. As Julie had been on the day she disappeared, he was travelling alone. Like Julie, he was driving a Suzuki jeep. From that day no one had seen or heard from Dr Southwell until almost exactly two years later when, just as Graham Searle and David Shipperlee were completing their investigation into the murder of Julie Ward on their second trip to Kenya, his jeep was finally found. The vehicle lay hidden in thick vegetation in Meru National Park, east of Mount Kenya. It had been gutted by fire and was completely empty. Of Dr Southwell, there was still no sign.

Back in September 1988, when Julie had driven down to the Masai Mara, she had been expected to return to Nairobi for dinner a few days later. When she had not returned, a search was begun. Her father flew out to Kenya six days after she had last been seen and immediately set in motion a massive air search, which before long spotted her vehicle and led to the discovery of her remains. Tragic though the search turned out to be, it was carried out not a day too late. A few hours more and Julie's possessions and remains could have been scattered or eaten by wild animals, or swept away by rain. Dr Southwell, on the other hand, had given nobody his schedule. He had arrived in Africa alone, for three months of travel through Kenya, Tanzania, Zimbabwe, Malawi and Botswana. He was thirty-eight years old and very independent of mind. As his brother-in-law Tod

197

Merson was later to say, 'He didn't like being shackled, he didn't want to leave a plan.' Consequently, it was nearly a month before the first doubts as to the doctor's whereabouts arose back in England. Southwell had hired his Suzuki in Nairobi for a week. When he had not returned it on time, the car hire company gave him a week's grace: tourists often extend their safaris. After that, they were forced to assume that he had stolen the vehicle. They began making inquiries through Barclaycard, since he had used his credit card to pay for the rental. Eventually, those inquiries filtered through to his family in England. By this time, Southwell was nearly three weeks late with the car. His family and friends had talked to him enough about his holiday to have expected him to have left Kenya by then. There was clearly something to worry about.

The Kenyan police were immediately informed, as was the British High Commission in Nairobi. Everyone seemed concerned, but nothing was done. Dr Southwell was nearly forty, a doctor and a man. Julie Ward had been younger, and a woman. It was, naturally, far more difficult to raise concern for the doctor than it had been with Julie. In November Tod Merson flew out to Kenya. Merson knew which hotel Southwell had stayed at in Nairobi, because it had been pre-booked. He also knew about the car hire company. At both places he found that the Kenyan police had not yet made any inquiries about his brother-in-law. Before Merson had left, the family had decided to offer a reward. In Kenya, Merson was advised that rewards were unlikely to lead anywhere, because people in Kenya were afraid to come forward and give information about a crime in case the police threw them in jail – not an unlikely scenario. But Merson printed up posters anyway and distributed them around likely areas. The initial reward was three hundred pounds, though this was later raised to three thousand pounds, some six years' wages for the average Kenyan. While in Nairobi, Merson met Deputy Police Commissioner Gitui, who assured him that everything possible was being done. Gitui said all the prisons, hospitals and border posts had been checked. He also told Merson that the records of all the likely game parks had been carefully examined. But the police had found no sign of Dr Southwell.

Tod Merson had just one clue. He knew that, at some point, Southwell had cashed an American Express traveller's cheque. For several days he waited to find out where the cheque had been changed. Eventually, the news came back that it had been done in Nairobi. That was no help. Merson had a farm to run back in Somerset, and after two weeks in Kenya, he was forced to return home frustrated. At this point, while Southwell's family and friends suspected that something terrible had happened to the doctor, they could not be absolutely sure. They had simply nothing to go on. The weeks passed until the crucial date: 29 December. This was the day on which Southwell had been booked to return to London. 'We still hoped that Peter might be alive,' Southwell's friend, Bill Cottle later said. 'It was not impossible that he wouldn't have communicated all this time and would just turn up on his scheduled flight. It was unlikely, but we had to hope. Truth is stranger than fiction, and all that. His girlfriend Vivien didn't want to go alone to the airport, so I went with her. We waited and waited, but he didn't turn up. It was really quite gruesome.'

It was after this that Bill Cottle decided to visit Kenya himself and try his luck. He flew out to Nairobi in February 1989 and on his first day there was taken to see Police Commissioner Philip Kilonzo by the British High Commission. Kilonzo was his usual charming self. He was extremely polite. He reassured Cottle that everything possible had been done. Cottle said that he thought Southwell would have gone up towards Mount Kenya, he had always wanted to climb the mountain. The Kenyan police asked Cottle if Dr Southwell had been a happy man. Might he have committed suicide? Could he have started a new life? What sort of man was he? In this case, as with that of Julie Ward, there was a marked reluctance to admit that anyone other than the dead or missing person could be responsible for the tragedy.

Frustrated, Cottle decided to try to retrace his friend's route, guessing where Southwell might have gone. He knew that

Southwell had wanted to visit Mount Kenya, so he made this his target. He also hired a Suzuki, hoping that he might be able to jog a memory somewhere along the way. But unwilling to travel alone, he did take a driver: 'It would hardly have been sensible to do the same as Peter.' Cottle drove north from Nairobi and up the east side of Mount Kenya, stopping at hotels and lodges along the way. Over the two days, he looked at the registers in more than a dozen hotels, but there was no sign of Dr Southwell. Cottle also stopped at the entrance to Meru National Park, but was told that they only had entry records going back to December. When he returned to Nairobi, Cottle told Deputy Commissioner Gitui about failing to see the records at Meru, and Gitui told him they had already been checked. Empty handed, Cottle returned to England.

Unlike John Ward, who had known all along where his daughter had gone, Southwell's family and friends could only guess which part of Kenya the doctor might have headed for. Searching the eastern corner of the Masai Mara was one thing. Searching the whole of Kenya was quite another. But in May, Peter Southwell's aunt and uncle took their turn to visit Kenya and make inquiries. They too drove around Mount Kenya, and there by chance met a farmer who said he had seen Dr Southwell on the road north of Mount Kenya, taking a photograph of the mountain. It was eight months since Peter Southwell had disappeared and this was the first breakthrough of any kind. If the doctor had been in this area, then perhaps he had tried climbing Mount Kenya and had had an accident there. By this time, Tod Merson had hired an Asian private detective to keep an eye on any developments in Kenya. The detective, who had been recommended by Byron Georgiadis, now arranged, on orders from Merson, an aerial and ground search of Mount Kenya. He found nothing.

Once again, there was little that the Southwell family could do. But finally, a full fourteen months after Dr Southwell's disappearance, the police came up with something. After all this time, someone had eventually bothered to check the records at Meru Park and had discovered that the doctor had signed into

the park on the evening of 20 September, the day that he had
left Nairobi. 'We were relieved that they'd found something,'
Tod Merson said. 'But rather appalled that it had taken so long.'
The park records also showed that Dr Southwell had camped
right next to a party of Germans. Through Interpol, the Kenyan
police contacted these German tourists, but while they remembered Southwell, they said that they had just chatted briefly to
him and had no idea where he had been planning to go. And
while the park records showed entries into the park, they did
not record exits. There was no way of knowing whether
Southwell had left the park or not. Moreover, the farmer who
had seen Southwell north of Mount Kenya could not remember the exact date, so at this stage the family were unsure
whether the doctor had been on the road before or after he had
visited Meru. But at least the area where he had probably disappeared seemed to be shrinking.

The next clue came in the form of a story that a jeep had been
seen being washed down the Tana river, which runs through
Meru National Park. Fishing at any chance, Tod Merson was
just arranging for an aerial and ground search along the Tana,
when the news came through that a ranger in Meru had finally
found Dr Southwell's Suzuki. The jeep was sitting right up
against a tree, about two hundred yards into thick bush from
the nearest track. There was a small dent in the front bumper,
which was resting on the trunk of the tree. The vehicle had been
completely gutted by fire. Forty feet away lay a punctured
petrol can. The dent in the bumper did not suggest a violent
enough crash to have caused a fire. Instead, the evidence suggested that the vehicle had been hidden and purposefully set on
fire. For Tod Merson, this information was enough. 'It looks
pretty likely to me that he's dead,' he said. 'Though some members of the family are hoping that he was abducted and he's still
alive.'

Less than three weeks before Peter Southwell had arrived in
Meru, a tourist in the park had been shot in the chest by bandits. Months later, a French couple were shot dead when they
stumbled across a band of poachers. Dr Southwell had, like

201

Julie, unwittingly chosen to go on safari at the height of the trouble with poachers, bandits and indiscipline among the park staff. It was quite possible that he had run into poachers and been shot as a result. Yet, one key question remained. Why would poachers have wanted to hide the car? By definition, the poachers and bandits would hit a target and then run. In the Masai Mara, the attempt to dispose of Julie's body had led the investigation to focus on the reserve staff. In the case of Dr Southwell, similar suspicions were roused. In Meru, as in Tsavo, the park administration had been rife with corruption: in particular, many of the wardens and rangers had been involved with poaching. Six weeks after Dr Southwell's disappearance, on 2 November 1988, five white rhinos were shot and de-horned in a guarded stockade just a few hundred yards from park headquarters in Meru. Park involvement was inevitably suspected. Perhaps Dr Southwell had come across a group of rangers pulling a tusk out of an elephant they had just shot. This might have led to his death. It may also have explained why his car had been hidden. It might even have been the reason why the park staff were so reluctant to show either the police or Bill Cottle the records for September's tourists in Meru. Comparisons with the death of Julie Ward kept cropping up, but for Dr Southwell's family and friends, speculation seemed unlikely to lead anywhere. Two years after his disappearance, they still had no body and it appeared unlikely that they would ever discover whether Peter Southwell had been murdered, or indeed who would have killed him.

The story of Dr Southwell served to show how remarkable John Ward's achievements had been. From the first moment that Ward had learned that his daughter was missing, he had acted swiftly and moved in the right direction. As he himself had said on many occasions, he had been fortunate enough to have had the money and the ability to free himself from work, which allowed him to fly to Kenya and rent, without hesitation, a fleet of aircraft to search for his daughter. It had taken two years to find Dr Southwell's vehicle. John Ward had found his daughter's jeep within little more than twenty-four hours of arriving in Kenya. And a few hours later, he had found her body. Moreover, John Ward's own instincts had persuaded him that, despite advice from all sides to the contrary, his daughter had been murdered. From that point on, he was almost unstoppable. Although his brusque manner alienated many Kenyans along the way – and their off-hand manner annoyed him – he forced them in the end to help him. The Julie Ward case eventually went right to the top: the Scotland Yard detectives were brought in because Kenya's President Daniel arap Moi asked Douglas Hurd, Britain's Foreign Secretary, for help.

In a country like Kenya, the authorities, and especially the police, are not used to being challenged. Had John Ward been a Kenyan he would almost certainly have ended up in prison for offending the people he did. Indeed, recent Kenyan history is littered with deaths that were brushed off as accidents because somebody within the Kenyan government wanted it that way. Two cabinet ministers, Argwings Kodhek and Ronald Ngala, were killed in extremely suspicious car accidents. Ngala's driver, who survived his crash, was initially reported to have said that a swarm of wild bees caused him to swerve. At the inquest, guilt was switched from wild bees to wildebeest. John Ward would have given short shrift to such explanations. The Kenyan government had even invited Scotland Yard in to investigate the murder of Robert Ouko, yet another cabinet minister, but the Yard detectives had had terrible trouble trying to unravel the events which had led to his death. But John Ward had pushed and pushed. He had managed to encourage a steady stream of reports in the foreign and local press. He had produced new post mortem reports and soil analyses. He had hired a private investigator and visited Kenya nearly twenty times himself. He had spent hundreds of thousands of pounds travelling to a dozen different destinations around the world gathering evidence. If his daughter's death had become an obsession, then it was a quite understandable obsession. More than anything else, it had been John Ward's dogged, shrewd, ebullient, money-no-object quest to avenge his daughter's death and find justice that had caught the attention of the British public. John Ward was not the first British parent to have been thrown into the public eye because of the death of a daughter. The father of Helen Smith, the nurse who died in Saudi Arabia, and the mother of Suzie Lamplugh, the estate agent who disappeared after going to meet a Mr Kipper, had both carved trails followed by John Ward. Yet of the three, John Ward had achieved the most.

At the same time, John Ward's campaign had also had a far broader effect than simply to lead him towards his daughter's killers. Together with the publicity given to other events in Kenya, the coverage of the Julie Ward case had helped in no small way to force the Kenyan government to acknowledge the dangers of a corrupt administration in its parks and reserves and, in a matter of months, to start to change it.

Before Julie's death, most of the attention attracted by Kenya's parks was focused on the slaughter of elephants. But the Julie Ward case brought home to Kenyans how the troubles in the wildlife system were starting to damage tourism and therefore the Kenyan economy. By the time Julie died, President Moi had already ordered the elite General Service Unit of the police into Tsavo National Park to try to counter the massive poaching. He had also announced a shoot-to-kill policy against poachers. Yet Julie's death showed that it was not only elephants but also tourists who were in danger from the poaching and indiscipline in the parks. If there was no control in the parks, then Kenya stood at risk of losing both its elephants and its tourists.

For several months after Julie's death, the government wavered on its policy over the wildlife system. Then, in April bandits launched two attacks on tourists on the Amboseli–Tsavo road. Coming at a time when the Julie Ward case was still very much in the news, the attacks swung the balance. On 20 April 1989, the day after the second of these incidents, Kenyan radio announced that Richard Leakey had been appointed as the new director of wildlife. It was an extraordinary move and one that was to have remarkable consequences. Richard Leakey was the middle son of Louis and Mary Leakey, the palaeontologists who had made East Africa a centre for the study of early man with their work at Olduvai gorge in Tanzania. Richard, a Kenyan citizen, was also a world famous palaeontologist, who had appeared on the front cover of *Time* magazine for his views on early man and had presented a series of popular television programmes. Yet he was also a wildlife expert. He had run a trapping and safari business when young and was now the head of the East African Wildlife Society. At around the time of Julie's death, he had chosen to speak out against the elephant poaching and corruption within the wildlife system. Then, it had led to his being accused of having a 'cheeky white mentality' and it had cost him his job as director of Kenya's Museums. But now, by Presidential decree, it had won him the job of director of wildlife.

Leakey was given not just the job, but also the necessary powers to go with it by President Moi. He would get army support, modern weapons, the freedom to hire and fire whoever he liked and to raise his own money. Moreover, as a white Kenyan, he was not subject to the tribal pressure which had crippled some of his predecessors. Within days, Leakey had hired as his deputy the assistant commissioner of the General Service Unit, Abdi Omar Bashir, one of Kenya's best military tacticians. Between them they set about shaking the wildlife system into shape. Hundreds of wardens and rangers were fired. Systems were installed to prevent ticket money scams. Bashir recruited two hundred and sixty illiterate young warriors from the nomadic tribes such as the Masai, Boran, Ndorobo, Samburu and Turkana to be moulded into anti-poaching squads capable of matching the Somali raiders. Dozens of Land Rovers were acquired and sent down to the parks and reserves. Petrol was suddenly made available. New uniforms were acquired, along with water bottles, radios, packaged food supplies and, most importantly, automatic weapons. Consequently, morale and discipline within the parks soared.

The changes began to have an almost immediate effect. Once the corrupt wardens and rangers realized that they were having to watch their backs, they stopped poaching and harassing tourists. Elephant deaths fell from several a day to a handful a week. For the first few months of Leakey's rule, the Somali bandits continued to attack the occasional tourist or elephant. But once the parks' new weaponry and morale began to tell, such incidents declined. In the year and more following George Adamson's death, there was not a single incident of tourists being held up or shot at in Kenya's game parks and reserves. Instead, it was the bandits who were on the run. Bashir's campaign was brutal. Bounties were put on poachers' heads. Suspects were shot on sight. In Tsavo, helicopter gunships were even used to flush poachers out of thick bush and then kill them. But the war on poachers and on the bad elements within the wildlife system did its job. For both elephants and tourists, Kenya's parks and reserves had become, by the end of 1990, a reasonably safe haven again.

Richard Leakey's appointment also gave a shot in the arm to a swelling campaign to ban the international trade in ivory. Kenya, led by Leakey, lent its support to this campaign and along with Tanzania was at the forefront of an African call for a ban. On 18 July 1989, Kenya demonstrated its commitment to a new tough conservation policy. A mountain of elephant tusks, worth well over two million pounds, was set on fire in the Nairobi National Park. Three months later, most of the countries of the world agreed to a ban on the ivory trade. Africa's elephants were being given a chance. Julie Ward would have appreciated that.

In northern Wales, near the village of Pente-llyn-cymmer, lies an area of forest and green grass around the banks of the Alwen reservoir. This was where Julie Ward used to come with her mother Janet to race their husky dogs. A track leads away from the B4501 between Cerrigydrudion and Nantglyn and passes a farm before arriving at an old stone building. Here Julie and her mother used to spend the night, sleeping on mattresses on the floor, on husky weekends. Jan Ward was back here in 1990 on her own. But she did not stop at the building. Driving past, she did a 'quick eyes right', looking out for something. It was a heavy wooden bench, made in medieval fashion from solid sycamore by one of the men who had raced huskies alongside the Wards. Carved into the wood was a portrait of a family of huskies: a mother lying and feeding two puppies, with the father standing over them. Inscribed into the bench were a few simple words. They read: 'In memory of Julie, a dear and beloved friend who is greatly missed.'

Index

INDEX